MANAGING EDUCATION

Managing Education

The purpose and practice of good management in schools

Joslyn Owen

LONGMAN
London and New York

Longman Group UK Limited,
Longman House, Burnt Mill,
Harlow, Essex CM20 2JE

*Published in the United States of America
by Longman Publishing, New York*

First published 1992
ISBN 0-582-08504-7

British Library Cataloguing in Publication Data

A catalogue record for this book is
available from the British Library

Library of Congress Cataloging-in-Publication Data

Owen, Joslyn, 1928–1992
    Managing education : the purpose and practice of good management
in schools / Joslyn Owen.
        p.   cm.
    Includes bibliographical references and index.
        ISBN 0-582-08504-7
        1. School management and organization--Great Britain. I. Title.
LB2900.5.094   1992
371.2'00941--dc20

92-34
CIP

Set by 7 in 10/12 Times
Printed in Malaysia by CL

7 104566 120164 7

CONTENTS

PREFACE

In the autumn of 1989, shortly after his retirement, Joslyn Owen came as Visiting Professor to the Rolle Faculty of Education, Polytechnic South West (now the University of Plymouth). It began as a strange arrangement. As Chief Education Officer in Devon, he had been the motive force behind the merger of four of its centres of higher education into a large regional polytechnic. When he came to work in one of those centres – the campus in Exmouth which, until only a year before, had been Rolle College in his own Local Education Authority – they were still in the early stages of learning how to live together within the new institution, and as the polytechnic found its new identity, so, in a way, did he.

At first, his arrival posed us with questions. How was the man who had so dominated the education service in the region, and who had been such an influence on education, nationally and internationally, going to find life working in the college? How would he cope with the pressures of no longer being in charge, in a college staffed largely by those who had, until so recently, seen him as the boss of their bosses? For a man who had the reputation of being so hard a worker, how hard could we reasonably ask him to work? Would he attend staff meetings? What sort of room should we – *could* we – provide him with? Could we match his pace? Would he find in us the anti-climax to the rest of his life?

But Jos Owen surprised us by his modesty. He listened and sought to understand. He spoke to many people and made it easy for them to speak to him. He taught on our Masters programme. He came to our staff meetings, listened, and said – briefly – a great deal. It was good to have someone with us, who had the long perspective of a life in education which spanned the distances from small rural primary school to the clamour of educational politics in Westminster. Gradually, he came to be a subtle presence in the place, a part of it; and this gradualness, this subtlety was a great part of his skill. We did not altogether realise how large and how important was that skill, and with what weight it influenced us, until he died, suddenly, in January 1992. We had known him as a colleague for two years only, but his loss left us unequivocally sad.

Shortly after arriving at Rolle (signing on for duty, so to speak), Jos Owen and I discussed possibilities for the development of his work in the Faculty. He was particularly keen to put his thoughts on paper and this is the result.

Michael Newby
Exmouth, 1992

ACKNOWLEDGEMENTS

I am grateful to the Governors of the then Polytechnic South West, now the University of Plymouth, Director, John Bull, and the Dean of the Faculty of Education, Michael Newby for appointing me as their first visiting Rolle Professor. Their generosity has given me much help and then allowed me the use of wide-ranging facilities.

I owe a particular debt of gratitude to Sue Austen for her skill and patience with the manuscript.

Joslyn Owen   Exeter 1991

INTRODUCTION

The aim of this book is to examine the elements which make demands on managers of education, particularly in schools. The immediate managers include heads, their teachers and governors. Near at hand are parents and employers, each with a voice. Further away are local authorities and central government. At the same level stand the teachers' unions, pressure groups of parents and governors and more special lobbies which are particularly connected with disabilities.

The managers who are in most close contact with a school's day-to-day work can work as colleagues or as a combination of the leaders and the led. The pattern of collaboration will change: different topics and different moments in the process of management call for different approaches. Those approaches have to be understood by every participant and much of the effort of management is directed to the sharing of commitment.

Each party in management, whether near or distant, wishes to see the emergence and the assurance of good learning. Much of the common ground between each party in seeking quality is now laid out by government requirements in curriculum and in the assessment of learners. But in addition schools (and colleges) still have their own preferences and priorities in providing the education which meets the needs of pupils, students, families, the locality, the field of vocational training and the worlds of employment and higher education.

Those who, whether as parents or as employers, assess the quality of education have to know about the procedures and guarantees which will sustain good learning. They therefore need to know something about the inner workings of schools and about the relationships of professionals to each other. In the same way, the professionals have to be attuned to what is expected from them by the outside world.

At a time when expectations combine the solidarity of tradition with newer emphases such as those which are placed on enterprise, economic awareness, citizenship and world understanding, managers can never safely assume that everything is known, understood and sympathized with to the same extent by each partner. At a time, too, when quality management is viewed by some parts of the education world as something which provides a marketing advantage and by others as an 'insidious attempt to impose bureaucratic standards derived from industry or academic departments' (*Times Higher Education Supplement*, July 1991:1) managers need to be clear, in schools as well as in colleges, that they are bound to be influenced by the near-contractual presssures such as those of the British Standards Institution's BS 5750 (Employment Department Group 1990, British Standards Institute 1991) as well as by the broader demands of total quality management (March 1991). They need to remember, too, that management training even in the world of business and industry has been reported to be 'elitist, sparingly applied and lacking structure and relevance' (National Forum for Management Education and Development 1991).

New approaches have much in common with the management-by-feedback which is implied in the wake of the National Curriculum Council and by the School Examinations and Assessment Council. Management review and the creation of a quality system go hand in hand. Both find a clear echo in the work of the School Management Task Force and in the School Development Plans Project.

Each, too, has a connection with the tenets of competence-based education. The guarantee of quality and of standards calls with increasing urgency for guarantees of competence on the part of those who manage and those who teach – who will, for most purposes, be the same people. Competence and the criteria of assessment which are associated with it can appear only superficially attractive to some, over-complicated to others and too impersonal to yet other critics. But at a point when within a very short time all teachers will be subject to appraisal and, more immediately, when open management and public accountability are a reality, managers and those who educate and retrain teachers have to come to terms with the task of defining competence, sustaining it and making use of it as a source of professional stimulus.

Behind this lie larger questions. How schools can maintain a broad perspective, how they decide on what to base their judgements about the quality of their initiatives as well as of their past practices, how they decide on and use their best sources of management information – it is answers to these questions which distinguish good from mediocre schools. At each stage managers need to know with which problem and with which objective they are dealing. They need to learn from past mistakes and to use their experience to form strategies which are proactive.

Repeatedly, the analysis of how good managers work and of how they can win allies who are also their accurate interpreters to the outside world emphasizes the place of trust, clarity of communication and a properly balanced confidence. Each of these three relies on good partnerships, and any study of management in circumstances which are relatively new must draw repeated attention to the need, when schools fend for themselves, to surround themselves with constructive critics and supporters. Such networks, in the context of the Education Reform Act, have virtually had to be created from scratch because teachers, parents and governors were not previously asked to share management. But without collaboration schools will emerge from the consequences of 1988, from the deliberate weakening of local education authorities in 1991 and their virtual dissolution in 1993, far less robust than they were after the 1944 Education Act.

CHAPTER 1

Education, its managers and the public

Despite the breadth of press coverage for education reforms, it is not the newspaper-reading public that will determine whether education is good or bad and whether this school shall survive and that one disappear. It is not the public at large, either, which seeks assurance about quality. That falls, instead, on parents.

The control of quality which lies behind assurances about its level is in the hands of governors, heads and other teachers. Governors know that their own position may still be largely nominal. Teachers have the power to provide quality but they – and heads too – choose to look upon the management of quality mainly as a matter of personal effort and personal trust. Procedures, the documentation of procedures, the revision of those procedures which can guarantee consistent quality – these are not regarded by heads as a main part of the tradition of management.

Instead of a detailed concern to produce a process of learning which is repeatedly, from pupil to pupil and from year to year, of good quality, heads and other teachers satisfy themselves that they are providing a good education which is suited to the individual needs of those whom they teach. Seldom is a longer-term aim described, an aim which will if realized improve life in specific ways. It is generalization and a broad brush approach which dominates. It starts with the public.

Of the three major events affecting schools between the Second World War and the turn of the century, the first was a piece of legislation. The Education Act 1944 brought into being the four-part system of primary, secondary, special and further education. It raised the minimum leaving age to 15. It modified the relationship between maintained and denominational schools. It put into practice divisions of responsibility between a Secretary of State and local education authorities (LEAs). How that Act's changes were initially put into effect and how their daily impact was managed has not been recorded – unsurprisingly at a time when a war was being finished off and when other major social reforms were afloat.

The second event was a report of the Central Advisory Council on the education of pupils of average and less than average ability between the ages of 13 and 16. This, the Newsom Report, published in 1963, led to the equalization of opportunity, to the enlargement of the curriculum and to a further lengthening of the period of compulsory education. How the changes that it brought about were managed is again unrecorded. Slow improvements and reorganizations, not very visible to the public eye, took until the early 1970s.

The third major change was the Education Reform Act 1988. A concern about how education had been managed had become more prominent for about two decades. This book is mainly concerned with seeing how a new approach to shared management can handle the complexities of legislation which then radically changed the scene which was shaped by the 1944 Act and which set out to build rationally on the reforms which the Newsom Report had called for.

How marked was the impact of reform on public awareness? To start with Newsom, education is not often the stuff of front pages and headlines. When it is, it is sometimes a matter of outrage: boys taking charm lessons, teacher expelled over a slap, an 11+ dunce for the university, girls in peril under the showers – each of these news stories was of the kind that was given generous coverage in popular newspapers in the same month as the Newsom Report was published. As though to balance things out it was allocated a two page summary in one daily and was given its own headlines elsewhere, with an emphasis on headlines which described a 'spotlight on our children' and articles which described how girls were given ten shillings to 'clear out and amuse themselves'. The example set by parents was described as 'shaky' and another approach was that everyone, children, students and teachers, should be required to work harder.

The Robbins Report, a week after Newsom, was interpreted in the headlines as a reproof to university teachers. Again the message was that dons and students should work harder and longer.

These represent part at least of what the country was to understand about two major reforms. Admittedly they coincided with the Profumo scandal, with the aftermath of the Great Train Robbery and with the comedienne Millicent Martin announcing that she was going to leave a popular television show, *That Was The Week That Was*. It was the time, too, when Harold Macmillan stepped down. The contest between Butler, Maudling and Hailsham ended up with Lord Home at Number Ten.

When that was all over, education's major reforms were scarcely remembered by the press and, perhaps, by the general public. Osbert Lancaster's cartoon aristocrat took a rest, now that we could all relax for a bit and give our undivided attention to pre-marital sex and the Beatles.

Thirty-eight years earlier the *Daily Mail* had been more zealous: it had offered prizes for the best curriculum which its readers could suggest. The largest prize (£500) went to Mr Ernest Melles, Headmaster of St Luke's School, Chelsea, who, in addition to a detailed outline of his ideal curriculum, also laid down the allocations of time which each subject and activity should be given. His suggestions do not make the national curriculum of 1988 appear very new.

What we do not know about 1925 or 1963 is what action was taking place in central government or in local authorities or in schools and training colleges. The Hadow Report, which provided a context for at least some public interest in education in 1925, said little about parents, nothing about governors and managers and nothing about education beyond the limits of schooling. Newsom had a good deal to say about the social and economic environment of those children who did not benefit from secondary education but, again, nothing about governors or vocational training after school — not that this meant that working life was not somewhere in the picture. John Newsom, the chairman, said that his mental image as he worked on his report was the boy in the leather jacket and jeans and the girl in the tight skirt and beehive hairdo. They would probably be married in five years' time — with the boy probably becoming a labourer and the girl a factory worker on the production line. His concern was that they should be helped to become full persons and to break through the barriers society had rigged against them.

Words into actions

Contact between any report and its surrounding reality used to be left in the first place to legislation and regulation (raising the school leaving age, introducing the Certificate of Secondary Education) which initially reached only some teachers and some schools. Changes until 1988 had not been implemented in such a way as to affect the inner workings of all schools and all colleges of further education at the same time. Nor had they given the impression that there would at some stage be a single moment when the benefits of change and reform would become obvious enough and powerful enough to influence the way in which people live.

In contrast, the intention that it should have a universal effect meant that the Education Reform Act 1988 should for once get over the difficulties of separateness and disparities of timing. It looked to the future in requiring that assessments of children's performance in the curriculum should affect the way they were taught in each phase which followed key stages at the ages of about 7, 11 and 14. The short-term effect of formative evaluation might be open to question since it was unlikely to contribute much to the picture of overall change which we might expect, for instance, in any period of two or three years. But the long-term effect was virtually certain.

Will education's effect change by the year 2000?

We shall know if the changes in education between now and the beginning of the next century are successful if we see that they establish at that time a previously undescribed view of what education should produce. It may be that we will then realize that an ideal of getting the majority of the population into higher education is practicable. It may be that education will produce a richness of mind which will not allow boredom to be the alternative for the type of employment which now takes a day's energy. It may be that education will produce a complete understanding of other people, of other parts of the world and of alternative ways of living.

As they stand, these examples themselves reveal some limits: the first ideal is that education should lead to more education. The second is that education is a source of activity which differs from work. The third is that education can alter feelings as well as enlarge knowledge. But the education system we already have makes it clear that education can only partially touch each of these. What has not happened is that changes have come about on a universal scale. Instead, we know that an experience of a little education may deter some people from seeking more, that some activities which are an alternative to work can become obsessive or unhelpful or dangerous. And as far as larger understandings go, we know that, for example, literacy may increase rather than diminish our prejudices.

Limited or not, our knowledge tells us that the more education we receive the more of it we want only if it is an education which suits us, which we find comfortable and stimulating and which above all fits in with a view we hold about ourselves and our future. And that view in itself is not always within the perspective of the person who receives education directly; it may be that of a parent or some other influencer – not least the teacher or tutor.

We know, too, that although it is a long way from being universal, education does have something to do with creating the desire to follow activities other than those of daily work. And, lest a glib comment about literacy destroys the real picture, we see that an educated understanding of world affairs is often accompanied by a sense of immediacy, a sense of the smallness of the planet and a feeling that the troubles of one country belong to us all.

Because we already have a limited experience of the benefits of education, it is difficult to think of benefits which might go far beyond that experience. Famine and cancer might become things of the past partly through education producing better systems of growing, distributing and affording food and partly through education creating a level of research and skill which allows either prevention to be total or therapies to be discovered and, again, made affordable on a large scale. More education or better education at the basic level, in these circumstances, is taken as the ground floor: more people have their intelligence fed and sharpened to a higher level and in numbers which have not so far been possible. But if education can do good because more people of intelligence can work to benign ends, it is also almost inevitable that some intelligence will be devoted to malign purposes – such as those of encouraging racism or of manufacturing drugs which are damaging and addictive. With 4-year-olds and 14-year-olds we do not know in which direction their education will take them – and at 24 the story is scarcely different.

At less dramatic levels of what is good and bad, education may domestically and in world terms lead us to live within our means. At the beginning, this would involve our being educated so as to be immune to some of the less helpful influences of commerce and credit finance. More broadly it would lead us to be unwilling to use and consume things which have a finite limit in the natural world.

At a very personal level, education would help us to live by good principles without being pietistic. It would, so to speak, make us realistic enough to see that the virtue of confining our diet so as to avoid eating meat might be balanced out by the harm done to the economies of those countries where wages and living-standards depend on providing meat for world markets. And even in the process of balancing the equations of harm and benefit, we would need to remind ourselves that always seeing both sides of a question can result in inertia: knowledge has to be connected with the exercise of will.

At another level, education may make us better at using and running a democracy. This would involve us in learning that not everything can be known, public, open and debated. But it would indeed assist us in reaching as full an understanding as we are capable of in those things which are accessible – and in transforming understanding into action.

These hopes for the future apply in the school and the classroom. Among members of a single group of teaching staff and in a single school, common understandings are sometimes hard to create. The questions are: how are they best sought and how is it known that one approach to a common understanding is better than another? How are differences to be reconciled?

Teachers

Major differences between individual teachers may at first sight seem likely to be their age and the time which has elapsed since they were trained. In a nine-class primary school it is not unusual to find two teachers who are fairly new to the profession and who see nothing too awkward about the requirements of the 1988 Act: ten subjects have not previously been explicitly identified in the curriculum of young children but teachers do know when they are teaching history and not geography or when they are teaching science and not history. On the other hand, when they move from teaching to assessing they do not find it easy to record precisely how much time they have dedicated to each subject. Nor do they find it easy to distinguish among, say, twenty-five children in a teaching group, precisely when they can be assessed as to their competence in geography rather than in their capacity to communicate what they know. And when English is being assessed, is it what they are writing about or their skill in the actual business of writing which can be the more readily gauged?

Even for the newly-trained teacher this difficulty of maintaining separateness about assessing what is being learned creates some hesitation. A teacher in mid-career who has taught in the same school and with the same age-group for five years or more will find it is slightly challenging (but perhaps no more than that) to ascribe a judgement about progress and development – or their absence – to children who, until the 1988 requirements for assessment, had been looked at in the round. The strengths of the past, such teachers believe, lay in their completeness of approach. There may be some nervousness that the sense of the entire child may disappear in the new curriculum and with new requirements of assessment. Nevertheless, even the diffident teacher admits that one is unlikely to be much of a teacher if he or she does not retain a sense of the personality of the children and of the totality of their capabilities and interests – even when the most detailed descriptions are hammered out about separate facets of development.

What does create nervousness, for those in mid-career as much as for those who are new, is the question of whether enough time is going to be available to record everything that is needed. Will the description be clear enough to provide a good jumping-off point for formative work based on one assessment in the term and in the years which follow? And, particularly if it is a teacher in another school or even in another part of the same school, will another 'receiving teacher' give the same weight and understanding to the assessment as the originator? If the answer is to be based on what is commonly said to have happened even at a time, such as the past two decades, when record-keeping and continuity received much attention, no one would be too optimistic about the formative uses of assessment. It will be a matter for persistence and good management.

Making use of assessment

Even if a continuous record of achievement, including the assessment at each statutory stage, is maintained in detail, who will use it? This question at the start of new schemes creates a puzzle rather than a deterrent. Those in secondary schools are accustomed to reporting in written form to parents. Most teachers, at the primary as well as the secondary stage, are accustomed to giving, from time to time, an oral report. But now the requirement is for a written record which will be open to the parent as well as to the next teacher – and open in certain circumstances to governors. No teacher has been accustomed to this last demand.

Any assessment can, if an individual parent complains, be used as the basis of a judgement about what a particular teacher has done for

an individual child. What is new here may be that the written assessment could be used rather in the same way as the policeman's note-
book. What has been said has been said. There could be no going over
it again – and it would not be for the headteacher solely to go through
the complaint with the teacher. The governors or the local authority
may also now come in – something which was admittedly possible but
rarely used in the past.

While it would be comforting to give the impression either to the
new teacher or to the teacher in mid-career that any extreme use of a
record and an assessment will be unusual, it does still present an edgy
new element. It is something to be anxious about – not least because
until the present it has lain in the realm of untested law and regulation.
What has been comforting, on the other hand, is that the earliest documents from the Schools Examination and Assessment Council (SEAC)
(notably Pack C of the 1990 *Guide to Teacher Assessment*) expressed
their guidance about access to information with sensitivity: assessment
records had to be used in providing information which was part of the
decision-making process within the school, between linked schools at
transition points and with the LEA and the community. In summary
the shape of access to information is that (SEAC 1990b: 75):

- Parents and legal guardians have a statutory right to view pupil
  records.
- Teachers who are to receive pupils at transition points need access
  to assessments of individuals to inform their planning decisions.
- Headteachers have access to the records in order to review and
  monitor the work of the school. They also require summary
  documents in order to respond to queries from parents.
- Members of governing bodies and LEAs also have statutory
  access to school records for purposes of review and monitoring.

This is clear enough until the time is reached when the first complaint
is made by any individual parent, interest group or local authority. It is
at that point that even the teacher who is a late entrant into the profession, who has previously experienced, let us say, the ways of industry
or commercial business, now has to keep his or her nerve. It is not the
diffident new teacher or the teacher who has been accustomed to matters being decided by different people in different ways who may then
feel alone in not knowing where he or she stands. It becomes a question of the management style of the head as well as of the personality,
choice of interpretation and tenacity on the part of both the head as
senior manager and of other protagonists who emerge at a time of
disagreement. How arguments are faced and won requires the same
armoury of skills as in the past. It is the tools of argument and new
rights as to their use which will decide a dispute.

Formativeness and the school plan

In contrast to the use of new information for settling arguments, a continuous and low-key use of assessments has to be part of the school's arrangement for ensuring that children make progress. The rate of an individual child's development is uneven. It tends to be slow at the beginning and to gain speed once the foundations of learning are laid and when connections are made between different elements of knowledge and experience.

This picture of development might not be the same when a whole school's pattern of change is examined; it would not be surprising if a school moved quickly in the early stages of using new methods of monitoring, quickly too in the first stages of putting information to a new use but then slowing down when it came to planning ahead. To build up a three-year perspective needs reflection and a very genuine sharing of judgements about what will be known about the allocation of staff time, the allocation of books and other materials to assist learning – and the effect which those allocations have on the general capacity of the school to meet the Secretary of State's requirements concerning the national curriculum. This must also include the task of meeting the expectations of governors, parents and the local authority.

Self-reliance, self-dependence in the classroom, a reluctance to act corporately – any of these on the part of individual teachers might make it difficult for the school as a totality to get things right when its plan for the future takes account of what has been monitored in the past. Anything which is to be achieved corporately in a school's development cannot be reached without most teachers expressing a view or an idea about the likely connection between time, money and the achievements of groups of pupils. Was more time needed in order to ensure that individual children gained a firm grasp of new concepts? Was more time needed in which to observe what they were learning? Was there enough time to try again when a method of teaching or even of assessment proved, in a particular instance, to be wrong? Could more time have been found for a teacher to sort out how to continue teaching, observing and recording without the last two processes obtruding on the first?

In the early stages of answering these questions both headteachers and their colleagues manage the adaptation to new requirements by using compromises, agreements and concessions. But as the early stages give way to a regular pattern of doing things, that pattern will be one in which each teacher knows how much time is available. He or she then plans the learning period in such a way that assessment targets are clear and the group of different children who are to be assessed each time are allowed to have their work and the assessment discussed. The teacher, too, needs to allocate enough time – if indeed there is elbow-room in the timetable – to examining the next teaching plan and to modifying the lesson plans which go with it.

Managing the plan

The evolution of a regular pattern has to be managed in which these six or seven elements of planning and assessment can be fitted. The pattern has to be such that separate difficulties do not make the work of a teaching team either tense or ill-balanced.

To manage the avoidance of division and collisions does not fit easily into either of the two main styles which are often debated: to manage a collegial system carries with it the difficulty that covert influences on the lines of leadership and direction from the top can continue to be felt behind the visible structure of democracy. And to lead solely from the top carries with it an unattractive aura.

To plan and to monitor views about the significance of assessments on a shared basis of colleague working with colleague has further risks than those of concealing one person's – usually the head's – overall influence. One such risk is that a head will depend on the advice of a small group of year-leaders or curriculum managers who themselves, whether junior or senior in terms of length of service, may be surrounded by slight tensions, resentments or disbelief in their capacities. Second, the collegial way of working does not itself guarantee that the decisions which are reached will be better than those which might be taken almost autocratically by the head. And it adds weight to favouring a single-leader way of doing things if we remember that it is the head alone who will most frequently be in contact, on behalf of the professional side of the school, with the chairman of governors.

How is the head to manage individual teachers' views about the feedback from classroom assessment? It is essential that there should be smooth progress into the next stage of planning both at classroom and school level. But teachers' differences and their feelings of assertiveness or adequacy may make it difficult for the dovetail to be perfect.

Sanctions and checklists

There are models for managing the task of sharing the formulation of new approaches to any task. In teaching and in the planning of different allocations of resource, few ready-made, managerial models from outside education seem to fit. Teachers are unlikely to be dismissed if their skill in linking monitoring to planning is below par. They will in law be accountable to governors and the local authority and, at one remove, to parents and to the more distant entity called community. But that accountability will only work if governors and the local authority make up, for instance, some form of check-list of skill, success and high performance.

This could be along the lines of the following:

- Is each parent satisfied in the broadest terms with his or her child's education?
- More specifically, are parents satisfied that their children are progressing satisfactorily in the core subjects?
- Have parents understood from teachers what is going to be taught in the foundation subjects each year?
- Have teachers given parents an indication of, say, three verifiable indicators of children's progress in the foundation subjects?
- Have parents been told how the school intends to review and if necessary modify its teaching plans and its allocation of resources in light of overall experience in the past year?
- Have parents been told how individual teachers will modify their planning, their action programme and their use of attainment targets in order to enhance the learning of each child in the light of experience?

This is the way in which some secondary schools already work – in their internal reviews, in their ways of preparing written reports for parents and in the information which is made available during parents' evenings. The approach is not universal. It is beginning to be more widely used among primary schools. And if the new requirements of review and planning are to be effective, an approach such as this to the process of accountability cannot be left as something voluntary, spasmodic or subjective.

You are a member of a team and you stay as a member if you contribute to the team's achievement. This is true of sport, of the Cabinet or of boards of directors. It is not true of Members of Parliament, local councillors, trusts, charities and quangos. It is not true of school governors or school staffs. However, even if a teaching team stays together as a team, and even if one member is retained despite a contribution which does not amount to much, it seems likely that the individual will still be affected by the influence of the head and other teachers.

A teacher in such a team is also likely to be at least partly influenced by parents, even though the confidence of parents in talking to the teacher direct – about his or her performance or to the head about the whole staff's performance – may be inhibited. And as to the influence which governors exercise over a teacher, this is always likely to be routed indirectly through the head. To merge the flow of assessment into the process of review cannot, if these examples are appropriate, depend simply on lists of performance indicators and, if performance is low, on sanctions.

Pride may be a stronger spring behind the action of the manager. Schools enjoy being at least as good as each other. There are long established local collections of opinion, favour, distaste or prejudice. Local opinion is not quickly changed but in an age of published results, competitive prospectuses and persuasive annual reports by governors to parents, the reputation and attractiveness of a school might change rapidly. Just as unfavoured primary schools become popular when they fall into the normal recruiting area of a good new secondary school, so schools whose pupil assessments at 7, 11 and 14 are respectable are likely to lead to their being sought out.

Pride or survival is likely to matter more at a time when schools compete for new entrants, for enthusiastic and potentially supportive parents and indirectly for a bigger share of a local authority's aggregated school budget.

To plan against this type of background is new. A starting-point must come from the self-assessment which teachers are asked to undertake in their classroom planning and in their handling of pupil assessment. For instance, teachers are asked whether, when they look back at a particular round of assessment, they think that any one attainment target allowed too little information to be gathered (SEAC 1990a:15). If so, was this because the statements of attainment were difficult to interpret? Was it that the particular attainment target needed the teacher to be with specific children at a time or for a length of time which he or she could not manage? Were there distractions? Did some children do one part of the task and some another part but with no-one doing the whole? Did children differ so much that the teacher was not sure what to record? Were there too few opportunities for assessment?

Check-lists on these and comparable lines are practicable – particularly since SEAC suggests where to look for help in putting things right. The superhuman element is, in effect, removed. So too is the element of leaving things to other people to sort out. And a head or a senior member of staff should know whether teachers are carrying out the self-checks. There is not too much about them which might be felt to be imposed from above and, if a school is entirely collegial in its management, each teacher can be relied upon to reveal his or her progress in self-checking without the intervention of the head.

A basis of self-checking should enable a whole picture to be built up of how a school is succeeding in the task of relating statements of attainment to attainment targets. It should also help in the task of producing records which can be summed up and, in turn, described to governors, parents, a local authority and to the community at large. Will it leave out the relationship of the teacher to the whole child? Will it leave out the effect which the teacher expects to have on the child's total development? Yes, if assessment and planning are allowed to become ends in themselves. No, if the management of assessment and feedback into the classroom and school and into the process of planning is seen as a way of enhancing children's learning.

The three points of approach adopted by the SEAC are the local authority policy statement, children's needs and parents' aspirations. These are reconciled in the school's curriculum policy and that has to be formulated, first, in accordance with national curriculum and, second, in a way which is capable of influencing the school's adoption of the national requirement. In time, too, the national curriculum itself can be reviewed and partly reframed. In turn, children's needs, the LEA policy statement, parents' aspirations, the school curriculum policy and the national curriculum have to reach operational form in each school's scheme of work for its teaching groups, through teaching plans or lesson plans and in a form which can apply to whole classes and groups or to individual pupils. These, in the best of hands, give weight to the performance of individual children and of whole groups. How can it be guaranteed that they will always be in the best hands?

Collective quality

To rely on the skill and dedication of individual teachers and to assume that all will be well is not part of central government's philosophy. We are a long way from the time when it could be said that the essential freedom of teachers was the freedom to exercise their individual responsibilities as trustees for the natural rights of individual children and their parents. Even at such a time it was acknowledged that the nature of the teachers' role required definition when they acted collectively to create the corpus of knowledge which made up a school's curriculum. Society, it was thought – particularly at a time of rapid social economic and technical change – also had a vital interest in securing that the curriculum was relevant to its needs. Even in the balmiest days of teacher autonomy it was not self-evident that shaping and delivering the curriculum was a job that teachers could claim to be exclusively their own.

Just as the traditional message insisted on shared responsibility and skill in re-creating the curriculum, so we still see frequent references to the tripartite nature of activity. But by now that activity is concerned with the process by which the assessment of children's attainments affects a teacher's decision, a school's decision about the deployment of time and other resources and national decisions about both curriculum and standards.

If assessment is meant to inform the process of planning, who is it who informs and who is informed? Sometimes this is diagramatically shown with five levels of activity linking the three parties who need and who provide information. Unfortunately, whichever way these diagrams (SEAC 1990b:4) are read, the descriptions of the levels of activity are, in their categories, disconnected. And, if the diagram is taken as representing inner and outer circles, it is impossible to say whether one is meant to work one's way inward or outward.

The only other view to take is that there is no core, that categories are bound to be mixed and that uncertainties and ambiguities are part of the nature of the task of linking assessment to decisions about curriculum modification and about the use of time, materials and other resources. An official acknowledgement about uncertainty and ambiguity is, however, not likely to inspire confidence.

National schemes and local practice

Even if we insist that shared efforts can lead to the new education being in the best hands, there will inevitably be anomalies. Schematic approaches by the SEAC to the management of assessment and planning may fail to fill all the gaps. But earlier theories of effectiveness are still valuable. For example, the Inner London Education Authority (ILEA) study of key factors in effective junior schooling, based on a survey carried out between 1980 and 1984, included items which still have a national relevance (ILEA 1986). In, for instance, the battery of factors which at school level made for effectiveness, five were regarded as inarguable: good physical environment, status, good management of resources, intake and stability. A further eight had to be handled as 'policy variables', again at school level. These were the head's style of leadership, the type of organization, the involvement of staff, curriculum, rewards and punishments, parent involvement and relations, equal opportunities and the school's atmosphere. Many later statements, by the SEAC and the National Curriculum Council (NCC), by the School Development Plans Project (SDPP) and by the School Management Task Force carry the same echo. A shared system of management can provide a child-centred system which respects both traditional verities as well as newer demands of a more closely defined curriculum and more closely defined levels of attainment.

The past and the present can coexist when the 1984 ILEA report is put alongside the 1988 statute. But two sets of views change frequently: teachers during a period of, for instance, industrial dispute will withdraw goodwill. Activities which depend for their success on a sympathetic voluntary effort are left to one side. And parents, although they more readily believe in the individual teacher who is most closely involved with their own children than in hostile media descriptions, can nevertheless, particularly at times of dispute, lose some faith in teachers. When there is any alienation of teachers and parents, new initiatives are difficult.

Since the 1987 Teachers' Pay and Conditions Act, headteachers are careful about going further than the 1,265 hours of a teacher's contract and about extending any activities (which would fit without embarrassment into directed time) into undefined areas of voluntary responsibility. And parents, once they are confronted with the example of a teacher who works to the rule book, can be discouraged from expecting more.

A headteacher has to gauge the degree of commitment which is shown by teachers, the degree of interest and urgency for development which is expressed by governors and the pointedness of what central government expects. When time and patience are likely to run out at the same pace, heads may be driven to hasty action. Because they cannot expect calm, reflective and time-consuming reactions from their colleagues they may risk snatching at incomplete agreements or understandings.

No government that seeks changes which depend on the collaboration of schools, teachers, governors, parents and local authorities can, after the 1988 Act, enjoy much of the certainty which was possible for two and a half decades after 1944. Uneasy though it was, the views of central government, the reactions and demands of LEAs (particularly through the Association of Education Committees) and the response of the leaders of the main teacher unions could be known in advance of public debate. Until central government's patience snapped there was at least the pretence of debate in the calm atmosphere of a club which had three types of member.

Heads and other teachers were not always aware of belonging to that club. They tended to be left in ignorance by their employers. Their assistance was invoked either as a formality or as a means of disarming those trade unions with whom not all heads were closely associated.

What has happened since 1988 is a long way away from that sedate scenario. Those who work in the system know this. In contrast the public probably did not know (or care very much) how proposals, agreements, changes and developments were negotiated in the past. Despite the exhortation for parent, employer and community involvement in controlling or managing education, have matters become very different since 1988? The answer is no, because not enough knowledge is shared. Managers at every level need good information but that information is still thin, slanted and selective.

An example of how sources of information have changed can be seen in the work of Her Majesty's Inspectors of Schools (HMI) during the period which preceded their terminal weakening in the Education (Schools) Act 1992. Between the late 1970s and the mid-1980s they were reviewed as to their efficiency, suspected of being too much hand in glove with the Department of Education and Science (DES), thought at the same time to be so independent of Secretaries of State that they were virtually at war with them and urged from time to time to work more closely with local inspectors and advisers.

Throughout this time their public reports on individual schools, their surveys and their curriculum publications retained a high quality – even if, during the 1980s, it sometimes became difficult to remember which publications were those of the HMI and which were those of the DES, of which they were still nominally independent. Their tone, however, was generally one of liberal protectionism for the work of schools.

This tone led some politicians to suspect that HMI were soft on teachers, particularly when annual reports on the effect of policies about expenditure on the condition of schools could be read as criticisms of undue economy on the part of both central and local government. However, when in the first weeks of both 1990 and 1991 the annual report of the Senior Chief Inspector said that a large number of pupils and students were getting a raw deal and that what was poor and shoddy was a worryingly persistent feature of English education at all levels, some parts of public opinion briefly changed. It was not HMI who were accused of lacking teeth. Instead, their strictures were taken as an attack on the government and at the same time as an attack on teachers. In the first of these two years the Prime Minister (in February 1990) claimed that the education service was in a far better condition than it had ever been before. In 1991 the annual report was published during the Gulf War and on the same day as the bombing of a civilian air raid shelter in Baghdad. No parliamentary questions were asked and no comparable ministerial reassurance was forthcoming.

But back in 1990, the popular press asked: 'When would the Prime Minister ever learn?' What was needed, apart from the truth, was less satisfaction and more investment. How else could the children of Britain compete against Europe, America and Japan? The press acknowledged, too, that reforms in the core curriculum and teacher training would in time remedy some of the deficiencies. What was urged was more pay for good teachers, a weeding-out of the duds, more talk from the trade unions about commitment and more talk from the government about cash. Elsewhere trendy theorists were attacked, along with those who wished to eliminate competition from the classroom. The public came to hear of what were described as our rotten schools. And not surprisingly, it was held in some quarters that HMI themselves who were to blame for recommending, in earlier years, the adoption of progressive teaching methods.

A third leader in *The Times* (7 February 1990:15) ended with:

There is clearly a good deal of dissatisfaction with the quality of books and equipment, with the condition of school buildings, with the size of classes. There is also still a widespread feeling in the profession that their salaries are inadequate. The underlying issue, however, is the matter of how the profession is regarded. Education is a matter of national concern. By moving closer to the aspirations of teachers in the matter of pay and status, the Government will underwrite the success of its reform programme.

Other press comments emphasized that the Secretary of State had seemed hurt by the concentration of all the media on the worst aspects of the report. It was hoped that the Education Reform Act would lead to improvements but two factors were highlighted as preventing things from changing, namely lack of money for buildings, equipment and books and the persistent problems of the bottom 40 per cent in the school system. It was thought that the new national curriculum would pass them by. Their needs would only be met when schools gave more priority to vocational and technical education.

There was a reminder here of the fragmented attention which some parts of the press had given in 1963 to the Newsom Report. Important pieces of information were left out. There was, for example, no press reference to the three initiatives of central government in the 1970s and 1980s, namely the Youth Training Scheme, the Technical and Vocational Educational Initiative and the Certificate of Pre-Vocational Training. Worse, the information in the media missed the point about the changes in the constitution of schools' governing bodies which had resulted from the 1980 Education Act, the 1986 Education (No. 2) Act and the 1988 Act. It paid no attention to the considerable efforts which schools were making in the first three years after the Education Reform Act to prepare themselves for the introduction of local management. This, involving school planning which reflected the national curriculum, the local authority's curriculum policy and the school's own curriculum statement, brought into focus the task of making local judgements about the distribution of staff and the movement of money between teaching staff, non-teaching staff, materials and equipment. In making these judgements heads, other teachers, governors and parents needed more than the superficial and limited range of information about national trends which the press had provided after the national annual reports of HMI.

This was particularly important in the first full trial year of the scheme of local management. Selected schools in many local authorities had practised the technique of testing a variety of management tactics and strategies. Governors had been involved and in some cases chose to lead the way. Training was offered not only to governors themselves but also to headteachers, deputy heads, teacher leaders of year groups and sub-departments, as well as to clerical assistants and secretaries. The only practical way to prepare a wide enough range of simulated alternatives in building up each school's plan was to make extensive use of hard information, shaped, juxtaposed and questioned by means of information technology.

As trial schools became more confident, they were anxious to go beyond the exercise of financial control and to use their new capacities for self management in order to implement improvements – not least along lines which they themselves, HMI or other monitors felt were needed.

Parent awareness

At a time, then, when schools were being publicly castigated through press coverage of one HMI report, the reality of good management lay in self-scrutiny, debate, realistic choosing of different approaches to school development and above all the creation of whole-school management plans.

In the process of building up these plans parents and school staff joined in working out what the school was good at. Typically, teachers and non-teachers thought well of their thematic approaches to the curriculum, the build-up of a purposeful working environment and a high level of parental involvement. But they knew they might do better at, say, music and design technology, at using each others' expertness, at being consistent in the way school policies were put into effect and at planning the use of their resources. Parents and governors, on the other hand, thought well of schools' skill in providing a creative education, in working out a good plan for home visits and for making the children's environment a stimulating one. But they also wanted schools to clear up the question of how (or whether) spelling was taught, how work set to be done at home could be better followed up – and they also wanted schools somehow to achieve more in the effort to reduce class sizes.

From these types of audit covering up to thirty or a forty aspects of school life, school staffs helped senior colleagues and then the headteacher to draw up a priority list of policies which should be followed while a management plan was developed. This priority list of policies was discussed with governors. Bit by bit agreements were reached about how changes of school management could take place – changes which were understood by every party.

Against the ever-present background of the national curriculum and programmes of assessment this process was a realistic way for schools to take account, as the 1988 Act required, of the feelings, wishes and aspirations of the community. In this constructive atmosphere it seemed likely that the HMI hope would be achieved, namely that the large-scale search for improvement in the Education Reform Act should be realistic.

The ground to be covered between the school and parents in reaching a common understanding of that Act was considerable. Some schools took relatively easily to the intricacies and challenges of local financial management. They knew that they had to budget for everything. They knew that each additional primary pupil for instance was then worth up to £800. They knew that the cost of teachers was increasing. As staffs became more stable more teachers would be in post long enough to push up the average cost of teaching any size of pupil group. Schools knew that the use and cost of supply teachers could be reduced by turning to what previously had been, for example, some part of a deputy head's non-contact time. They knew that limited switches were possible between money for very minor capital work and the budget for teachers, non-teaching staff, books and materials. More important, those who took part in early schemes realized that handling finance with confidence required good information technology, an expert school secretary or clerical assistant, the availability of a support team from the local authority and a firm, trusting undertaking between the head and other teachers and between the head and governors.

But most important of all was the understanding that a money plan, a capacity to monitor, review and change a school budget was only one part of the process of enhancing children's learning. There was no single bottom line. There were questions of the quality of teaching, the quality of staff development and in-service work, quality in making assessments of children's performances, quality in interpretation and, again and again, quality in the relationship which allowed the process of making a management plan and putting it into effect to become something which was genuinely shared between heads, other teachers, governors, parents and the local authority – as well as other parts of the school's own community. The answers to these questions lay in what has been described as a post-bureaucratic organization (Jenkins 1991).

To organize how plans and assessments, initiatives and reviews are to be shared needs work which is detailed and sophisticated. It is, in its importance, critical. One or two substantial mistakes in a budget plan can damage a school's teaching capacity. But financial mistakes have the advantage of at least being visible. It takes time to get things back on the right lines and that time, whether it needs one year or more in getting a budget balanced once more, constitutes an unrepeatable period of time in a child's education. That is bad enough. Less visible is the error which gives too much or too little emphasis to one piece of learning, one unit of curriculum or one stage of assessment. Where mistakes occur in these three activities it will take longer for them to be spotted. They will ultimately become visible but the time which has to elapse may have to be measured in terms of several years, for instance, while the moderation of assessments is cross-checked. And the task of putting a finger on what went wrong could itself, if it is exhaustive, take much longer than in the case of a financial mistake. This is the reason for teachers putting accountancy low on their list of necessary skills in developing their school's management. They place more importance on interpersonal skills and on the negotiation of relationships – largely because they choose to see that trust in each other and open sharing are the keys to good management.

Conclusion

Education is something in which the public is in general only moderately interested. It is presented to that public by the press and broadcasting on the basis of official and professional documents in the form of fully detailed reports, commissions and reviews.

The public's impatience with education is matched by the impatience of those who work in the education system with press and the other reports which are selective and eye-catching. The legislation of 1986 and 1988 made it important that scepticism, on both sides, was minimized. Lengthy apologias, bouts of inquisitorial witch-hunting and a stream of bland official interpretations satisfy neither the media nor the educators. Nor do they satisfy parents. Families may believe that things are unwell with other schools but they know, they say, that their own children's individual schools are different. And at the secondary stage and in the world of further education, employers, too, are likely to say that generalized criticisms made on their behalf by their own professional organizations are accurate but that they seldom apply to their own local school or college.

There is no future in a continued gap between providers, professional evaluators, publicists, parents, users or employers. The work being done to create new and shared understandings needs to be better known and encouraged for a very specific purpose, namely to assure parents that what is promised is being provided. If parents can see that a school is promising to achieve certain standards of learning, understanding and behaviour, if those promises can be tested and if the school can show step by step how it works to fulfil its promises, the school is more likely to survive and to thrive. Survival comes first: everyone who is working for the school must know that.

CHAPTER 2

Managers of development and change: the shift from expecting to requiring

The product of a school is not a pupil to whom this or that has happened nor is it a qualification held by a pupil or student. Instead, the product is either the value which has been added to a pupil's or the student's life in specific terms or it is the process of learning through which the pupil will have passed.

In order to give an assurance to a parent that a child has had value added to his or her life the school must define the terms in which that value is to be described. It must also define the process of learning which it is guaranteeing the pupil shall have gone through. In defining what is to be added and in defining what is to be experienced the school has to deal in firm descriptions of what parents will want and will understand. The school must define how the product is to be worked for and must give promises that everyone in the school knows what his or her job is. It must also demonstrate that it can control each teacher's contribution to the work and that the definition of contributions and the monitoring of the quality of those contributions is part of a documented requirement. Anything less will not allow a school either to claim that it can assure quality or to promise that it can control quality.

Until the early 1960s schools made their own choices about what to teach. That choice was not unfettered: in some primary schools there was still 11+ selection to concentrate attention on mathematics, reading and English. In secondary schools, the General Certificate of Education (GCE) drove both comprehensive schools and unreorganized secondary modern schools to concentrate on producing successes in public examinations for pupils in the fifth form. Parents hoped that their children might do well at both these stages but they could only wait and see. What emerged might be predicted by teachers and parents on the traditional basis of whether or not a child came from a well-motivated and literate home. But predictions were a chancy business. Not much was said about children who entered grammar schools as a result of their 11+ performances and then failed to produce academic certificates of achievement. More was heard about young people who had failed the 11+ exam (for that was how the selection at that age was often described) and who nevertheless did well, later, at

GCE O level, at A level and in the competition for entry to universities. This was still a time when colleges of advanced technology – let alone polytechnics and institutes of higher education – were relatively unknown.

No one outside a school could do more than hope and expect: the rest was in the lap of the teachers, good or bad, of chance and of the rapid or slow development of children's capacity. Whether that development was produced under pressure from the child's school or left simply as something which was uncontrollable and unpredictable lay, it was assumed, beyond the influence of teachers and beyond the ambitions of parents.

Helping teachers to expect more of themselves

The Nuffield Foundation funded the production of schemes by which primary teachers might bring themselves up to date with new mathematics. The tireless work of a member of the central inspectorate, Edith Biggs, began to reduce the difference between schools. No one paid much attention to whether schools could be compared as to how much their pupils knew, but the main purpose was to even out the chances lest some children in some schools were given less opportunity to learn the new maths. The way to approach this was seen as a task of making all primary-school teachers' grasp of mathematics expert and confident. Teachers were expected to share their knowledge as well as their diffidence, their confidence as well as their uncertainty. The mask of privacy between teachers began to drop.

The mask of privacy between teacher and parents on the other hand remained in place. Neither Nuffield nor Edith Biggs pressed for the understanding of governors and parents for what was going on. There were other movements (led for instance by Michael Young and Patrick McGeeney) to involve parents and to recruit their understanding of what schools were doing, but that was a separate campaign, related more to reducing social differences than to creating a more open support for the curriculum.

The 11+ fell away. Plowden in the late 1960s pressed for individualization of learning: this moved the idea of what children should be able to do away from tests and selection and put the seal of approval on child-centred learning. They would also learn better, it was thought, if they were encouraged to enquire about things and to make discoveries on their own. Teachers would be more likely to achieve what was sought by teaching children on an individual basis or through the organization of small groups in which children learned together.

Whether these ideas were good or bad mattered less, in terms of the practical organization of schools, than the question of whether enough teachers were available. Until the late 1960s LEAs were rationed as to the number of teachers they could employ (the quota system).

Favoured authorities were thus prevented from scooping the pool of newly qualified teachers to the detriment of local authorities which served less favoured localities.

Those cautious first steps towards producing common opportunities in the curriculum were helped by new ideas about in-service education. At the same time they were hindered by problems about the supply of teachers. Forecasts of how many teachers would be needed in three, five or ten years were almost always wrong; the school population continued to grow.

By the middle of the 1960s, however, the picture changed. The government of the day required, in the secondary school sector, the establishment of comprehensive schools. The 11+ lost significance and at the same time there were changes in the examination of the fifth year of secondary education. The Certificate of Secondary Education (CSE) was aimed at expanding the 'qualified' section of fifth formers from 20 per cent to 60 per cent. The organizational changes of comprehensive secondary-school systems and the alteration of the height of the fifth form hurdle began to take education away from firmly established and unquestioned sets of requirements. The idea gained dominance that children and young people should be allowed to reach levels of achievement of which they themselves were capable and in which their schools could support them. It became less a matter of other people making all their decisions for them.

There was a reaction to this: by 1981 and in succeeding years the National Council for Educational Standards (NCES 1981, 1983, 1985) was analysing secondary school examination results, making the point that more was being spent per head of the school population than ever before and that the public was not given access to basic information. In two reports (*Standards in English Schools*) spokesmen for the NCES asked that the 1980 Education Act's school information regulations should be amended so as to require LEAs to send to any person, on request, copies of examination results for state schools within an authority's jurisdiction. The NCES also urged that regulations for the Assisted Places Scheme should be altered so as to require schools taking part to send copies of their examination results to anyone who sought them. It was asked, too, that there should be more school-based research and that primary data on examination results and other measures of attainment which were collected by the Assessment of Performance Unit, by HMI and other publicly funded research organizations should be brought together and made public.

The NCES in its 1985 report drew attention to the absence of well-organized study of those educational factors which were associated with social class. It was anxious to see connections drawn between a child's general educational environment outside school and what he or she achieved at school itself. This meant that the number of factors which had to be taken into account in managing schools was increasing, as too was their breadth and long-term significance, but they still did not amount to a systematic collection of activities which could be defined and controlled. Management was still a long way from giving defined assurances of quality and from controlling the steps to deliver a specific quality product.

Official approaches to assessment

In addition to the concerns felt by the NCES, there was another worry – about children's ability to read. From 1948 to 1964 regular national surveys had been commissioned by the DES from the National Foundation for Educational Research (NFER). In 16 years, there had been a 17-month advance in the reading age of 11-year olds and between 20 and 30 months for 15-year-olds. In 1970 a further test, which was said to be open to technical criticism, produced results which were interpreted as showing that standards had ceased to rise. This was regarded as so important that it led more or less directly to establishing, in 1972, the Bullock Committee with its inquiry into the teaching of literacy and into means of improving the way in which language development could be monitored. The report, *A Language for Life* (1975), gave as its first recommendation the need to set up a system of monitoring which could assess a wide range of attainments.

In 1975 too, worries about one individual school added to the feeling of unease: parents' complaints about their children's learning at the William Tyndale School in Islington led to an inquiry as a result of which the headteacher and several staff were dismissed. Later, in 1976, the then Prime Minister spoke at Ruskin College, Oxford. The education profession should be made accountable to society and non-professionals should have a greater say.

Alongside these developments, a working party which had been set up by the planning branch of the DES in 1970 set in train feasibility projects which were directed at measuring attainment in mathematics. Reading was the other field of concern. In April 1974 Reg Prentice, then Secretary of State, referred to the Assessment of Performance Unit (APU). Its terms of reference were spelled out in an annexe to the fall of the Conservatives and the return of a Labour government in the General Election of October 1974.

There had been an expansionist White Paper in 1972 (*Education: A Framework for Expansion*), but the rise in oil prices in 1972, a miners' strike in the same year, followed by a further strike in 1974 led to the fall of the Conservatives and the return of a Labour government in the General Election of October 1974.

By 1979 the Conservative Party manifesto found it useful to refer to children's performance in school: 'We shall promote higher standards of achievement in basic skills. The Government's Assessment of Performance Unit will set national standards in reading, writing and arithmetic, monitored by tests worked out with teachers and others and applied locally by Education Authorities' (p. 25).

Although the APU had a fairly long life – it changed its title and purpose in 1990 – it did not set national standards. Nevertheless both main political parties found it useful at a time when the call for consumer control over education became louder. The APU itself was from time to time referred to in language which had an inevitable echo of the lobby of those who called publicly for higher standards (DES 1980):

Everyone wants to raise educational standards. But how do we know what the educational standards are? How do we measure standards in education? How can we monitor progress? There is not enough information available at present. There is plenty of hearsay, hunch and opinion. The last ten years have seen changes in school organisation and curriculum. We need to be able to monitor the consequences in children's performance in school. We need to know how our schools can service the changing needs of children and society.

In its early days the APU was criticized because it was feared that it would force an artificial accountability on to schools and teachers. There was concern, too, about so-called blanket testing. Above all there was a fear that the APU was a DES instrument which would lead to the introduction of an assessment-led curriculum. This would, it was feared, come into being through LEAs using the APU framework and in that way bringing into operation their own core curriculum. The instrument for this would be the Local Education Authority Schools Item Bank (LEASIB). This came to little. No link between national and LEA testing emerged. A question remained unanswered: why did the DES, if that was its intention, not create a policy – or at least underwrite a set of priorities – for the APU? Was it that in the end the APU was not needed by the DES as an instrument with which to influence curriculum policy (Gipps and Goldstein in 1983. 166)? Yes, because central government was moving rapidly in the 1980s towards new requirements about educational standards, imposed by law and intended to be managed uniformly in each school and locality. This was in line with one of the tenets of the DES, described by Ball (1990) as a belief in the efficacy of assessment-led control and typified by an attitude which he described as reformist old-humanism (p. 211).

Assessment and home influence

The home and the family can enhance or diminish what a school produces. If the quality which is promised is to be consistent, the ways in which it works have to maximize home support or to compensate for what is missing. In planning how to guarantee consistent quality the manager is entitled to remind parents of the well known connection between home and school. One commentary on attainment – but less well-known than the work of the APU – emerged in work carried out by Gilbert Peaker, HMI. Working with the Plowden Committee, he seemed to confirm that the patterns fixed in early childhood influence everything which came later. He added (Peaker 1971:5–6):

The evidence from the study about the importance of background and early learning strengthens the case for nursery education, particularly to supplement the resources of the home where the latter are meagre. On the other hand the relatively small part played by the teaching variables seems at first sight to be a warning against expecting very much. There are however three reasons why this may be unduly pessimistic. In the first place it is hard to get anything like a full measure of the effects of teaching, chiefly because all methods of measurement hitherto suggested are themselves inhibiting. Secondly the range between the best and the worst teachers is small in comparison between the best and the worst parents, chiefly because very bad schools are not allowed to exist. In the third place, since everybody goes to school from the age of 5, the existence of schools is part of the general background of the study which compares the effect of different schools. But the case for nursery education rests not on the difference between various nursery schools, but on the difference between the effects of some nursery schooling and no nursery schooling. In 'parental circumstances' the literacy of the home is the largest constituent. For each of us the major accomplishment of our lives occurs in the early days when we learn to talk. We learn by imitating our parents and we learn well or badly according to our parents' command of language. This explains why 'literacy of the home' plays the major part.

How can managers take account of home influence? Not to give it weight makes attempts at universal assessment spurious but there is no certainty that it is a factor which means the same thing in every school. Whether teaching can outweigh home was a question which preceded the Plowden Report and it was one which remained unresolved after the researches of Rutter (which are referred to in Ch. 9). What weight, if the home accounts for a great deal of a child's educational growth, should the manager allow for the relationship between the teacher and child? In addition, where should that weight be placed? The quality statement has to be specific and has to refer to what the teacher does in the classroom. In particular, when the focus moves away from the background of children outside school and on to the classroom itself the manager should take note of the abiding lessons which were learned in the research programme of Observational Research and Classroom Learning Evaluation (ORACLE). This threw considerable light on teacher–child relationships, but Galton and Simon (1980) found that, for example, the use of more open-ended questions did not of themselves guarantee greater effectiveness in learning. Open-ended questioning needed time and the teacher had to organize the classroom and the teaching time which was available in order to allow for lengthy discussions. The conditions which were created in this reordering of teaching led to the relationship with pupils changing. But teachers had choices: they could increase the amount of whole-class teaching and while this increased the amount of teacher–pupil interaction it still left some pupils mainly passive. (This was one of the reasons for Plowden having said that there had been too much whole-class teaching.) As an alternative individualization was favoured. If teachers sought to increase individualization through discovery learning they could try to intensify the probing and questioning nature of their own role but their style, found Galton and Simon, was in the majority of cases still didactic rather than exploratory. Individualization of learning needed a range of intellectual and social capacities on the part of the children, as well as appropriate resources from the teacher. There had to be tolerance and a willingness to listen. The sequencing of tasks was crucial (Galton and Simon 1980:205–10) and attention to this and to other details must be part of those activities, under a teacher's control, which make up the specification for guaranteeing quality of learning.

If the rigidity of too much specificity is to be avoided, the manager must remember that their study led Galton and Simon to conclude that the practice of different teaching styles should be encouraged. They felt that a correct balance should be sought between different forms of organization which would permit an increase in the use of more interactions but would still need to take account of an individual's personal qualities and the context in which the teaching was done (1980:212). To lose the weight of teachers' personal contributions would diminish the value of what a school guarantees to provide. But in this the quality which is assured has to be on the positive side.

Reducing the guesswork

The personal qualities of teachers and the context in which school work is carried out matter to a child's quality of learning. The responsibility for managing these factors effectively has to hinge on a combination of four factors: more effective learning can be expected if home conditions are favourable, if teachers are skilled in using different approaches, if the school's physical context is right and if enough time is available for the teacher to do the job properly.

In contrast, the language of the political manifesto does not take account of variables: 'we *shall* promote higher standards' in much the same way as it was said that the APU '*will* set national standards'. These are not sensitive expressions of intent but the language of that kind of expectation and requirement which came increasingly into view in the time running up to the 1988 Education Reform Act.

Between the Plowden Report and 1988 there had been a series of moves towards stating requirements. One of the broadest-ranging of these came with the open publication of reports about schools by HMI. Instead of being confidential, HMI reports had, from January 1983, to be considered by LEAs in open committee. When inspectors pointed to matters which needed attention, time was allowed for improvements to take place. And a short period within that time was set for local authorities to indicate what they intended to do.

To study the way in which reports are couched and to look at the ways in which schools and local authorities respond gives an idea of how the process of assessment has expanded since the 1980s and of how education has become more openly accountable – in terms which are exact rather than a matter of guessing how they should be interpreted.

All HMI reports cover uniform ground: the organization of a school, its curriculum, its accommodation and its physical resources. The school's internal community is made a matter of comment as too is the connection with the communities of the outside world. The governors of schools had always been given an oral report by HMI before the written version was published. This prior knowledge is still provided, with publication following on. It gives headteachers and governors a chance to marshal their thoughts and in particular it gives the head the chance to make clear what he or she will be doing with staff colleagues in response to specific comments.

Not surprisingly heads sometimes question or rebut the views of inspectors. Equally unsurprisingly their governors support them in those rebuttals when the moment comes for them to make their views known to the local authority. The public part of the response tends to concentrate on the quantifiable aspects of each report. And, as often happens, when HMI point to a deficiency in accommodation or books or equipment, the criticism is passed on by the school to the local authority. But not everything which lies at the heart of quality is a question of buildings and money. There are other matters: some parts of the curriculum are not covered by appropriately trained teachers, some opportunities for connecting different parts of the curriculum are not taken, too little response is asked for from pupils, too little oral work and too little classroom interchange takes place between teacher and pupil, schemes of work are sometimes ineffective and occasionally appear not to exist at all. Often they need to be brought up to date.

Heads volunteer to their governors information about how they are tackling each issue. Their reports occasionally refer to individual members of staff who have long been at the school and who are soon to retire or to the appointment of new, freshly trained graduates who will show their true worth once they have settled down. Such qualitative comments about staff experience and about the organization of improvement are not left simply at the level of comment. There usually lies behind them discussion and exchange between the head and his or her senior colleagues with the inspector or inspectors who wrote the report. There has in the past also been a detailed working through of what can and what will be done between the school and a local authority's own advisers and inspectors.

In the publicly reported parts of any inspection and the response to it, these internal discussions are generally regarded as professional and, without defining that word, better left to the headteacher, other teachers, inspectors and advisers. They are an essential part of management. They involve accurate information and provide a review which has to be given a structured response within a limited time. They form a proper part of the process of defining and assuring quality and of setting out the steps by which it is to be reached.

Feedback from assessment into organizational change

HMI reports are a well-documented and long-running example of how assessments go through the stages of report, discussion, acceptance, positive response and improvement. Rebuttals and negative responses are few. And there was until recent years often some good to be gained from reports in terms of extra funding, capital improvements and, always, the chance of sympathy and understanding.

In large schools heads and their senior colleagues (deputies, heads of department, heads of upper and lower schools) manage the response and the feedback in ways which they regard as part of their normal duties despite the fact that few job descriptions include the management of responses to external review. If matters need to be improved, they are discussed with the staff at large and, also, with individual teachers who have already been involved by the inspectors in an analysis of how they themselves need to change or improve their work. In small schools the same principles apply although there is often little opportunity for the head to distance himself or herself from other teachers. Without distancing, objectivity is difficult, as too is the exploration of genuine criticism. Nevertheless small schools are expected to respond as constructively as any other to the plus and minus points of inspectors' reports.

Behind the management of external assessment lie unwritten rules: to what is reported as being good, everyone makes a modest acknowledgement. To what is less good each school in the first place is expected to rely on itself in making things better. This assumption used always to be made by local authorities about heads and it was assumed that heads would pass this on to their colleagues. Self-awareness, self-correction and self-improvement are so obviously the part of being a good teacher that there is no need to draw attention to it.

Behind this there can be responses which amount to unjustified self-satisfaction or reluctance to criticize oneself. There can be an unwillingness or incapacity to improve oneself. If so, there are few if any corrective steps which can be taken by those who are finally responsible. This means that the assumption that self-awareness and self-improvement operate automatically is a weakness in schemes of management. Some will argue that what is needed is the knowledge that there are sanctions as well as rewards in the offing. This does, however, have the difficulty of over-simplification. In the end, the tell-them-where-they-stand approach is not a substitute for the effective management of self-awareness.

Attention to the importance and complexities of the teacher's self – particularly in primary schools – has been drawn by Nias (1989). Her analysis of the teacher's position as a person first and then as a teacher, her disentangling of teachers' dependence and interdependence and of the significance of their relationships to each other as adults, underlines the difficulty of missing out the prime position of self awareness in any school-wide strategy of improvement and development. Her exploration of what it means 'to feel like a teacher' suggests that this feeling emerges from having

learnt to feel relaxed, whole, natural in the exercise of one's job and that these states in turn rely upon a sense of being in control (of oneself, one's pupils and their learning, one's environment, one's destiny) which enables one's relationship with children to be responsible and loving. Yet these states are attained in the face of endemic dilemmas, tensions, uncertainties, inconsistencies, paradoxes and contradictions (Nias 1989:201).

Almost as though to admit that inconsistencies and dilemmas are, in the end, insoluble and unmanageable, HMI reports show that there is no final stage to which matters will move if that which needs improvement has not, after a lapse of time, changed for the better. More usually the response, if there is no clear movement forward, is that of noting that certain matters are better or that at least some attempts at improvement have been put in hand. Things are then left – or so they have been until now. But if they are to guarantee a stated quality of education, schools cannot risk inconsistency in one vital area. They must, without taking the humanity out of teaching, reduce to a minimum the degree to which tensions, inconsistencies and dilemmas are deleterious to teaching. In the short term, admittedly, it is doubtful whether anything better can be achieved in the management of feedback even when the long-range effect of inefficiency is described in terms of a poor market image, a drop in popularity in the eyes of the parents, a loss of pupils and a loss of the funding which accompanies pupils. Admittedly bad teachers can now be moved out of a school more readily than in the 1970s. But it is generally achieved at high cost (and with the use of euphemisms such as early retirement in the interests of the service) and always on the basis of individual cases. This may change if government advice about the wider use of existing powers to delay the payment of increments to poor teachers hardens into a policy which employers might welcome. And it would require a clear use on the other side of a 'fast track' policy of extra allowances and discretionary payments for outstanding teachers.

A more positive management tool is the rescue and retraining of teachers who are given the chance to rehabilitate themselves or to change direction in their teaching. Here, in whatever way the disciplining or the stimulating of different qualities in a teacher is handled, the definition of standards and of the effect of assessment in improving education must become more than a matter of conscience and good fortune.

Knowing what supports progress

Management can alter the organization of teaching. Where that change depends on simple funding it is more straightforward than a change which asks teachers to achieve some previously unattained expertness. And managing an improvement of organization is more straightforward in a secondary school with 60 teachers or a primary school with 16 teachers than in a primary school with a staff of only 3 or 4. What supports or holds back progress in individual parts of the curriculum works more easily – but not necessarily better – when the institution is large enough to make its different parts visible. That visibility enables managers to identify what is weak and what is strong.

This process of identifying what needs attention is normally entrusted to the head. The action which is taken depends on his or her capacity for what is sometimes described as instructional leadership. In working through the task the head's tone can be expected to be a major factor in influencing the school's organizational climate even though it was said as recently as 1990 that there had still been no large-scale investigation of, for example, the primary school head in British schools (Saran and Trafford 1990:101). More tangibly the input of the chief manager can be analysed on the basis of the success or failure of any strategy which is initiated in reorganizing an institution (Ranson 1990: Ch. 3).

In the broadest terms this brings into play influences on the part of the manager which relate to, for instance, a vision of educational merit. Outside the manager's control lie the influences of demography and financial constraint. When both sets of influence are brought together in the work of an individual school it comes down to the number of pupils or students who will be affected by change, to the ease or difficulty of winning arguments about educational quality and to the capacity to attract additional money.

How the manager works inside such a framework requires agreements to be made. How that is done depends on sensitive negotiation. This in turn involves people exchanging support for mutual gain. It involves give and take. Nevertheless in the management of schools – and particularly of primary schools – negotiation receives less attention than the exercise of the head's leadership and the process of carrying out top-down consultation (Coulson 1990:106–7):

Paternalism remains in many schools but many heads favour a management style which combines direction with consultation. The relationship between headship and school culture is a reciprocal one. Hence, though a diversity of headteacher styles can be effective, certain personal attributes and competencies are associated with successful headship. Paramount among these is the ability to engender the commitment of other members of the school to shared goals and values. Since this is achieved predominantly through the head's personal example, primary headship reflects a fusion of the personal and the professional.

When one reverts to the original question of how a school should organize its teaching against the background of knowing what it is that specifically supports or holds back progress in individual aspects of the curriculum, the answer is unsatisfying. Good management depends upon the personality of the head and, *pari passu*, of the senior staff. It also depends upon the readiness of teachers to be stimulated to take another view of their teaching and to alter both their aims and their practices, upon there being enough time for teachers to retrain or to re-plan and upon there being money to hire substitute staff to take over the teaching role while permanent staff get on with the task of co-operating in, and launching, new initiatives.

This approach leaves out of account the question of whether pupils' education will be set back while teachers take time to define their objectives and to lay new teaching plans. It leaves out of account, too, the understanding and agreement of parents who may look upon staff training as yet another hour a week lost from their children's education.

Managing predictable and unpredictable changes

Predictable changes are those, typically, which accompany modifications of well-established public examinations. When secondary schools and colleges of further education plan the time and other resources for courses which lead to examinations and qualifications there is a near-certainty about the repeated pattern of what is achieved each year. Thus General Certificate of Secondary Education (GCSE) and A level can be planned for securely, as can Business and Technical Education Council (BTEC) and City and Guilds of London (CGLI) courses.

On the other hand, the outcomes of the Technical and Vocational Education Initiative (TVEI) and Alternative Supplementary (AS) levels are both less certain and more open to argument about their significance. Such evaluations as have been attempted of TVEI, for example, have stopped short at the end of the compulsory school attendance period at the age of 16. We lack both information and accurate judgement about the effectiveness of the transition to further education and of the bringing together of academic and quasi-vocational aims. Research has been promised but until that arrives, in the words of Colin Morgan: 'we do not yet know how young adults in occupations, further education, on YTS or as unemployed connect their perceived abilities (or lack of them) with earlier formal education . . . until there is good qualitative data on this issue it must remain an act of blind faith that schools and colleges are influential in establishing social and occupational identities' (Saran and Trafford 1990:94).

In AS levels there is a comparable uncertainty; Jewell (1990) was able to say that although 47 per cent of those who were entered for AS levels in 1989 failed to reach their targets, the idea of a new examination which was worth half an A level was nevertheless attractive. He saw it, as did others, as a way of broadening the range of post-16 choice in the curriculum. The same argument, but again untested, supported the initiative of the Associated Examining Board in making a post-GCSE one year ~ertificate available before AS and A level. Also the introduction in mathematics of modular examinations and a series of equivalences (Mathematics in Education and Industry) was in a comparable position. At the introductory stage the equivalences which were suggested were less important than the intention of establishing a modular qualification at the age of 18.

To handle change even within well-founded parts of the system requires that managers should both open up new ground and probe previously unexamined certainties. As attempts to look at matters anew, those examination initiatives which have been described shared the promise of what was, in the early 1980s, offered in the Educational Counselling and Credit Transfer Information Service (ECCTIS). This might have established in Britain an approach to accreditation and advancement comparable to that of the transfer into higher education from US high schools – flexible, aimed at improving predictability and well suited to the exercise of choice. It proved to be a difficult innovation to publicize and for which to attract broad support. It was well managed but, like TVEI or AS level, it was not without its critics.

Each of the examination changes in GCSE or AS was described at the same time as radical, threatening and complicated and also as conservative, ill-thought-out and impractical. Those inside education who managed them had to accept that reluctance expressed through the media could lie behind those local and individual difficulties which were brought forward by school and college staffs. And perhaps the only moral was that managers need to be aware of the way in which the outside world can seem sometimes to legitimize an internal lack of enthusiasm.

To overcome or take account of that reluctance may seem to need a choice between prescription from the top or of arguing the way through to a consensus. To achieve the latter might mean, with all the recognized chances of misunderstanding, that every member of staff in either a school or a college is to be seen as a co-manager. But to pursue consensus can mean that the head or principal cannot be certain that he or she can, in the end, manage the school or college in such a way that it will provide what is required by law or regulation. It may, admittedly, not ultimately lead to a school or college foundering but there will nevertheless be a call for the skill of – and the allocation of time to – management by diplomacy. Only that can allow an organization to withstand shocks and amend its position in small details while at the same time it stands its main ground and makes headway against unforeseen problems.

The importance of managers moving from the predictable to the unpredictable and responding to what has not been foreseen has not been given enough attention – nor in the analysis of their shifts of power has enough significance been attached to the effect of those shifts (Saran and Trafford 1990:149–55). But if new management does not take account of the unintended consequences of action, it fails. As things stand, the managers of new schemes, surrounded by national publicity and media debates, should be aware that unexpected transformations may arise. And in handling large changes managers cannot be sure who will influence them the most or which argument will be the weightiest.

However good a management plan is, however accurate and detailed the description is of those steps which have to be taken in order to guarantee quality, a parent is unlikely to be reassured if a school can be thrown off balance by unexpected events – whether they are opportunities or crises. Even at the simpler level of day-to-day management there is a comparable pull on any manager between different interests and understandings. In particular, differences in the interests and understanding shown by teachers call for continual sensitivity of management. In analyses such as those of Noel Entwistle (1987:97) descriptions of contrasting characteristics of formal and informal teachers are known to those who manage schools and colleges. They know that they must take account of and make allowances for teacher differences and they will agree with Entwistle (1987:101) when he summarizes one aspect of the process of managing learning:

Approaches to learning are influenced by assessment procedures, by dependency on the teacher, by the time available, and by the quality of teaching. Techniques have been devised to help pupils to become more aware of their own learning strategies and also to reflect on their own experience. Thus a deep approach depends on the teacher providing a suitable context and the pupils taking more responsibility for their own learning strategies.

He goes on to underline the fact that a teacher's own personality and style of thinking will lead to a preference for a particular way of teaching but that it is important for teachers to avoid adopting a style which will create difficulties for pupils who flourish only when they are taught in different ways – but ways which are congenial to themselves.

Exactly how learning is influenced by differing modes of assessment will become clearer when more is known about the effect of standard attainment targets. In guaranteeing quality of learning it is as important for the manager to reconcile differing styles of learning and teaching with the need to reach specified learning targets as it is for him or her to make sure that everyone knows what is going on. In other words, the manager has not only to be sure that members of staff will recognize each others' differences and will work, within those differences, to create and implement an agreed management plan but also to be sure that parents understand that differences are important.

Despite the tightness of a quality specification, it is unlikely that any body of governors or more than a few parents would expect a school to organize its teaching in a uniform way. But when a parent wants reassurance that his or her child will progress equally fast in future years or will accelerate the pace of learning there is bound to be a comparison in that parent's mind between what happened in his or her own education and what is happening now. There is also likely to be a comparison between the ways in which different children in the same family have been taught and between the ways in which it is reported that the children of friends or neighbours have been taught.

In responding the manager must show that a school is providing an education which is consistent with national requirements and that a certain level of quality is guaranteed in *this* particular school. And however skilful the manager may feel that he or she is in the process of reconciling and giving rein to healthy internal differences in the school's teaching capacity, the outside world must always be satisfied at the level of the individual child and the individual family.

It would be regrettable if that satisfaction was bought at the cost of ignoring the difference between deep and superficial learning (Entwistle 1987:60). Nevertheless the temptation is undeniable – to match the surface approach with a series of assessments concerned with a type of education which differs sharply from that which requires depth. Indeed, in keeping with an end-of-the century view of education as a matter of enterprise and effectiveness is Entwistle's third category of approach (strategic), marked out by an intention to obtain the highest possible grades, using previous examinations/tests to predict questions, being alert to 'cues about marking schemes', organizing time and distributing effort to greatest effect and ensuring that the conditions and materials for studying are appropriate.

The manager must make it clear to parents that he or she is responsible for deep, surface and for strategic learning. What is provided will be different for different ages and stages of pupil and student. It will differ, too, according to the individual capacity of the learner, but it will at all stages provide a consistent quality of learning. Account will have to be taken of what Neville Bennett described in terms of pupils' quality of attention and differing levels of comprehension (in Entwistle 1985). He pointed out that problems of matching learning tasks with ability levels are severe among the top and bottom thirds of the ability range. Along these lines there are those whose studies underline the argument that pupils of lower ability should have less taught to them and should have it taught 'redundantly to the point of overlearning and proceeding in small steps that they can master without undue cognitive strain' (p. 260).

To make sure that the assessment of each pupil's attainment is fed through for the next key stage calls for routine management efficiency. To determine which pupils need to be taught repetitively and slowly is nothing new. Explaining this to parents is something to which most teachers, at all stages, are accustomed. But when the manager has to explain to parents that their children are travelling at different speeds because their teachers have, perhaps in contrast to previous years, different styles of teaching and that further differences of pace are made necessary by the children's differing ability levels, it will need patience and trust, as well as understanding, on the part of the parent.

Will he or she have to digest, too, the fact that despite the virtual standardization of attainments which was promised as a result of the Education Reform Act, differences from teacher to teacher and class to class may still leave what appears to be an unexplained hole in a child's education? No: in a scheme which guarantees quality there has to be consistency.

Managing a consistent message

Although schools cannot be managed so as to exhibit uniformity in the approach to teaching and learning, there remains the task of making sure that parents receive information about and form an impression of the school which is consistent, regardless of who it is who last spoke to them. It has to be a matter for management that teachers do not contradict each other.

More important than what they say is how they act. If a school has to organize repeated staff sessions simply to make sure that a consistent image of its activities is transmitted, it will be unlikely to be treated seriously unless activity and obligation go hand in hand with statements of purpose. Good work ought to speak for itself without the stage management of meetings and votes but good work which is part of a compact about quality assurance has to be tightly organized.

There need be no over-zealous concern with image but Duffett's comment (Everard 1986:102–4) should not be ignored when he says that heads appear to have no difficulty with parochial identity but find it hard to define a corporate image. Whether this is a sufficient response to the demand for consistent (and constructive) statements to be made about an organization becomes more clear as the power of parent choice makes itself felt. Since the first publication of school prospectuses (Education Act 1980) that choice has come to mean more and more. As key-stage assessments become universal and as the word about their significance goes around, parents use other sources of cross-reference in their wish to find what they regard as the truth. Managers and those with whom they work need to reinforce the description of what a school does with an openness about the steps which they take to reach the level and quality which they promise. And the effectiveness of each step must be capable of being traced back to the teacher or manager who is responsible.

The other sources to which parents turn will almost certainly be made up of reports about behaviour, discipline and the setting of personal standards. It seems unlikely that what schools simply say about themselves will satisfy the questioning parent: every boast of being a friendly and caring 'family-atmosphere' school may be cancelled out by anecdotes of harshness, ignorance or insensitivity.

Parents want two types of information: one about the personal and social way in which their child is emerging at school and the other about what the school can do to correct or compensate. In face of this no school finds it easy to turn to the parent with the statement that children are only as good as their parents wish them to be. Although a school might wish to make that comment and ask why parents do not set a better example, they themselves are vulnerable to the same question. As institutions they are expected to set an example and if a school accepts this it has to look for the right lead from each individual teacher.

Social learning has important implications for individual teachers. Thus Docking (1980:55) underlines the message that 'unacceptable behaviour which has been learned outside school can be modified inside school through observational learning. This is why it is so desirable for teachers to avoid adopting primitive attitudes towards children and instead to present themselves deliberately as models of socially desirable behaviour'.

The alternative is to attempt to ensure that all teachers share between themselves and transmit to others (parents and children) a single ethos. Each teacher's personal values are then reinforced by those of the staff as a whole (Docking 1980:221). This requires a defined and consistently monitored staff policy which in turn can make sense to those who observe and provide partnership for the school outside its walls.

New relationships among the partners

Past partnerships consisted of the churches and central government, of central government and LEAs and, for the past forty years, those two together with teachers' associations and local authority associations. These broadening steps took account of organized interests, served by powerful secretariats and made up of parties with an interest in funding (whether in central taxes or the then local rates), in terms of teacher salaries and in terms of capital assets. The question which was constantly addressed was that of who really controlled state education. Later on to the scene came governors (National Association of Governors and Managers), parents (well served by the Advisory Centre for Education, who have also consistently given a high profile to governors) and more recently still lobbies with more specific aims such as those who concentrate on special education needs, on gifted children and on minority groups.

To manage a partnership at school level consisted, until the latter part of the 1980s, of a head getting on with the chairman of governors. The shift in responsibility, particularly for the curriculum, to head-teachers and governors in the 1986 Education (No. 2) Act meant that governors became more than simply the nominal approvers of matters which the headteacher attended to on their behalf. The same legislation gave more prominence to parents. The piecemeal and isolated efforts of local authorities and their schools in the two decades before the 1980, 1986 and 1988 Acts were given official approval. Local authorities themselves lost their role as those who had previously been regarded as having a large say in curriculum, in staff allocations and in the appointment of headteachers.

Although there is in some schools still a tendency to regard governors as being a body who should be kept at arm's length from the management of the place, their role as the representatives of the community is inarguable. Important, too, is their capacity – if they are thus equipped – to bring individual members' special professional skills to bear on long-term planning. They are required to approve and therefore to know about the curriculum. And they are permitted by regulation to know the outcome of regular assessment of individual year groups of pupils.

Four concerns lie at the heart of the relationship between heads, other teachers, governors and parents. These are the definition of where the school now stands and the direction in which it plans to go, the managing of resources and the process of matching outcomes with the allocation of those resources, the managing of the autonomy of the school in a manner which allows it to compete healthily with those other schools to which parents might alternatively send their children and, fourthly, managing the relationship with those services and people who can support a school. The latter includes librarians, curriculum advisers, educational psychologists, educational welfare services, social services and community health services.

The broadening of the network for some heads only reaches (and then stops at) the relationship with governors. Thus there is a visible and regular contact with governors and a less visible and regular contact with the professional supporters. This is partly because not all services are regularly needed (psychologists and community health workers, for example) and partly because external advisers are thought to be limited in their usefulness. When much of the curriculum is shaped centrally by the Secretary of State is there scope for anything other than the expression of a very local interpretation? Thus Everard (1986:208) comments, in connection with the development of school management:

Not only is there a dearth of advisers who are competent and practised process consultants but their inspectorial role acts as a major constraint. They are widely perceived as 'task consultants' working on concrete and recognisable problems such as the teaching of reading, the evaluation of pupil performance or curriculum development. They are not perceived as people to be involved in helping the school with less obvious problems like its underlying decision-making and problem-solving procedures or in the processes of departmental and staff meetings, of communication and of the exercise of power and authority in the school. Yet these areas of organisational life are central to school effectiveness and difficult to work on unaided.

This leaves out of account the traditional role of advisers in reviewing each school and in keeping the local authority informed. The relationship between inspectors, advisers and local authorities inevitably changes under the requirements of the Education (Schools) Act 1992. But there are still three questions: if a school is examining its present position and deciding in which direction to go in future, does this do away with the need for external review? Should a school devise its own review and, within that, should the processes of school review and staff appraisal be integrated or separate? Third, how is school autonomy to be squared with its accountability to the outside world?

The manager who underplays his or her use of any member of those who should be consulted about the condition and running of the school risks losing a potentially significant contribution to management planning, to the continuous process of monitoring and to maintaining its assurance of quality.

Diplomacy

In contrast to the grouping, in the years before the Education Reform Act, of external supporters as those who fell into the category of carers, parents, governors, sometimes employers and often that difficult-to-define entity called the community, the essential outsiders whom the manager must serve are nowadays more specific. Each age-group of pupils has a different set of parents behind it. Some of the differences depend on which levels of assessment come next and how the earlier assessments of individual children have turned out. Other differences relate to short-term changes in parents' preoccupations or longer-term expectations which are shaped by public debate and media exposure.

Equally specific in their interest in assisting or questioning a school are those governors, first, who have the skill and experience to look objectively at the use of resources. Their objectivity may be expected to cover an interest in different per capita expenditures on children of different ages. Second, if learning begins at home, those who believe in the particular value of early years education may want to see more spent on 4- and 5-year-olds than on 9-year-olds. Third, those governors who think that the ability to read is the most important part of primary education may want to see resources being concentrated on the teaching of reading. Fourth, governors, again, who represent the parents of children who are gauche, disturbed or disabled may, to different degrees, prefer to see a school's management plan as a scheme which has a predominant interest in equalizing chances.

The list of governors' interests can be long: some want a painless transition between primary and secondary schools, others want to look at post-16 education as a period of constructive and shock-free change-over. Others believe in the value of education up to the age of 18 but will be unable to make up their minds as to whether this be a matter of part-time or full-time education and training. They may also believe in breadth of study at the 16–19 year stage, but, again, without much knowledge of what might prevent this.

In giving an assurance of quality, a school must satisfy its governors that each interest, each type of education which leads into or which is led into by the school has been taken into account when the *method* of securing that quality has been planned. Each support service of education – social services, education welfare, educational psychologists – must be involved and each aspect of community life which works through or depends on a healthy school must be remembered. Everyone who is involved has to contribute to the delivery of quality and each must see that every supporter, agency or ally of education can benefit from the trust which comes from truthful assurances of quality. Those who provide teachers with their professional education are part of this network – not least those who wish to combine the vocational training of teachers with an involvement in community education and a steadily broadening general education.

In facing a considerable variety of external relations, the diplomatic skill of managers goes beyond the capacity not to offend. A more positive view is that they should be able to persuade other people to adopt points of view which are sometimes very different from those with which they normally feel comfortable. A manager has to handle this kind of conversion against a background of different circumstances and influences with one common theme, namely that of improving the school or college and of proving to the world that it can provide a high quality of learning.

Improvement can be treated as a matter of overall strategic development or of smaller-scale and discrete changes. Overall strategies are not part and parcel of most people's working lives. Governors who face such changes under the influence of a head or principal who propounds a large vision of new opportunities may feel worried until they can see what the institution will have to undertake in detailed matters of organization and planning. Teachers, too, are often more consistent about coping with change in their own curricular discipline or in their own field of traditional responsibility outside the curriculum than with all-encompassing changes which affect departments, subjects or levels with which they are not directly familiar.

The scale of improvement

How successfully the manager will engineer both overall and discrete improvements will depend on whether he or she makes it clear on what scale change is to take place. Success will depend too on it being clear whether changes are emerging from open debate, from the manager's own mind or from outside sources. Of these the first two may be linked, so that what is originally a product of the manager's mind is handled in such a way as to become a matter of consensus. The third – change from the outside – will only have the appearance of external imposition if fellow-managers (staff, governors, parents) have not been prepared for it. The most damaging aspect of imposed change emerges when those who are responsible for implementing it have not struggled to understand and adapt to it. For staff, parents and governors to internalize the implications of change before the procedures or mechanics of improvement start is something for which managers must allow time and assistance. Questions must be stimulated and answered and both sides of any question must be acknowledged even if they are not deeply debated. In all this, successful management needs a good mind. This, however, may be regarded differently by those who manage and those who are managed. If there appears to be a gap of reason or intellect between the manager and other people, suspicion and a reluctance to co-operate can set in.

If the distance between a manager and other people is seen not as a matter of thinking but as a matter of personality, there is little chance of any allowance being made for this except in a corporate management style which is based on debate among equals and on the emergence – rather than the fabrication – of consensus. The effects on management of an over-strong personality are diminished when there is a sharing of responsibility between all parties. Otherwise, insensitive management will stand in the way of parity.

Corporate management can also bridge other gaps. In addition to differences of mind, differences of intellectual approach and differences of personality, a distance between manager and managed can spring from features inside the organization itself; it may be hierarchical and formal – and priests and acolytes are intended to stand apart from each other. It may be rooted in a neighbourhood whose social milieu demands that distances be maintained between different levels of those who are functionaries. If traditions of difference in social environment do not make shared management acceptable to the outside world, the head is unlikely to work smoothly with those who expect internal management to be a matter of direction rather than discussion.

Attitudes

Just as attempts to reduce distance can be tackled in more than one way, so dissonance of attitudes can be taken into account by different methods. Again, the management of acquiescence is unlike the management of commitment. The manager must decide whether commitment on the part of those with whom he or she works stems from relief that long-awaited improvements are finally being put in hand, relief that the changes which are in progress are not daunting or relief that what is planned is not as severe as what was expected. The acquiescence of those who put improvements in train has comparably diverse origins: quiet-lifers and non-stirrers-up differ little in their outward behaviour from those whose previous experiences have made them into resigned but dogged workers.

To manage those who are committed is not the same as to manage simple enthusiasts: the former are likely to see their own way of doing things but nevertheless act on the basis of sharing the wish to put improvements into action. Enthusiasts may be less well informed, less aware of alternatives and potentially briefer in their loyalties. But committed or enthusiastic, each represents one positive aspect of an institution.

Attitudes which are less likely to assist dynamic movement are those of diffidence (which carries the same innocence as acquiescence but which may conceal valuable and yet untapped strength) and the dubious twins of scepticism and cynicism. Well-managed scepticism is healthy and a manager who has a sense of reality must cultivate an appropriate level of wry laughter. Too much scepticism on the other hand turns into the corrosion of cynicism. For a manager to try to eliminate cynicism may lead to working out how long the cynical colleague or governor will stay connected with the school. All that the manager can do is to try to insulate other people – but that, too, can carry the stigma of paternalism. The effect of a cynical teacher or a cynical governor on others within the network can not only throw doubts on the values which a school proclaims and on the quality of learning which it promises but can also call into question the bond of loyalty between those who regard themselves as a school's allies.

The strength of external alliances needs to be regularly assessed by the head. They may be measurable in a range of attitudes (acquiescence, commitment, relief, enthusiasm, diffidence, scepticism) or they may be regarded as ties whose strength and weakness rest on feelings – of understanding for, sympathy with and warmth towards the manager or distrust either of him or her as a person or of the management methods which are used. Self-delusion in assessing these can be ruinous.

Rational planning depends on the capacity to reconcile attitudes, to maintain values and to remember differences. Inside a school a comparable bringing together of directions is necessary: the separateness of the curriculum has to be managed at the same time as cross-curriculum links are organized. The academic curriculum has to be managed alongside a school's pastoral organization. Ideally they will feed each other. A good deal of a school's pastoral organization takes account of a pupil or a student in the process of personal development. There can be no easy distinction between personal development in the terms in which it is seen at school and personal development at home. In both contexts it will not be self-conscious. The style of family life is often reflected in the geographical neighbourhood of the home, and the home, along with the type of influence it exercises on a young person's personal development, takes some of its colouring from that physical neighbourhood. But the family and its members are part of a range of communities as well as part of a neighbourhood. They bring to bear upon each other the influence and values of the community of work and play, of youth and age and of ambition, of satisfaction or of failure.

Sharing knowledge

Because governors and parents bring a considerable range of experience to bear on the school the good manager needs to allow space for their influences to work. Providing that these influences are benign the manager must trust them to work their way through to the school in their own way. But the important message which the manager does need to make clear is that five spheres of activity (curriculum; cross-curriculum; pastoral; personal education at home and school; home, neighbourhood and community effects) need a strong network of support and understanding from the outside.

The unofficial but major providers in several of these spheres are parents and governors. In return for their support they need a response. The best way for a school to do this is by giving a properly worked out assurance of quality. In other words, managers need to acknowledge the assistance they receive and to pay something back, i.e. 'schools must be held accountable not only for educating their pupils but for informing their communities on a continuous basis about the content, process and practice that are central to curriculum, about personal and social education and about education objectives, programmes and performance' (Sayer and Williams 1989:155).

Sharing knowledge with parents, governors and the community has a counterpart among the professionals. Within that framework lie those who were responsible for education before and after the child's or young person's time at school. Playgroups and nurseries are always taken into account by well-run infant schools and departments. The infant and first school stage has always been treated as formative by junior schools and departments and by middle schools. The hand-over from primary to secondary has an uncertain past but is nowadays generally better organized. The development of thorough record card systems, the evolution of records of achievement and the systematic manner in which assessments are now required to affect the next state of a pupil's schooling – each of these is a sign that the mid-school link is well managed.

The hand-over to post-16 education is not difficult to manage if the prime information is that of academic achievement. But neither examination results at 16 nor records of achievement based on the national timetable of assessment can take full account of personal, social and moral aspects of schooling. Even so, sixth forms and colleges of further education (FE) have in general developed a method of working closely with those who have provided education up to 16. Efforts must be made by both national and local managers to make sure that the quality of that link is not lost when FE is, in its funding, separated from schools.

It used to be employers to whom it was difficult to pass a coherent and constructive picture of what the young person had gained from education thus far. The effect of the separateness between schools and the careers service was always something which could be reduced by good management but by now, as the number of people entering employment at 16 diminishes year by year, the manager can concentrate on providing information which will bear upon vocational training up to the age of 17 or 18 and upon pre-higher education studies up to the age of 18.

There was in the 1980s a particularly valuable development of co-operation between careers services and educators. As that service, too, moves towards a separation from local school systems, managers need to take care not to lose past benefits.

Behind the problem of giving information to each next stage and using the information which comes from preceding stages of schooling lies the management of that information in building up the picture of what has been – and what can yet be – achieved. The management of feedback between phases is comparable with managing the feeding of assessments through to the next teaching level. And although at present there may appear to be little scope for the manager at school to organize information about a person's career in a way which will benefit that person at the level of higher education, that sector's expansion and the coming together of the Universities Central Council on Admissions (UCCA) and the Polytechnic Central Admissions System (PCAS) will no doubt underline the continuing importance of informational feedback.

With good network management both broad and specific understandings can be encouraged for teachers as well as governors. Teachers are sometimes thought not to have a broad grasp of the total education enterprise. This, in the past, may have been understandable. By now, however, it is essential that everyone who contributes to education should possess an awareness of how it interconnects within its own system and with those other systems which take over even after formal education has been left behind.

Conclusion

The combination of governmental requirements, pressures from active interest groups and the continuing call for self-review on the part of schools and teachers leads to a choice of management approaches. One, based on the explicit use of pupil and school assessments, depends on the organization of agreement about criteria and purposes and on feedback at each stage when assessments are completed.

Other approaches rely on external reports, internal goal-setting and on the reconciliation of demands which range from the easily acceptable to the suffering of impositions. Managers have to be clear about the influences to which they respond, whom they treat as their fellow-managers and how information is communicated between those who manage and those who use education.

Inside the service there are new obligations to be met, notably on the part of parents and governors. They need to be encouraged to share judgements about the weight which is to be given to tightly organized professional activities and to less definable influences from a neighbourhood and a community.

Managers are under other obligations to be consistent, credible and intelligible. They need to make it clear to others how the unpredictable effects of change can be handled. They also have to be clear about how they can take account of differences of attitude, mind and personality on the part of those with whom they work. Above all managers need to ensure that the long-term and large-scale aims of education as a whole are kept in sight at every stage of development and of that evaluation which makes up the guarantee of quality learning and the step-by-step control of providing that quality.

CHAPTER 3

Training

When it assures parents about the quality of its education a school must define those elements of its work which contribute to that quality and must define the steps taken in order to guarantee it. Everyone who works in or for the school needs to know what his or her contribution has to be. This contribution needs to be stated clearly enough for its consequences to be traced back to the individual teacher.

The head has the main responsibility for making the plan but other teachers must take part in its formulation. Although it will be a shared task it is the head who must take the lead. The making of management plans is an activity to which heads became accustomed in the 1980s. They are detailed and open to review and revision but they are principally designed for the inner working of the school. In contrast, assurances of quality and their supporting documentation are designed for those outside, for parents and employers.

Governors must understand and support what is done to control quality and the first steps towards explicit planning and the giving of account came in 1977, with the Taylor Report (DES 1977 xii) recommending that a governing body should invite the headteacher in consultation with other staff to prepare papers setting out the means by which they proposed to pursue the aims adopted by the school. The report emphasized the educational value of the process:

Teachers would have an opportunity to discuss, explain and justify their decisions in terms which could be understood by people not belonging to the teaching profession; their skill as professionals can only grow from such an experience. Lack of confidence may often have been behind the reluctance of many teachers in the past to discuss their work with people from outside the school. The latter also would come to recognise the importance and difficulty of reconciling the different objectives of the school.

The 1980 Education Act revised the constitution of governing bodies and laid down standards of information which local authorities would have to provide about each school. A new freedom was given, in the same Act, to parents to choose between schools. Very quickly, central government made possible several improvements which had for long represented the platforms of unofficial groups and bodies. In the 1960s, in the words of Kogan (1975:72),

Policies as perceived by the newer interest groups which formed in the 1960s emerge very differently from those of the established groups. The role of parents in decision-making, the enhancement of the role of governors and managers, the status, contractual rights and participative power of students, the right of teachers to participate in institutions' decision-making, the belief that schools should help mould a more equal and undifferentiated society – all these values came from outside the system and cut deep into the institutional policies and values.

Not everything made the same impact and some concessions (particularly those related to the participation of teachers) were later modified. But it meant that from the 1960s through to 1977 and then into the legislation of the 1980s explanations came to be required.

As a result of DES Circular 6/81 schools had to prepare a statement of curriculum objectives. Comparable to the way in which this requirement brought headteachers and governors closer, there was a bringing together, in the local authorities, of senior education administrators and locally elected politicians who formed the major part of local authorities' education committees. This coincided with the reorganization of local government in 1974. In education it had meant that

by good fortune and, no doubt, because this is one of the things at which local government reorganisation aims, the gap between layman and professional is narrowing. We are living through a stage at which major policies are being reviewed, made or done away with and at which both committees and officers know in detail what they are handling. Things have had to be revised or learned anew, the grasp of those who run the show is therefore a firm one. In time this grip will slacken somewhat. (Hughes 1975:162) .

This was prophetic in more ways than one. The onus of accountability moved steadily towards the managers of individual schools. This brought with it what Sayer (1989:90) described as sets of consequences for the way schools are run. 'One is that they are no longer going to be organised as though they were complete in themselves. Another is that their organisation and its members will be facing outwards to meet other outward-facing organisations, groups and individuals. A third is that those who work from a school base will do so with a professionality trained to be explicitly open and co-operative. A fourth is that such open sharing and co-operative modes of management will be part and parcel of the school learning experience.'

The shift has tended to emphasize the autonomy of schools and to couch the task of a school's accounting for itself in the language of competitive marketing. This had been a predictable movement even in the late 1960s.

Those parents who pay for their children's schooling, and those who are in a position to choose in which state school's catchment area they will live, are involved all the time in making decisions based upon some criteria of success. It would be naive to assume that such parents always define this solely in terms of examination results; a variety of other factors enters into parental, professional and public estimations of what constitutes a good school. We are beginning to document the way in which the school can exercise an independent influence on the educability, career assumptions and out-of-school life

of its pupils, to recognise the kinds of facts to the importance of which parental behaviour and attitudes have long been testimony (Baron and Taylor
1969:113–14).

The importance of the head

Against this background of hope and history, little has been done to
train managers in education to give an account of themselves. There
have been short courses provided by DES, higher education and local
authorities. Bodies such as the Institute of Personnel Management, the
British Institute of Management, the Industrial Society, the British Association for Commercial and Industrial Education have been noted for
their work (Everard 1986). There are also the efforts of official and
quasi-official bodies such as the DES School Management Task Force
and the National Development Centre for School Management Training together with the British Educational Management and Administration Society.

One theme which most of these bodies emphasize repeatedly is that
of Sayer's professionality trained to be explicitly open and co-operative. They also go beyond the professionals since they call upon governors to contribute to finding the balance between institutions
working together to provide a better service than any one of them
alone could offer. This lives up to the Taylor Committee's view about
structured involvement: 'The decision-making role of the governing
body is only part of its functions: equally important is its responsibility
for promoting and protecting good relationships both within the school
and between the school and its parents and the wider community'
(DES 1977:xii).

In the partnership with governors the head, as prime mover, must
ensure that the school's management plans contain a substantial
enough element of staff development in the field of management to
make sure that the business of being explicit about quality is handled
thoroughly. But the manager must also provide an example, by going
through the process of training and by undergoing both the pains and
the rebuffs which accompany change and development.

In initiating open and shared management the head will find that
some colleagues will still prefer a hierarchical chain of command. Not
all staff will be clear at all times as to whether they do wish to share
responsibility (Glatter, *et al.* 1988). At those times leadership must
come first. And the outside world, it has to be said, does not always or
easily accept that assistant teachers should share in management responsibility. This was borne out in experience-based studies reported
by Briault and West (1990: 97):

The Head's role as chief professional must clearly be maintained, but exercised
in such a way as to allow the maximum involvement of the governors in
making the decisions which are within their responsibility. The role of the

Head as manager will undoubtedly be enlarged as financial delegation comes into effect and Heads will wish to develop their own skills and perhaps buy in special skills, possibly on a part-time basis, from other professionals. In all areas which will have become the governors' responsibility, the Head will remain the chief executive, answerable to the governing body as a managing director is to the board of directors. The Head's leadership role is more important than ever in these changing times. One who can be alongside colleagues, part of a consensus; one who takes initiatives and encourages others to do so as well; one who brings a wide vision to the school's role in the community as a whole; one able to help others to overcome weaknesses and is prepared to recognise his or her own.

These expectations raise the profile of the head. He or she is not simply responding to that which is required by law and regulation or to that which is sought by powerful governors. The Head has – and needs fully to exercise – a proactive role, spotting the opportunities as well as the hazards which lie ahead and aware at all times that he or she will have with fluency and credibility to explain and justify what is being done for the benefit of the school's pupils – and why.

Regular reporting

Although it may meet the formal requirements of regulation it is not enough for a head to provide one account a year or one each term if a detailed policy of quality assurance is to be followed. The organization of every school is radically changed by, and will continue to react to, the 1988 Act. Managers will continue to learn not only how to handle the accountancy side of local management of schools (LMS) but also how to use it in order to bring in alternative part-time teachers, a limited range of new resources and the occasional contribution of non-teaching assistance from a range of helpers other than those who work voluntarily. The head is already in a position to make a judgement from year to year about those matters which need reinforcement and others which can, for a time, be played down. Changes of emphasis and the need to alter the financial feed into one part of the school or another depend on how effectively the curriculum is being provided and on the messages which emerge from successive stages of pupil assessment.

These alterations must be thought about by the head, put to (and if necessary altered in light of discussion with) other teachers and both presented to governors and justified to them. The reactions of governors may lead to more information being needed or to a change in the detail of the principal proposal. The process takes time: experience which is summed up at the end of the autumn term of one academic year needs a further term of planning and discussion among staff before it is a matter of firm decision by the governors. To reach a decision at the Easter of any year is too late for a large alteration to be made in the allocation of funds in the financial year which starts that April. New arrangements when they are needed must, following the governors' approval, either be brought in piecemeal between autumn and the end of the academic year in the following summer or, if a large-scale change is made, it will have to be delayed until the following financial year can take it into account. By then the change will have seen through several stages of discussion, agreement and approval.

Quality assurance is unlikely to be believed if changes are made frequently, piecemeal or in a way which appears to be random. The process of managing any particular change extends over a period long enough (staff may have changed, new teaching materials may have become available) to necessitate adjusting and adapting the original process on its way through. But in addition to allowing something to develop further in the course of managing it, there is also a need to recognize that a period of eighteen months or two years lead-in is likely to have given the head, other teachers and governors new experiences and insights. Some lessons will have been learned from the way in which other schools handle their policies and practices. Some lessons will have been learned about how to interpret parts of the process of, for instance, pupil assessment in daily operational terms. Lessons will have been learned, too, about the speed which accompanies staff's and parents' understanding and acceptance of change. Above all, important lessons will have begun to show through in terms of whether and how children's learning is being improved. All this will mean not only that the time dimension of management has had its effect but also that the experiences and insights of those who manage will change and deepen. The development of management must expect these awarenesses on the part of each participant to become more profound and must not only allow but also encourage the process. This means that development cannot be left to a series of regular, fixed moments. Instead management has to depend on the co-operation of other people over a substantial period of time and that co-operation has to be earned by explanation and understanding. In particular, it can be argued that a time allocation for work with parents should be available across the age range (Jowett *et al.* 1991:144).

This means that the formal annual meeting of parents and the presentation of the school's report to them is just one event in the course of the management year – an important event and one on which several threads can be drawn together, but still only one item in the manager's programme. It has to be a moment in the year when a complete report is provided about what it is that the school has planned to develop and about its success or delay in completing this or that development. It has to be a moment in the year, too, when as much as possible can be presented and proposed to parents about changes and developments both in the next academic year or in two years' time.

If parents disagree about or cannot understand what is proposed, they can require the governors to satisfy them. If governors do not, parents have a right to appeal over their heads. Although this is unlikely to happen often, the sanction is valuable. It means, too, that unilateral, quick and visionary changes of direction cannot be put in train by a head without there being the need subsequently, even if it has been missed out at the stage of prior planning, to give a detailed account. The process of justifying and assessing is an essential part of the effect of the 1988 Act.

Schools which entered pilot schemes of local management early were in the position described by Nightingale (1990: 112): 'When we entered the pilot scheme, we did not sit down and describe the management and resources of our school. That makes it difficult to say clearly what has changed over the past three and a half years. There is no doubt in my mind that there have been changes, but they have occurred slowly and have resulted in a better school.' The school was better resourced and the children did have, says Nightingale, better educational opportunities. As LMS develops and as quality assurance as well as quality control take root, these improvements will need to be regarded as quantifiable.

Vision and intuition

It used to be repeated that a school was only as good as its head. By now that has to be amended: a school is only as good as its management. That goes beyond the head into the area of sharing, where other partners need to know, to agree and to criticize. The individual skill of the head is still important but it now faces risks. It can be distorted if it is asked to provide too complicated a style of accountability. Even the stimulus of greater freedom can be disturbing. Briault and West (1990: 73) quote an example of a head who complained to governors about inadequate funds but who was unable to give an adequate answer to the question about where the need was greatest. They go on to say: 'local management schemes . . . have been valuable stimuli to heads to make a much fuller and a more careful analysis of the sources of money available, the existing material resources of the school and the more effective allocation and use of these resources'.

To be professionally stimulated by new approaches to the job of providing education differs from having an inborn capacity to go beyond the organization's demands. Reliance on inborn capacity is relatively dangerous – not least because of differences of scale. Is a headteacher in the same league as the head of ICI? Lessem (1985: 201) had no doubt about the task which Sir John Harvey-Jones had set for himself. It was 'to bring back a personal and charismatic presence into an organization that had become depersonalised and rule-bound' . What he did was not to rely on personal and isolated gifts but to alter his own position inside the organization. 'He did not see himself at the top of a pyramid. He shifted to the centre of the organization, at a point where all channels of communication met' (Lessem 1985:209). Charisma came down to calculation.

That calculation is not an isolated event. Lessem (1985:209) points out that the industrial manager 'instead of focusing momentarily on the management of change, regards the present as a snapshot on the path of development'. Again, 'instead of pursuing business, technical and organisational change as separate goals, he strives to integrate business, technological and personal development within a transformed business and social framework'.

The business and social framework within which the school manager works has to include calculations and judgement about colleagues. Teacher appraisal is important (West and Bollington 1990: 55): 'As an aspect of management, appraisal can make a significant contribution to the motivation, development and effective use of staff. Given that the staff of a school are its most important and indeed its most expensive resource, an effective appraisal system is highly desirable to school managers.' In the list of verifiable assessments on which the manager must base the justification for change, teacher appraisal is now as important as pupil assessment, and for the same reasons.

Any alteration in teaching and learning which is needed by the pupil becomes clear at each stage of assessment. Each time a teacher is appraised he or she becomes aware of how much has been achieved and what more needs to be done. Staff development is a continuous process. In the words of Jones, Clark *et al.* (1989) 'they will experience a variety of forces which will produce change in knowledge, understanding, skills and, probably, attitude. . . . Just as pupils are entitled to a broad, balanced and relevant curriculum, so teachers have the same entitlement to professional development support.' And, in the description given by Dean (1991:190), professional development is a cyclic rather than a linear process.

The battery of attainments which will matter to a manager in deciding what needs to be strengthened, reintroduced or played down include, thus, the position of other teachers as well as the position of pupils. The head, too, will be appraised – not least against the background of changes which have to be put in hand. 'If the headteacher does not understand the dynamics of the change process, then individual teachers within the school can often feel a sense of confusion or a lack of direction. It is not enough that Heads provide a general endorsement to change: specific support is needed that is active, direct and interactive' (Jones, Clark *et al.* 1989:261).

It is those with whom the head must interact outside the daily work of the school who fall outside the reach of assessment. Governors are not appointed according to verifiable standards of their capacity to govern. Active parents are not questioned about their effectiveness. The neighbourhood does not have to justify its favours or its prejudices. These three are powerful sources both of support and criticism. Will other agencies be equally powerful in future – such as inspectors and advisers? Their worth matters even if it is not formally assessed. Those who give faulty advice will not last long. On the other hand, those whose standards of inspection are easy may find, in the so-called privatised period of school assessment (that is after the enactment of the Education (Schools) Act 1992) that it will be some time before their own faults are exposed.

The larger question about advisers and inspectors must now be that of how powerful they will now be in what they report to other people. And how useful will their advice be to the managers of schools when the managers themselves have to contract for the services of inspectors?

In calculating the capacity of all those who can assist a school's work, the manager has to recognize that advisers and inspectors were responsible to local authorities in conducting reviews of schools until the role of those authorities themselves was sharply diminished. Local advisers and inspectors became increasingly distant from schools, as too did HMI. The balance of the HMI workload in particular altered: they studied aspects of schooling and of educational organization rather more than individual schools. They reported on the implementation of policy and most particularly they inspected and reported on the efficacy of the national curriculum.

Some criticism of the position of advisers was voiced in Everard (1986: 207–9). That was echoed by the School Management Task Force in its comments about the role of local authorities in the introduction of the national curriculum and assessment: 'At this stage LEAs saw their role mainly in terms of providing advice and materials though a few LEAs have developed support teams of advisers working directly with schools. Schools were less optimistic about the type and amount of support, recognising that the LEA often knew little more than they did' (DES 1990a: 10–11).

If local authorities and HMI remain part of the team by whom heads may at one moment be assessed and at another assisted, those agencies must make clear what they expect, how they will use what they learn from or about the school and what they can give to it. If they do not make themselves clear, they will matter less and less.

In contrast, teachers are still the essential contributors to the daily quality of what is achieved. Governors are less directly involved but nevertheless their support and the range of decisions which they can make about the school's strategies and resources matter enough not to be treated as merely nominal power-sharers. Parents have to be satisfied. Their unpredictability has to be taken seriously and their need for plain information about the achievements or plans of the school means that a head has to give a thorough and patient account.

Frequency, as has already been said, will be one of the marks of a head's reports to governors and thoroughness and clarity will be the marks of the reports which go to parents.

Conclusion

The position of a headteacher as the sole manager in quality assurance is not tenable but the development of management schemes needs skill and clear perception from one source.

The support which is available to a head has to be paid for in terms of openness and accuracy of feedback to other teachers, governors and parents. Tardiness of feedback has to be avoided as much as excessive haste. All the parties to corporate management have to have time to absorb new roles and requirements.

Miscalculation about the importance or reliability of partners in management has to be avoided. Although this created particular difficulties during the period when local management became established, the continued acceptance and extension of managerial responsibility call for insights into teaching and learning, into social organization and into interpersonal structures.

CHAPTER 4

Corporate management

There is a three year cycle in the creation, testing and modification of school management plans. The stages overlap with each other and the process is both continuous and deliberately visible. Each part of it needs to be revealed and shared by the head and governors with other teachers, parents and those who have an interest in the school on behalf of local or central government.

In this process of revealing and sharing the head must manage the activities which add up to accountability. This is not a matter of communication skills alone despite the emphasis which is placed on the open dialogue between schools and parents and on the need for active publicity. If account is to be taken of what has been described as concern with the well-being of the system, then 'the best way of earning public confidence is the most direct: to be clearly seen as doing a good job' (Becher *et al* 1981:156).

Performance should clearly speak for itself but the English and Welsh system for some time lacked (and now needs) evaluation and evaluation which can be clearly expressed. In other words heads, governors, teachers, advisers, inspectors, researchers and evaluators (whether these come from education or from a broader world of audit) need to be trained to provide 'the sort of information evaluatory mechanisms might provide . . . there is an informational feedforward and feedback need affecting all those personnel, both professional and lay, who make decisions associated with the system' (Watson 1980: 194).

How reports are couched is important. If heads' statements to their governors are the key documents which they ought to be, they deserve all the care which drafting and redrafting can confer on them. They are the raw material of governors' discussions. They can be bare records of numbers and events or they can be windows on a living school and

most heads will be able to think of ways in which reports can be used to enrich governors' perceptions, prompt good questions and solicit positive advice and support as soon as they have made a breakthrough into a sense of their responsibility for creating a favourable climate. A good starting point is to think of how closed and impenetrable a school's affairs, particularly its curriculum, appear to governors and to visualise the report as a series of entry points. Again I should emphasise the helpfulness of sharing problems and asking difficult questions (Sallis 1988: 158–9).

Reporting and questioning

The readiness of governors to ask constructive questions depends on how well the school can do its job. If a school has to be defended in a head's report, the defence may take the form of not providing as much information as governors would want. In the words of Sallis again, 'If we know that the head's motive is to protect the school, and especially the more needy in it, from questions which are ill-informed, destructive or selfish, we have a clear objective, which is to make sure we don't deserve or unwittingly attract such accusations' (1988:17).

The ways in which heads reported to governors before the 1980 Education Act, when there was less community representation, and after the 1986 Act which required governors to report to annual parents' meetings (and for which the reports were largely written by heads), differ from the task after the Education Reform Act. The changes of 1980 left local authorities in what was still a strong and, if they wished, an influential position in determining what it was that governors and schools should put their name to. The changes of 1986 placed governors and parents in the front of the picture, with LEAs losing some of their power to central government and some to schools and their local managers. The 1988 Act emphasized this shift by increasing the autonomy of schools both in making and implementing their own management plans and in organizing the balancing of finances behind those plans.

Helping governors and parents to see how well a school is doing and explaining or defending the school has now taken on another dimension: comparisons with other schools leads to one set of questions while the extent to which the school is organized in accordance with the national curriculum and within the national framework of pupil assessment leads to different, inward-looking enquiries. Both approaches are reflected in the report to annual parents' meetings and both require a looking back at a school's achievements in order that differences or improvements can be headlined. Thus Anderson may have been more prophetic than was realized at the time (Earley 1988:61):

Parents are basically looking for reassurance about their children's schools and teachers. They want to have confidence in what the professionals are doing for their children. If I were a head teacher or a chair of governors now, I would use quite blatantly the annual meeting and the annual report as ways of sounding the loudest and brightest clarion calls about my school's performance and achievements. . . . Major or sudden change creates uncertainty. Implied dismissal of past achievements creates a lack of confidence. I would make it clear that I was seeking to build upon a solid platform of achievement – whether true or not – with gradual developments that can be understood and accepted from the outset.

'Whether true or not' does not stand up to what is needed in the formulation and review of school development plans and in the assurance of quality. In the four processes of that planning (DES 1989e and DES 1991a) the starting-point is audit, followed by and fed back from successive stages of construction, implementation and evaluation of a plan. In answer to the question of how a school is further to improve the quality of its pupils' education, more plans can be laid. They need to be the product of shared work between head, governors, staff and, as far as possible, parents, but the main responsibility lies on the head.

Self-evaluation from which review and audit can begin has been at the heart of a long-standing national project, Guidelines for the Review and Internal Development of Schools (GRIDS). The questionnaire connected with this review is aimed at identifying a school's needs in terms of the strengths or weakness of its individual parts. This is an important aspect of the process of developing a school's strategy of in-service education but it also enables other parties to share in the awareness of what has been achieved and what needs improvement.

The GRIDS self-questioning approach has been analysed as to its advantages (Jones, Clark *et al.* 1989): on the plus side, all staff are involved in decisions about priorities, the enquiry provides a system for moving from discussion into action and both stresses the importance of monitoring and evaluation and emphasizes the cyclical and ongoing nature of staff development. Among the disadvantages, there may be an artificial limit of activity imposed by the need to work within pre-identified categories, and confusion both between the identification of broad as against specific needs and about the 'invitation to identify weakness implies a deficiency-based model for staff development' (Jones, Clark *et al.* 1989:43).

The School Development Plans Project (SDPP) broadens the basis of audit to include not only the aims and values of the school but also the policy and initiative of central government and the LEA. It includes recent reviews of the school in the shape not only of self-evaluation but also of inspections and reports by the local authority and by HMI. More difficult but, if practicable, very valuable are those views and perspectives (again acknowledged in the SDPP) which reveal how the school is seen by governors, parents, pupils and the community (DES 1989e).

When the manager extends his or her self-evaluation to the encouragement of others to reveal their own views as well as their estimate of their own capacities, the notion of self-certainty and self-esteem is crucial. With the right kind of self-certainty goes sympathy with others and a sane balance of mind. In the language of self-concepts, 'self-esteem refers to personal feelings concerning one's own value, importance and competence. It is a result of a long process of appraisal which is influenced by self evaluation as well as evaluation by others. These evaluations of, for instance, values and capacities, vary over time and continually affect one's self-esteem' ; (Oppenheimer 1990:121).

The emphasis here on the length of time over which sound appraisal is built up, and the linking of self-evaluation with evaluation by other people, points to a broad approach to appraisal. Also, the humanity, strength and potential for fallacy which lies behind the notion of self-esteem makes the idea of training for it appear mechanistic when, above all, it is sensitivity which must be shown towards all levels of expertness among partners in management.

The poor performer

Governors and teachers vary in their capacity to join in the management of a school. If there are noticeably poor performers in the task of co-operation, the manager has to notice which form of inadequacy is revealed. Withdrawal, deterioration in relationships, slowness in joining in, waywardness, emotionality – these and others are listed by Stewart and Stewart (1982). A variety of causes can lie behind the poor performer's difficulty – low threshold to boredom, poor verbal facility in professional discussions with adults, inadequate job knowledge (whether or not as a result of inadequate initial training) or stress. The work group in a school may exercise detrimental or divisive pressures, a school may have a history of tolerating poor standards, working conditions may be dispiriting and, after long neglect, may indicate that the manager does not notice or does not care. Putting right the poor performer may need an approach from several directions. Dilemmas can always arise since, while people are more likely to improve if they get feedback about their skills, 'unless they have a sensitive or trained manager they are likely to get feedback on less relevant topics'(Stewart and Stewart 1982:169).

This is true of the manager inside a school. But a head does not manage governors or parents in the same sense. He or she knows how, and can be trained, to manage fellow employees; helping people to manage themselves is an essential core of management and managing relationships between people has to be concerned with always taking account of their attitudes and capacities.

In any management group its members have to disclose themselves. No one member should always be the sole person to reveal himself or herself, nor should it be forgotten that there is no consistent pattern of when the process of disclosure is desirable and beneficial (Chelune *et al.* 1979).

When confident awareness is not available to managers, they have to rely on intuition, judgement by analogy and the informed reports of other people. These are shared by those who appoint heads and other teachers, who nominate governors and who entrust the representation of the views of a parent body to two or three of their number. As the basis for shared judgement their views are as important as more formal criteria. Although they carry the risk of overemphasizing the subjective and personal make-up of a team they have to be taken into account in any scheme of training.

Training from starting points which are different towards an end which is uniform is not a unique aspect of voluntary partnership. The work which has, since 1986/87, been achieved by Action for Governors' Information and Training (AGIT) took its beginnings from a very wide range of agencies: both through its original base at the Community Education Development Centre in Coventry and through its non-governmental funding, it has been able to take account of differing interests and pressures.

The training which has emerged from AGIT and from other less comprehensive but nevertheless comparable providers in LEAs, in the churches and in higher education means that Joan Sallis's prized ideal of 'the precious light of ordinariness' has been allowed to shine. It has come from people who are well informed about the governors' aspect of management, who know how to take the influence and information of parents into account and who, because they have taken part in one specific but widely shared exercise in adult education, have had the chance to understand and contribute to a wide field of public and community affairs (Sallis 1988).

It would be too much to hope that, once ordinary people became governors and once ordinary parents became involved in what (and why) a school chooses to do, then the process of improvement and development would look after itself. There are others to take into account, namely those co-operators who come from the teaching body, from LEAs' advisers and from HMI. Attempts in the past to ensure that the latter two groups shared their views about quality achieved worthwhile ends. They were seen to be working in the same direction and although it has not yet been possible to gauge the extent to which they help in the task of managing new education, their contribution to quality assurance should, by tradition, be valuable.

Reviewing

At national level HMI customarily look back two years when an overall survey of progress is made. When the restriction was lifted from the Senior Chief Inspector's annual report about examining the effect on maintained schools of local authorities' financial and finance-linked resources, it became a report about national quality. Had local authorities still the influence over schools which was diminished by the Education Reform Act, it would have been commonplace for each authority to compare the performance of its own policies and of its own schools with a national standard. Much the same impulse had been felt in the early years of reports by the APU. Going further back again, local authorities had made good use, on a comparative basis, of national reading surveys.

In each of these contexts – HMI reports, APU exercises or national reading surveys – to move from national assessment to a local authority assessment and then to a school's performance (summed up in the achievement of its individual pupils) provided a method of finding out whether, in some of the measurable parts of schools' work, matters were standing still or edging forward.

If earlier national and local links still existed it would have given a helpful criterion to governors to know whether their school was being managed well. But two things have happened: schools must now be uncertain in comparing themselves with each other because the Education (Schools) Act 1992 has created dilemmas about the mediation of inspectors' and advisers' reports. Second, they have to work harder than in the past to find out how they are faring in quite basic parts of the curriculum. Schools now compare themselves (or have themselves compared, by parents and others) with other schools within one neighbourhood or one sub-area of a county. They have to handle quite parochial comparisons without enjoying much sense of how they stand in the national scene. This may suit the trend to treat education as a local activity but quality assurance needs a comparison with broader standards. Governors, parents, teachers and heads themselves cannot now take their eye – for too long – off their pupils' achievements in the basic curriculum. They need to know how their standards compare with those of other providers but in ways which are less traditional and restricted than through the five key documents required by *The Parents' Charter* (DES 1991b:2–7).

As an example, personal, social and moral education was from the 1960s onwards a field where schools shared their experiences, their approaches and their materials. It was an appropriate part of the curriculum for learning from each other. Similarly, environmental education and world awareness were studies which fitted into the interstices of the main curriculum and were, in different ways, organized on a cross-curriculum basis. This is still possible and it can also go further by sharing and co-operation between schools. But in terms of comparison and competition the professionals who are responsible for one school's management may now have to justify to governors and to parents a consumption of time which some people might think would be better spent on raising pupils' performance in a limited field and in ways which are visible, competitive and market-orientated. If quality is to be controlled in a tight and limited way, the price can be that of narrowness and aridity.

Present-day comparisons

There is little to be gained from looking at the past achievements of a school if the head and the governors treat their task as having been totally defined by the Education Reform Act. A corporate view, instead, has to be taken of the school's comparison with others – and expressed in terms of measured attainment. Nevertheless there will still be inter-school sport and competition at music festivals, chess championships and inter-school exhibitions of art. Out-of-school behaviour will be a matter, as always, of comparison – as will the obligation to wear a uniform or the regular obligation to do homework.

These are traditional areas of distinctiveness and competition. But there was, quite recently, a time when co-operative organizations of schools with titles such as academic councils brought primary and secondary schools within one area (sometimes, in country districts, quite a large geographical area) together for the shared planning of curriculum. In other vicinities, clusters of schools shared some part of their staff in pursuit of a common curriculum entitlement for all those pupils who would transfer from, for instance, distant and isolated primary schools to a single country-town secondary school. In schemes of sharing such as these, there had to be some form of common management. Governors of individual schools needed to be at the same level of understanding and acceptance of what was being planned. Parents, too, needed to know that their children's education was being enhanced by this system of sharing.

Some aspects of shared planning are valuable enough to survive regardless of the competition for school admissions. This means that co-operation and competition will go along at the same time. Only one form of training in managing this double act is likely to succeed: staff and governors need to be encouraged to support every movement which makes the best of their own school.

This joint commitment moves away from the idea of loyalty solely to a single school and from the idea of out-and-out competition. It moves towards the acceptance of belonging at the same time to a larger enterprise which combines the strengths of sharing and collaboration and the sharpness of keeping an eye out for one's own survival. When this is translated into personal terms, it means among other things that at some point in his or her career a teacher will have to look at its pattern and will have to pay attention to changes which ought to be made in his or her work-role. This involves a difference in teachers' perception of themselves and of other professionals.

Governors, in trying to handle collaboration and competition with other schools at the same time, will not face a disturbing change. There is, after all, a tradition of some governors serving more than one school and the bond between a governor and a school is less compelling than that between the teacher and the daily commitment to one organization and one ethos. Parents, too, particularly when their freedom to choose and change their children's school is a central tenet of the organization of post-1980 education, will feel less difficulty in understanding a school which is an effective competitor but which nevertheless co-operates with others for the sake of ensuring a wider curriculum.

Working with, while at the same time competing against other schools, raises questions about management which bear on a point made by Rutter *et al.* (1979): a school can choose its values and norms. In school, teachers show what they expect of children in terms of work and behaviour, they provide models for children by their own conduct and they feed back to children what they judge to be acceptable performance. One commentator, while accepting the importance of Rutter's finding, then asks whether we have the means by which deliberately to create a planned organizational ethos in a school. If we do, does this mean that the use of coercion, enthusiasm or the encouragement to be involved are equally acceptable? (Reynolds 1985).

When the issue is not of a split in attitudes ('I will compete but I will also borrow and lend') the head is unlikely to find enthusiasm or coercion an appropriate tool of management. Instead, teaching colleagues need to be asked – with encouragement, admittedly – whether they wish to be involved. The answer is likely to be more predictable if they are continuously kept informed of what the head and governors are seeking from other local schools and how they assess their own school's effectiveness.

In the picture

Keeping colleagues in the picture is more important than keeping parents informed about the minutiae of school management. Ignorance and distrust go together. To keep a large staff informed requires that senior staff are used by the head to spread information, to note reaction and to ensure feedback.

The process by which colleagues are kept informed may differ from what is expected of them in building up either a school development plan or a scheme of quality assurance. Preparation for the latter may be regarded as a matter of self-training: it needs a comprehensive and co-ordinated approach to all aspects of planning, one which covers curriculum and assessment, teaching, management and organization, finance and resources. From this type of starting-point the SDPP expected two things to flow, namely the capturing of a long-term vision within which short-term goals were to be set and, second, a relief in teacher stress. Instead of feeling under pressure from the pace of change teachers would come to exercise greater control over it (DES 1989e: 4).

That the preparation of a development plan should be a matter of self-training follows from those steps which the SDPP suggests, for instance, in auditing the curriculum:

- check whether the planned curriculum meets the statutory requirement;
- identify possible gaps or overlap between subject areas;

- ensure that where two or more subjects or activities are concerned with the same range of objectives, this is recognized and used positively;
- analyse the curriculum for each year group in terms of curriculum objectives within and outside the National Curriculum;
- decide in which part of the school curriculum to locate work leading to the National Curriculum and other school curriculum objectives;
- assess how much teaching time is available and how best to use it;
- compare planned provision with actual provision;
- judge whether curriculum issues need to be among priorities of development (DES 1989e: 7)

This range of tasks is within the capacity of a large secondary school's staff. It may be beyond the capacity of a 12- or 15-teacher secondary school, a 10-teacher middle school, a 10-teacher primary school or an 8-teacher first school. These eight tasks of audit cannot be carried out in smaller schools – schools in which it has never been possible to develop subject differentiation to the same degree as in larger schools. The three- or four-class primary school is left well behind.

However, if staff led by a head and one or two senior colleagues worked their way through these tasks (and it might be more likely that senior staff themselves would have drafted the audit and put it forward for discussion, alteration and approval by others), they would be familiar with most of the important issues concerning the national curriculum. When confronted with the head's and the governors' account of the financial and other resources with which to achieve its implementation, few members of staff would feel able to contribute to the debate. This can isolate the head; and the School Management Task Force has commented that 'the absence of any direct supervision leaves the head vulnerable in making judgements about personal development and in locating support. This has always been a problem for heads because the structure of the service puts them in an isolated position. Heads have operated without a clear managerial line of accountability' (DES 1990a:18).

Whichever approach is adopted (that of the SDPP or of the School Management Task Force) the head has to decide whether it is practicable in his or her school to assume that the more that teachers are asked to do in the way of auditing, laying plans, implementing them and reviewing them, the more they will understand about the effectiveness of pupils' learning. Will they know more about that than they do when they simply carry out what the curriculum requires of them regardless of how it is supported, budgeted for and described to parents by the governors? And, if the line of the School Management Task Force is followed, how long will it take teachers to appreciate that what they are going through is an assessment 'of the opportunities in each individual's working routine for acquiring positive experiences of good practice and receiving support and advice. Each individual needs to understand and share the purposes, goals and values of the organization, and feel able to make a positive contribution as a worthwhile part of the whole' (DES 1990a:8).

Separation of training

In contrast to the government's approach to school planning and management in 1990, a report six years earlier aimed its message at heads and at an LEA. It concentrated on the curriculum and organization of Inner London secondary schools and focused on those pupils who were underachieving, took few or no public examinations and showed their dissatisfaction with school by absenting themselves or by behaving in an uncooperative manner (ILEA 1984).

Good practice was described and 104 recommendations made. These suggested changes in organization, assessment and teaching and recognized the key role of teachers. The Report pointed at the level of resource needed in order to achieve improvements and it sought to improve the management of schools by making them more meaningful to a wider range of pupils.

That it was addressed to teachers and their employers and not to governors or parents mattered less when the report was published than it would now. Most of the steps which are required in creating improvement are, after the 1988 Education Act, under school control. That was not the case when the Hargreaves Report was published and was one reason for its being welcomed as being ahead of its time.

By now it is accepted among teachers that

it is within the individual school that curriculum innovation and development, the implementation of whole school policies and the continuing development of professional skills must be initiated. It is at grass roots level that teachers can best foster the development of existing good practice, identify specific professional needs, challenge their own attitudes, assumptions and values and analyse their practice. Corporately teachers can plan and develop strategies, translate them into practice and monitor and evaluate their effect. We believe that a prerequisite of this co-operative and corporate activity is a climate of open discussion and dialogue among the teachers, a willingness to share experiences and expertise and, most importantly, relationships of trust and mutual support (ILEA 1984: 111–12).

If radical alterations are to be debated and believed in by heads, staffs, governors and parents and if the management of improvement is largely in these same people's hands, the task is broader than the School Management Task Force's concern with national curriculum – and broader than the SDPP's recommendations about planning.

The preparation (it is difficult to think of it in terms of training) of those who put radical reform into action requires vision, strength of mind and persistence. Can attitudes and dispositions be summoned up at will? Can they be trained for? Above all, are they a reliable basis for believing a school's assurance about quality?

Conclusion

Preparation for the task of managing by means of a partnership is less a matter of structured training than a process of growth. Each partner has to recognize his or her position and that he or she represents a group who have a legitimate voice. This is a particularly slow matter for parents, who have a voice but who are only gradually being empowered. For heads, other teachers and governors partnership needs, as a first step, self-awareness, self-esteem and a capacity to tolerate something less than perfection.

The aids which can be used in preparing for joint management are those of information derived from comparisons, clarity of purpose and a readiness to undertake corporate self-assessment. Energy has to be devoted to making sure that the assumptions which lie behind these activities are genuinely shared; mistaken judgements can lead to ambiguity in the way in which people outside a school view its managers. While uniformity of view between the managing partners cannot always be achieved every effort has to be made to avoid discrepancies.

The largest questions the members of a management partnership must answer are whether sharing is practicable, whether its members believe in it and how long – if it is a reality – it takes the outside world to believe that it can provide the promised level of quality.

CHAPTER 5

Marshalling attitudes

Those who take part in change usually want it to succeed. If they do not, they must leave the system in which it is taking place. Those who do not want change are, however, unlikely to wish to leave a system in which they are already working. The choice then lies between staying in and going through with the change despite initial disfavour or staying in and changing either reluctantly or superficially.

The initiator of change cannot, in the face of reluctance or merely token activity, be confident that every participant will end up as an active and confident partner. Nor, in an atmosphere of reluctance, can the initiator be confident that a participator's initial dependence on other people's ideas and energy will in due course be turned into well-informed independence. Reluctant participators who start off with a limited range of interest and involvement in management are unlikely to find it easy to commit themselves to new and broader aims.

Because training other people's feelings is not available as a method of reducing reluctance, the manager in a school has to choose which elements of the process of change will in themselves bring about changes of attitude. Will the partners enjoy exercising new powers? Will they be confident in reading between the lines? Will they wish to look upon their school as a robust institution? Above all, can they run the risk that it will not be able to deliver quality?

If change is treated at the large-scale level, teachers, non-teaching staff, governors and parents cannot deny the consequences of local financial management: 'Pushing management decisions – for instance, about staffing complements and who should be appointed and dismissed – down to the schools will make it extremely important to know what they will do with their new-found power' (Maclure 1990:9).

In exercising that power, managers have to be ready to debate the issues. In the shift from 1975 to 1990 away from 'concerns about equity and fairness and a concentration on more practical and immediate questions of efficiency and relevance', discussions have to 'lie at the heart of the democratic debate between and within the parties, and a constant flow of messages, coded and uncoded, ensures that the discussion is never far below the surface' (Maclure 1990:14).

Debate and questioning are only threatening if an organization is weak. The school may be a strong fortress:

Most schools are robust organizations with many good management practices from which anyone in industry and commerce could learn; yet those same schools are likely to miss aspects of elementary motivation of staff and good housekeeping that are elsewhere taken for granted. Many industrial companies devote considerable energy and funds in the development of organizational culture to overcome deep-rooted problems such as them-and-us alienation and a lack of commitment to organizational goals. Most schools accomplish with ease what these companies seek, because schoolteachers know that their efforts can only succeed within an organization that is a community with ethos, spirit and individual commitment (Torrington *et al.* 1987:23).

The process of building up the strength of shared commitment can seldom be consciously managed in a schools. Instead there is what has been described as 'the glue of schools'. By this teachers are bound together in a whole school, managed by a head and others who can

create moments to hear and see all aspects of the school. Get togethers, huddles, working parties, visits, chats and the like, become the occasions when more is learned about the school. At the same time the process of meeting and getting together does not simply afford times for the head or deputy to gain insights; because everyone participates, everyone's awareness is extended and engaged. Whole schools do not happen because the head alone has a greater view of the school, they occur because everyone's view of the school is extended and embraced (Southworth 1988:327).

Another way of extending everyone's view of a school and of diminishing the opposition to change within it, is to acknowledge one of the less fashionable aspects of management and to make a virtue of it. Packwood (1989) pointed to the bureaucracy of educational institutions. He argued (1989:14) that since institutions, largely regardless of the wishes of their members, have retained a bureaucratic organization, it is important to use the bureaucracy well,

to maximise opportunities for institutions to achieve their objectives and for individuals to succeed in their careers. The underlying assumption has been that bureaucracy is desirable as an organizational principle because it attempts to clarify authority and accountability while depersonalising their application. Work is too important and too unsure to be obstructed by the uncertainties of not knowing what is expected and by whom, and by having to continually negotiate what one can do with individual power players.

Avoiding long-drawn-out negotiations and yet ensuring that everyone is in the know is part of the task of governors. When they were, by one LEA, advised about how to produce a management plan, they were told that there was probably 'much information already in the school which would either be part of the plan or would help in the process of producing specific documents within it.' The advice (Devon County Council 1990:12) was that

Each school must decide for itself exactly what to include but it is likely that all schools will want to include the following documents:

● a statement of the school's aims and values;

- a statement of priorities chosen for development in the current year;
- a list of objectives to be tackled in the next two or three years;
- an outline of how the curriculum will be developed and specially of how the National Curriculum will be introduced;
- staff development plans, including the in-service education and a training plan for the current financial year;
- plans for the use and development of the school's resources;
- the school's approved budget for the current financial year.

Of those seven aspects of planning it is likely that all members of staff will have been previously involved in at least three. Their involvement in those parts of the management plan in which they have not been previously interested will be taken on and driven by the possibly irresistible surge of the whole school's development.

As well as being influenced by what is required in local terms, schools are also bound, on a national scale, to be affected by statements such, for example, as those of the Secretary of State for Education and Science. He set out his views, for instance, about the report of the 1989 Records of Achievement National Steering Committee. He endorsed the aims of contributing to the raising of all pupils' achievement through and beyond the national curriculum, of improving pupils' motivation and increasing their participation in education, of preparing pupils better for the transition to further education, training or employment – and, all important in the preparation and review of management plans, of helping schools to consider how well their curriculum, teaching and organization enabled pupils to develop their all-round potential (DES 1990b).

Every picture of the broad purposes of a school's plan is drawn from a particular viewpoint. When that viewpoint is outside the school it is of assistance to corporate management to weigh up its authority and seriousness. To be given a steer saves time but regardless of whether the head or the local authority regards change as being large scale, well publicised, hotly debated or self-evidently necessary, it is still necessary, behind every broad picture, to make sure that the purpose and implications of specific change are explicit. It must not be assumed that everyone initially agrees about the implications.

Teachers need to be clear about the way in which different issues are decided. They need to know how senior managers set about making decisions. In that process it is not the style as much as the consistency of those managers which is significant. 'Nothing is more confusing to staff than not to be able to foresee with reasonable certainty how a significant issue is likely to be resolved' (Earley and Fletcher Campbell 1989:184).

Teachers will understand and support the way in which management decisions are made if they are fortunate enough to receive any management training and any assistance in their professional development, especially if it is linked with their working experience (DES 1990a:9):

Training opportunities increase in value to the degree that they are planned to integrate with and enhance the experience of management in school. Wherever possible, the project and surveys undertaken in training should be drawn directly from the working life of the participant and selected because they will contribute to the better management of the school.

If schools are to be better managed, the making of decisions in the course of managing has to be understood and shared by as many people as possible. Simply to understand how a decision is made requires a positive interest, an awareness and a wish to see how the management process works. This is partly a question of attitude, partly a matter of training. But in reality there is little or no training for the assistant teacher's role in school management. Attitudes of interest and awareness therefore are highly important and that importance will persist throughout the teacher's career.

From planning to implementation

The process of change is not something which is done once and then stops. Four activities, in particular, matter: the way in which teaching and learning are conducted, keeping up to date in a subject, applying a new technology and managing the sequence of review, improvement and change. Particular parts may move more slowly than others. Not all subjects are changing at the same pace although the national curriculum will in time no doubt reach some kind of consistency. Other parts are continually on the move and the way in which teaching and learning are organised, in particular, has to be the subject of regular review and continuous overhaul.

The application of new technologies will not take the form of a constant challenge. Management, in contrast, must be a continuing process – always ensuring that the best use is made of time, human resource and money, taking up some slack, reinforcing successful practices, reviewing the state of staff development and offering encouragement: 'Successful implementation needs continual support. Sustaining commitment is a key task for the head, senior staff and team leaders. The enthusiasm of even the most committed staff can flag when routine work and unanticipated events distract teachers from the targets and tasks' (DES 1989e:15).

The movement from planning into implementation has to be smooth. The Development Plans Project commends the practice of senior staff showing interest, making themselves accessible and joining meetings. But they need to make sure that implementation is evaluated. It concedes that 'many progress checks are intuitive, a 'feel' for whether things are going well or badly. This is a normal part of the monitoring of one's activities: it becomes more systematic if these intuitive reactions are shared within the team' (DES 1989e: 15).

Intuition is not enough when a school has to give assurances of quality and has to prove that it can control that quality. In addition to intuitive judgements a head, deputy and other colleagues need to make sense to outsiders. There is little point in trying to transmit a professional's 'feel' for something to a parent who is anxious about his or her child's education but does not know very much about the intricacies of teaching and learning. For this reason the manager must go beyond the internal handling of colleagues' enthusiasms and transactions. Unexpected difficulties which have prevented things from going well need to be identified and put right. There are eight other lines of action which the Plans Project has identified as a means of recovering ground or of preventing mistakes from being compounded. Some depend on the ability to find or switch extra support, to seek outside help or to use the skills of new staff. Others are a matter of reassigning tasks, adjusting the timetable of a plan, scaling a project down or postponing the achievement of one or other of the targets which had originally been identified.

None of these is intended simply to mollify reluctant staff: each is intended to provide more time, to allow a fresh look to be taken or to try out different approaches when there are setbacks. The management leader's understanding of the complexities and challenges of a school's work have to be displayed clearly.

Not all the attitudes which precede a review will survive once a management plan has been put into action. This is because the process of planning has no alternative to that of moving continually forward and, in that movement, applying methods and ideas which have previously been untried.

The methods and tools which are available to the manager have been comprehensively reviewed by Earley and Fletcher-Campbell (1989). The manager needs to know – and to make sure other people know – whether what is being practised is what has been described as transactional leadership (fixing and dealing) or transforming leadership (involving partners in raising one another to higher levels of motivation). Transformation is preferred over transaction by those who believe that participative decision-making is crucial, but most managers – and the Earley and Fletcher-Campbell study underlines this – prefer to operate in both styles according to the nature of the task and the attitudes of those with whom they work.

Working with partners

Because the effective leader must perform two functions successfully, namely the achievement of the task which has been set and the fulfilment of colleagues' needs, he or she must develop a role in which those broader needs can be taken into account.

In defining those needs it is important to pay attention to the teacher's self in the amalgam of teaching, managing, initiating, following and criticizing. Nias argues that the description of what the primary teacher puts into that amalgam is incomplete 'if it does not make room for potentially dangerous emotions such as love, rage and jealousy on the one hand and intermittent narcissism and outbreaks of possessive dependence on the other'. And although we may concentrate attention on teachers' socially regulated selves, 'their own descriptions of their feelings about pupils, and their relationships with them and with their colleagues remind us that the regressive, passionate and unruly aspects of human nature are always present in the classroom and may sometimes escape from rational control' (1989: 203).

The truth of this does not make it easy to define the teacher's role in management. But if the human component in teaching is important in securing a 'substantial ego-reward', it should be asked how heads can acknowledge that colleagues will endure low points in their morale (and there are certain numbers of compensating highs) and how, in taking account of this, they can work on assumptions about other people's attitudes. Do the assumptions of heads have to attach less weight than might be reasonable to, for instance, a colleague's attitude of reluctance? No, because the personal strategies which allow teachers to enthuse about one activity, put up with another and resent but simply get on with yet another can indeed be taken into account by heads. Those strategies do not, however, normally form part of the plan of campaign of governors and parents. Reluctance and misunderstanding must in their case be dissolved as far as possible by rational persuasion. If after that the prime manager finds that there is still opposition to a management plan, losses must be cut and the required action put in hand, come what may.

For a head to override governors and parents in one sense contradicts the spirit of the manager as consulter but it still underlines the need to realize that consultation is not endless and that consensus cannot always be achieved. If governing bodies set up finance committees as part of a school's organization to meet the requirements of local management, governors and parents are more likely to be able to be involved in management decisions. 'This is not the case of the head surrendering his responsibility but [of his or her readiness to consult] more and thus [enhance] his or her managerial role. In this process of consultation, the emphasis moves from deciding how to spend available resources to identifying needs, establishing priorities and then deciding on the budget' (Nightingale 1990: 110).

There will be a difference between management by consultation within the school's staff and management by consultation with governors and parents. In the first, if consensus is not achieved, more effort needs to be made to find how to agree a plan.

To treat governors and parents – and ideally non-teaching staff too – in a way different from teaching staff raises the question of why there should be differences if the process of management is a democratic activity which is conducted between equals. Their starting-points, their work backgrounds and their position in the education system as users and receivers make it likely that the criticisms of non-teachers as well as their expressions and acts of support will differ from those of teachers. And because the nature and significance of these differences are even now not fully appreciated by all heads there is a risk that the relationship will be treated in an over-simple way. In other words, some heads may think that it is desirable and right to devote much care to management through the corporateness of professionals but, within the same code, to achieve as much agreement among the non-professionals as one can and then to stop trying. If this is the approach which is adopted it means that when a certain point is reached the word of the head is final.

This will not always stand up to present day expectations about democratic management. It was not, for instance, the intention of the Education Reform Act. Yet there are unlikely to be many governors or bodies of parents who would disapprove of the more or less traditional approach of putting class teachers first, and there would be few who would persist in wanting the headteacher's draft management plan – his or her daily manner of organizing and managing the school – to be changed as the result of open and equal argument between staff of all categories. There is, as reported by Baginsky *et al.* (1991:118) very little governor involvement in the production or implementation of management plans.

Visible democracy

Public disagreement about a school is sometimes said to be bad for the education of its pupils. It is used as a reason either for not dissenting or for not admitting to differences in public.

If the disagreement is about a trivial matter it will be forgotten. But the idea of shared management is not trivial and dissent will therefore either be camouflaged – but still be there – or the party whose views are overridden will feel that it was, after all, only a nominal attempt at agreement and partnership which was intended. Governors, parents and others might become sceptical about the other people's intentions.

It is likely that most schools at some stage or another will fail to achieve managerial unanimity. Compromises might be sought and the true weight of governors' opinions then known. However, the weakness of setting out to find a compromise is that each side assumes at the start that its own view is the one to be preferred. Each side then loses something if there is an attempt to meet at a mid-point.

This picture of the grudging but well-intentioned patching up of managerial differences is some way away from an ideal of quality control which relies on teamwork. This represents a homogeneity of effort but is criticized because it is some way away from full partnership. This is because those who are inside the system recognize that as potential sharers they are not equal. Thus teachers, on one side, can know everything about the technicalities of curriculum, pedagogy, the use of resources and professional standards. Parents and governors, on the other side, know what they are told, what they sense through adult contact with schools or through the reports of children and the family. Teachers claim that they deal in facts, measurements, definitions of aim, standards of attainment. The other side concedes that it deals in reputations, gossip, intuition and the ambitions of private families. Apathy is usually ascribed only to one side – the parents – and that is sometimes thought to give a sufficient reason for teachers and schools to give up the struggle of recruiting them as allies. The Hargreaves Report (ILEA 1984) showed that schools can achieve a great deal on their own and that they can outweigh parental lack of interest. But equally if a school does not matter to a pupil because the school itself does not try hard enough, there is as much risk to the achievement of a sound education as would arise if all the fault lay with the child's own family.

There has to be a new evenness of balance between parents and schools when it comes to making judgements about how schools should be managed. To which activities should priority be given? How can pupil assessments affect the organization of the curriculum? Will staff development make a difference in improving the quality of team planning?

Balance

Four elements of interest and influence need to be weighed against each other, namely the effect of the parent as the educator who is helped by the school, the school as the institutional teacher who is helped by the parent, the school as the manager and decider (with the parent being kept informed) and the school itself as the only 'real' provider of education.

The fulcrum of this balance has shifted. A report of the Consultative Committee of the Board of Education in 1931 (*The Primary School*) contained words which were repeated by the Plowden Report in 1967, 'What a wise and good parent would desire for his own children, that a nation must desire for all children.' In 1968 Michael Young and Patrick McGeeney invented what they described as the 'syllogism of parental participation: a rise in the level of parental encouragement augments children's performance at school, teachers by involving parents in the school bring about a rise in the level of parental encouragement and teachers by involving parents in the school augment the children's performance' (p. 107).

It was on the basis of that syllogism that the connection between schools and parents developed for another decade or more. The 1980 Education Act increased parental choice and the 1986 Education (No. 2) Act increased parental representation on governing bodies.

To supplement, strengthen or, as some think, to contradict the legislation of 1986, the 1988 Education Reform Act made it possible for parents directly to intervene in their children's schooling through a complaints procedure (Maclure 1989:22–3):

In terms of a market ideology, this gives the consumers (i.e. the parents, who throughout the Act are seen as surrogate consumers for their sons and daughters) a chance to act if they believe there is a failure to deliver the curriculum to which they are, by law, entitled. In an ideal market system, pressure by consumers would be all-important. Under the Act is seems unlikely to be of paramount significance but dissatisfied parents who might otherwise feel impotent are given a weapon with which to fight back. It may also open up opportunities for barrack-room lawyers. Its main significance is likely to be to keep heads and their staff – and governing bodies – on permanent guard against the possibility of local challenge. They will watch their flanks with caution.

In contrast, Jones (1989) argued that 'only the most myopic enthusiasts for parent power can believe that this constituency [the total number of 100,000 parent-governors] will, by being placed in a quasi-market situation, automatically start operating as agents of that system'. He does, however, acknowledge that though 'Conservative rhetoric is fundamentally consumerist rather than democratic, it has served to put the issue of school-parent relations near the centre of educational debate and has led to legislation which increases parental involvement' (Jones 1989:120).

Future policies of parental involvement were also examined by Macbeth (1989). He outlined a basic professional minimum policy of twelve points. This should be supported with a professional code of practice for teachers. The aim should be to recognize that parents are consumers as well as clients and their schools and local authorities are the agents for implementing a closely knit policy of collaboration.

Several signs from differing sources point in the same direction. Sexton quoted in Ranson (1990:115) argued that 'it supposes that the wisdom of parents, separately and individually exercised, is more likely to achieve higher standards more quickly and more acceptably to the public than the collective wisdom of present bureaucrats, no matter how well-meaning those bureaucrats may be'.

Conclusion

To manage education through a partnership requires that those who are untrained and whose views and reactions are unpredictable must be treated nevertheless as full contributors rather than as nominal collaborators. The process of consultation carried out by a head must take proper note of their doubts, resistances and rejections. Finding a way in which fully to involve parents and governors takes time. To regard them as a formal but irrelevant accoutrement of educational reform would be a severe managerial mistake. Each party has to be treated as an unambiguous, properly informed and fully participative element in the process.

Clarity, trust and a constantly explicit readiness is needed in seeking a view, a criticism or an improvement on the draft of any plan.

A development scheme which is produced by the senior manager may first produce disbelief or scepticism. Consistency of attitude and a degree of persistence in time creates confidence. Matters have to be handled on a basis of equal awareness between numerous potential peers in the management task but it is the school alone, led by the head, who can give an assurance of quality. The school and its teachers alone can control the steps which produce quality.

CHAPTER 6

Managing connections within education

The manager has to be clear about the purpose of improvement and will use knowledge and support which can be brought from other places into the field which he or she can directly manage.

For instance, a young child's capacity to read is improved because a parent or a playgroup or a nursery class gives a good start. The primary-school headteacher then ensures that a clear message goes out to the effect that an early, informal, friendly or affectionate discourse in which printed words play a part is a welcome foundation for any school's reading programme. Mothers, fathers, playgroup leaders, nursery teachers and nursery assistants who respond to this are accepted as initiators and supporters in the process of learning to read. Beyond these, who are almost automatically involved in the process, stand librarians who make efforts to ensure that early reading is given prominence in both public and school library collections, social workers who know the importance of gearing the mind and interest of parents to the needs and interests of their children, and health visitors who encourage new mothers to talk and play with their babies in ways which allow growth and development to be marked by natural milestones of awareness and understanding.

In this example almost everyone knows what his or her task is – without very much management. If there are problems with illiterate families or reluctant parents, their difficulties can be tackled not so much through decisions about resource and direction as through guidance and persuasion.

If a class teacher is unduly censorious about reading difficulties or if a parent who, in school, listens to children reading but shows impatience, all that is required of management is the gentle touch.

Phase to phase

By contrast, how is the primary school to manage what it is that passes to the secondary school? If this were a simple and one-way movement, the answer would lie in ensuring that the record of achievement is up to date and intelligible, that assessment records are accurate and that the pastoral record, if any, is both just and constructive.

To manage a primary school, however, requires more awareness of the secondary school than is covered simply by passing on a record. Just as those who at the pre-school stage help children to learn to read know that a structured effort to consolidate all the skills connected with reading will be made in the primary school itself, so teachers in primary schools need to know what will be built on the skills, knowledge, interests and attitudes of the children whom they will pass on to the next stage.

Secondary schools do not always tell primary schools in detail what they do in terms of pupil development on either the curricular or the personal plane nor do primary schools always set out to learn what comes next. Where combined schools exist, usually in areas where primary and secondary schools have been replaced by first, middle and high schools and whole first and middle schools are occasionally run into a single (combined school) organization, there is some continuity of teacher programming from the age of 5 through to 12 years. Even then there can still be a gap between the combined school and the high school.

To avoid the waste of pupil time which arises from duplication of teaching in differing phases of schooling when the gap itself creates discontinuity, a variety of organizations have been used by LEAs to make sure that primary and secondary schools make clear to each other, first, what is being provided and later, as achievements and the needs of learning change, to help them to plan together to create a complementary or continuous curriculum between the phases.

The advantage of this type of planning is considerable and, if the organization involves teachers other than heads and deputies, it can permeate a whole school without difficulty. If only the head and deputies, on the other hand, can be involved (a limitation which is sometimes unavoidable unless lengthy and massive planning subgroups are to be put to work) then they, as managers, must make sure that the decisions about sharing are understood within their schools.

There is, even with a relatively sophisticated system of cross-phase planning, the difficulty that the children who are directly affected are those who are at the top of the primary school and at the youngest end of the secondary age range. What happens in the middle part of each phase may seem – mistakenly – unimportant.

Two factors can improve this limitation of effect: government documentation about programmes of study and statements of attainment are available. In theory, each phase of schooling can see at a glance what is to be built upon it – and can see the size of that future building. There are bridging organizations too which already exist between primary and secondary and have ample outline information. Neither a system of documentation nor a local bridging arrangement can change the national requirement but both have the opportunity to adjust to and to accommodate local preferences, strengths and developments of the curriculum.

The second factor lacks the structured objectivity of programmes of study and common statements of attainment. It comes in the shape of parental and family information. As information it is far from perfect but it draws its significance from the weight and faith which parents place on their view of which items constitute the stepping-stones of their children's ambitions. They know that there will be subjects to choose between at the right moment (or, sometimes, subjects for which their children will not be chosen) and they associate the chances of doing well at, for instance, GCSE level in mathematics with being good at maths in the primary school. They know that efficient reading is essential for all subjects other than physical education and they will in consequence watch very carefully the primary school's success with their children's capacity to read.

From bare bones such as these parents are able to relate questions about other types of learning: whether their children will do well in science in the secondary school can scarcely be judged if the primary school's own efforts in science are nervous or dull. But the science programmes which are set out in the national curriculum can be of realistic value to the parent as well as to the primary teacher. A foreign language, in contrast, carries the problem that there is virtually no evidence of capacity at the primary level – and a judgement or prediction based on an analogy with a proved capacity in a native language is open to doubt.

If the national curriculum and the process of assessment is intended to work through from Stage One at the age of 5–7 to Stage Four at the age of 14–16, there can be no reason for the primary and secondary phase of schooling to be in ignorance of each other. Indeed the need to know about the earlier and later stages of a child's education becomes imperative when schools have to plan the next stage of learning on the basis of achievement so far, when teachers have to evaluate and – if appropriate – change their own teaching, when parents have to be told in detail how their children are progressing and when LEAs, parents and governors have to have information which allows the performance of the school as a whole to be evaluated.

The parents' part in the continuity of learning has to be recognized. It is not a matter of simple sufferance on parents' evenings, with their lingering conventions that parents should not be encouraged to ask too many questions. Nor can teachers any longer be allowed to say that they do not know what will be required of their pupils three, six or eight years later. Being aware of what lies ahead is not a matter, that is, for teachers simply at the cross-over point. Every teacher, from the reception class upwards to the age of 16, needs to have a confident grasp of what the *whole* process of schooling and education can provide for and require from the pupil.

If managers fail to ensure this confident grasp – together with an equally confident openness to questions about the future needs of their learners – they will betray the ideals of that type of schooling which requires the co-operation of partners rather than the criticism of consumers. They will, too, have little to contribute to managing the total quality of the education they provide.

Beyond schools

The primary–secondary continuum has the advantage that it can be managed by people who are at home with schoolteachers, parents and families. The continuum between main secondary and post-16 education is more doubtful. Certainly schools which have sixth forms try hard to make use of prior knowledge about each student's performance and information about his or her potential. Such problems of internal management as may arise are likely to come from unfamiliarity on the part of individual teachers with the changing requirements of examinations and assessment.

More difficult for a secondary headteacher to manage is the feed-through to non-advanced further education (FE). Both schools and colleges give prominence to the near-autonomy of their subject departments – and indeed heads of departments are sometimes regarded as those who really run an upper school or a college.

Organizations for linking, such as those which many LEAs provide for the primary-to-secondary move, have also done much to encourage the pooling of detailed information about the curriculum up to the age of 16 and the curriculum either in the technical or vocational context up to the age of 17 or 18 or in a tertiary college up to the age of 18. When the non-school element of education and training after 16 is, in 1993, placed in a different part of the education system – even if it is only different for the purpose of separate funding – care will have to be taken not to lose the benefit of previous links.

Those links were particularly strengthened when a major test of the management of information which bore on student's continuity of study came with the Technical and Vocational Education Initiative (TVEI) in 1982. It was regarded as a way of forcing the emergence of a new curriculum (Jones 1989) and covered the last two years of compulsory secondary education and two years in FE. Technology at work, the world of business, personal and caring services were all, in one version (Ranson *et al.* 1986), to be included – combining an orientation to the world of work with strategies for learning which emphasized relevance and inquiry.

The TVEI programme required clear management at the point of input, at the end of each of the years of a scheme's work (particularly at the cross-over from the main secondary school stage to the college phase) and at the stage of evaluation. Not all the evidence about its early years pointed towards good management. The question of how far TVEI ultimately succeeds or fails has yet to be answered. So too an answer is needed to the question of whether the failure to manage the transfer of information and the joint planning of a continuous four-year scheme between two different phases and organizations of education has led to the achievement of less than was hoped for, regardless of the fact that it has been very heavily funded.

Another example of the need for sound management between two phases of education comes with entry into higher education. Schools and non-advanced FE colleges know the standards and the A level performances which will get their students into universities and institutes and colleges of higher education. In the case of the universities there is still a tenuous connection with schools in the broad context of A level examination syllabuses. There has been no comparable link in terms of examination syllabuses between schools and polytechnics. The only real connections are those which are associated with selection and admission (the Universities Central Council on Admissions (UCCA) and Polytechnics Central Admissions System (PCAS)) and not with continuity of curriculum. Higher education, like FE, is part of the total system of education. Guarantees of quality have to extend *through* the system rather than at separate points and junctions.

Partners in the community

Governors, teachers, parents and the earlier or later phases of education need to belong to a partnership which is managed directly for the benefit of children and students. Despite their all falling within the group of people who, trained or not, have like minds and common aspirations for the improvement of education, the management of even that partnership is not straightforward.

More complex still is the management of partners who form nine other agencies and influences. Some have connections which are so close to education that they can be regarded as falling inside the group of like-minded supporters. But their distance from the point where contact is directly made between teaching and learning is important. They are not on the whole involved in direct teaching and, second, each of them has to have a separate viewpoint because the focus of the job is mainly outside that of any school.

Thus, health visitors have a specific interest in some individual children and a broad interest in, and view of, the local communities which each school serves. Social workers in the same way have a specific involvement with some individual families and children. Where they are still organized separately from social services, education welfare officers can sum up an area's state of mind as well as help – or question – individual families, at least up to the time when centralized social work services are cut back. One effect of the local management of schools (LMS) might, ironically, be that no school can choose or afford welfare officers. Their sole task would become that of the LEA duty to keep truancy in check (*TES* 1991e).

The police, in early schemes of proactive community work, also took an interest in a locality and its population at all ages. The narrower role of school liaison officers to some extent diminishes the usefulness of the police in building up a cross-community view. Housing officers, too, will provide important links between some parts of a local community and its schools but notably less than in the period before the privatization of subsidized housing.

Probation officers are less often in contact with a whole school. In the secondary sector they may from time to time be concerned with defined localities and with those young people who come to their attention from specific communities. But it is in their generalized role as the preventers and headers-off of criminality that they give the greatest value to schools as well as to young people and their families.

Local businesses are more directly involved in school affairs since the 1986 Education (No. 2) Act's change in the make-up of school governing bodies. In the secondary sector they have a long history of influence as local employers. The same connection exists in FE. They are also suppliers of goods and services. There can be an ambiguity about their standing but they are very often sponsors and supporters, in material and financial ways, of schools' programmes.

Two other types of body fall into a final category of partners: counsellors whether in Citizens' Advice Bureaux or in RELATE (the earlier Marriage Guidance Council) are often drawn into school connections – through parents rather than children. The latter, however, also benefit from the type of counselling which schools, usually together, wish to provide or which churches on their own or through dioceses and joint ministries are ready to fund. Other voluntary bodies, in youth services or adult education, can also be relied upon as partners but more often in the secondary and FE sectors than in primary schools.

With these nine potential partners in addition to teachers, parents and other phases of education, the manager has to decide whether to seek a broad partnership or the separate involvement of individual co-operators.

For the direct benefit of pupils it will be individual partners who will matter more than a grand design of co-operation. But if a school sees itself as a community school, giving out as much as – or more than – it takes in in the shape of benefit to individual pupils, the manager must decide with some or all the partners on which aspects of community education to concentrate. Later will come decisions which hinge upon the manager's having identified points of dissent or resistance. Funds will then need to be found or diverted and teachers trained or retrained in their understanding of community education. In the process of its development the manager must define the purposes of community education, identify the steps by which it can be provided, define responsibilities at each stage and operate some form of continuous monitoring.

It is a big move to concentrate not on the co-operation between a school and one useful ally but on taking an active position in, for instance, needs-orientated community education for the benefit of the community at large. In the latter, the school which sets out to democratize education in its geographical or moral area (that is, in a context of those who share beliefs and values) or to enable more people to help themselves, brings with it a set of beliefs which go beyond the Plowden idea of the community making use of the physical amenities of a primary school. They come nearer to the views of A. H. Halsey about educational priority areas (DES 1972). And they go considerably beyond such statements as the government made about the connection between community and schools in the 1988 Education Reform Act.

To choose between individual partnerships which feed benefit into the school and large associations which have potential value for a larger community is a matter not of managerial choice from day to day but of planning and drafting at the level of the institutional development plan. Those who draw up that plan should include – and not only because they are nominally represented on governing bodies – a wide range of community interests. But the first move must come from the school itself. This is because it is only the school and its daily managers who can assess what it can afford – and what it has to afford – to do in terms of staff time and money and because it is the school which has, in the end, to initiate any assessment of the type of community assistance which will provide its partners with the benefits they seek.

Appraisal and training

In contrast to the immediacy of assistance which can emerge from well managed relationships between phases of education and between schools and colleges and the external community, longer-term connections need to be created and nurtured. For instance, primary schools are now involved, on a thin representational basis admittedly, in providing feedback to teacher educators. This involves an awareness of the activities and requirements of the Council for the Accreditation of Teacher Education (CATE) and of the validation processes in higher education (particularly, until its demise, of the Council for National Academic Awards (CNAA)) which control courses of teacher education. It means that the initial education of teachers has to be more open than in the past to the understanding of those who employ new teachers.

A broad awareness of the details of initial teacher education will not be of great assistance to a school other than to bring into some kind of focus an activity which used to appear to be both distant and unrelated. However, when teacher appraisal is a firm part of educational reform, it would make better sense if certain aspects of management in initial teacher education could consciously be brought together with the assessment of teacher capacity. This linking of two aspects of a teacher's professionalism would prevent appraisal being regarded as simply a tiresome extra and could, on the positive side, help the process of planning (West and Bollington 1990:9–10):

Planning for appraisal . . . . needs to be carried forward in the light of the full range of the demands confronting the particular LEA, the particular school, the particular teacher. The introduction of the national curriculum, for instance, could be significantly eased if the appraisal process is used to identify what changes will be necessary at school and teacher level and how and by whom these can be achieved. Similarly, appraisal is capable of providing much of the data necessary for the production of a realistic School Development Plan, since the important part of the planning will not be identifying appropriate curriculum development goals but identifying who will be able to deliver these, and what preparation and support will be necessary if they are to deliver.

In a management plan which guarantees quality, those who manage are able to make a systematic connection between differing aspects of initial teacher education and differing types of teacher performance in the school. It is possible, too, to link the implementation of a school plan with a ranking of priorities between a school's teachers and their needs for in-service training.

In the still longer term it would be possible for national planners and institutional managers of initial teacher education to adjust the mix of curriculum, pedagogy and school-based learning in such a way as to narrow avoidable gaps between initial and in-service teacher education.

Vocational education

While it may be straightforward to think of school development planning, teacher appraisal, the identifying of remediable faults and the training or retraining of teachers as one set of loosely connected but manageable disciplines, it is less straightforward but equally urgent to expect that other connections should be more systematically organized in order to give assurances of quality. In particular, schools need a better working knowledge of the link between their own level of general education and the requirements of vocational education and training.

While one argument against expecting schools to carry an additional load of knowledge is that such knowledge, particularly in the vocational field, rapidly becomes out of date, two arguments from the other side have some lasting weight. First, even at the primary-school age, parents are thinking ahead to qualifications and jobs. To wait until their children are in the secondary stage may seem a long time for delay. Second, the connection between the national curriculum and assessment at Key Stages Two and Three ought to show an understandable link not only with work at Key Stage Four but also with the examinations and qualifications which are either directly relevant to the final stage of compulsory schooling or into which work at that level immediately leads.

At that stage the equivalence between the final level of attainment in the scheme of national assessment with the grades of GCSE will for some years leave questions to be answered. Nevertheless, because GCSE was planned for a decade before it was implemented, the debate about equivalence started early. Those who managed it had access to information and carefully sifted opinion.

Less clear is the equivalence between the upper levels of attainment at the age of 16 and the exemption of a student from some of the requirements of qualifications which are administered by the Business and Technician Education Council (BTEC) and by the National Council for Vocational Qualifications (NCVQ). There is confusion too about the future place of the Certificate of Pre-vocational Education. The school manager, in contrast to his or her experience of GCSE, here has to struggle for clarity – a struggle which is made no easier by the over-simplified statements of policy about the unification of general and vocational education which are made by central government and by its political opponents.

This is because the fine detail of equivalence and exemption in the world of FE and vocational training is being handled by those who have a direct involvement in that field alone. It does not, for instance, impinge on the fifteen or so criteria for sound initial teacher training which come from the CATE in its guidance about the professional education of those who teach in schools.This can partly be excused on the ground that there is already a great deal for those in initial teacher education to do. The student has to benefit from up-to-date practical experience on the part of the teacher trainer. A broad range of non-classroom experience is also expected from the student. He or she must know how to exercise pastoral care, what to do in order to observe requirements of health and safety, how to handle links with parents, how to weigh the significance of community connections, what to understand about the world of work and how to regard a teacher's individual position within the structure of the education service at large.

These have a practical usefulness. They are not matters solely of philosophic awareness. They are valuable parts of the network which the manager must handle. But are they so important that the teachers should not be expected to know about technical and vocational education, about an important part, in other words, of the education service towards which many of their pupils will, in time, be moving?

However slight the contact may seem to be between certain levels of government policy-making and the work of teaching, managers of education at school level would be better placed if teachers were at least aware that programmes such as those connected with the TVEI can be altered by ministerial will – and can have their funding reduced. It helps managers when teachers know, for example, that ministers in one government department (the DES) blame those of another (Department of Employment) for shifts in a national scheme of vocational education. It matters, too, that teachers should grasp the fact that the DES can lay down details of a policy but that the Department of Employment funds it. Even the struggle for the control of the FE sector from 1993 between those same departments is not without significance for those who teach in schools.

Knowledge which teachers possess about other parts of the world of education and training allows managers to rely on a broader set of reference points when new policies are developed. It also requires them to guard against their own tendencies towards myopia. Managers need to feel, for example, that for teachers, maybe not directly involved but who, perhaps in primary schools, know that parents are aware of TVEI and expect some of their children to benefit from it, nonetheless know about any significant lack of governmental co-ordination. For a teacher not to know which national policies exist and how financial considerations affect those policies creates – as far as parents are concerned who want information and advice – an unreliable ignorance.

Primary-school teachers have to work harder at reducing their remoteness from large aspects of policy than those at the secondary or FE stages. It is secondary-school teachers who need to know how, in practical terms, reduced funding affects the work of a TVEI team and, more seriously, how it can affect a TVEI consortium. Consortia reduce isolation, encourage curriculum planning across schools and colleges, allow joint in-service training and common timetabling and stimulate good marketing of courses for post-16s. They also move well beyond simply the delivery of the TVEI programme (Cohen 1989:16):

While . ... . consortia were initially viewed as vehicles for 'delivery' they have, in the extension programme, quickly incorporated other concerns which relate to the whole gamut of educational concerns and particularly those relating to the new curriculum changes of the Education Reform Act. Moreover, as schools across the country have already discovered, curriculum changes initiated for 14–19 year olds inevitably impinge on the curriculum of younger age groups.

Hence national levels of support for what is essentially a late-secondary or post-secondary programme, the local organization which supports it and the commitment of teachers who contribute to it at more than one level – all these matter. They matter, too, to the curriculum of younger age-groups – and it is difficult for any manager to justify omitting the primary school teacher from the long term planning of vocational education.

This last point is repeated in a study of the work of those who have co-ordinated TVEI clusters in Leicestershire (Edwards *et al.* 1990:48):

The introduction of the national curriculum requirements for primary science and technology emphasise the importance of primary/secondary liaison. The cluster co-ordinators were beginning to find a role here, drawing on their experience of secondary/tertiary links. Co-ordinators' ideas for improving links included a suggestion for staff exchanges for finding better methods of publicising choices for courses.

The effect on the education of younger pupils has been specifically highlighted by the Association of Science Education as a task for management. Science as a vehicle through which the national curriculum's concerns can be met for equal opportunities, the heightening of economic awareness, the creation of links with industry, the enhancement of knowledge about the technological aspects of science and the effective use of information technology – these all mean that the principles of TVEI can be embraced at one and the same time. And if the management of secondary school science departments includes the management of review and of staff development then the effect of a whole-team approach to TVEI and the sharing of ideas, expertness and good practice will be better than the effect of teachers accepting TVEI principles on an individual basis. Beyond the team in the individual school 'it is important to note that TVEI funding is aimed specifically at the 14 to 18 age range. However, it is impossible to attend to approaches to teaching and learning for this stage without attending to how students are learning prior to this' (Versey 1989:23).

Helping to breach barriers

Most messages about the significance of the TVEI programme for the education of younger children come from the secondary sector or from those who speak for the ministries, either of Employment or of Education and Science. It is disappointing that a comparable awareness of the inter-phase link is not commonly recorded in the primary sector itself. Is that the fault of initial teacher education? No, at least not as far as that will have been changed by CATE. Is it the fault of an overburdened teaching force, for whom full time class teaching is the norm? This is more likely, but there must also be some responsibility on the part of heads and governors. Academic councils, professional resource centres and curriculum 'clusters' all acknowledge the need to diminish isolation, but they do not all look forward with the same clear-sightedness further into any young person's life. This being so, who, outside the schools, can provide assistance?

The most obvious answer lies in careers services and counselling. The careers service works for secondary schools and, up to a point, for FE. It does not penetrate the primary school although it is acknowledged that the earliest thoughts – mainly in the form of fantasy – about one's choice of life-work do formulate themselves when children are between 8 and 12 years of age.

In place of an external adviser drawn from the careers service, the primary school draws on the build-up of a pupil's capacities and potential as assessed by teachers in the traditional way and by the national system of assessment at two stages. The secondary school can rely on further stages of national assessment together with recourse to a record of achievement which has to be provided for every pupil at the age of 16.

The putting together of a record of achievement and the formative use of assessment at every stage of schooling should mean that such patterns of feedback as well as prediction would in time be developed as would cross the divide between primary, secondary, sixth form, tertiary college, FE and higher education. The manager at both secondary- and primary-school level, would, when that development is complete, find it possible to adapt to school use recommendations about the wholesale management and regearing of both policy and practice which is needed in FE in order to create a comprehensive setting for the introduction of new vocational qualifications (Haffenden and Brown 1989). This in turn might be assisted or hindered by the treatment of vocational education as well as FE colleges, sixth form colleges and tertiary colleges as entities which are to be separately funded and managed under the Further Higher Education Act 1992.

As matters stand, the development and negotiation of student action plans point to the need for college staff to be aware of what happened before the age of 16. It also requires that teachers in schools should know the purposes to which their assessments and predictions will be put. And it is significant that, in the Association for Science Education, an introductory report (Billings 1989) drew attention to the particular importance, in the framework of new vocational qualifications, of the assessment of prior learning, an importance further underlined by Slusarchuk & Nicholl (1990:112).

Taking account of what has already been achieved by a student and breaching the barriers between separate sections of education and training calls for conscious management. Careers advisers and counsellors can help. But there are now other large sources of potential assistance.

Although the flow and use of information about TVEI and NCVQ have been patchy and limited, the aims, in contrast, of Training and Enterprise Councils (TECs) are all-embracing. In trying to ensure that every young person has access to education and training leading to recognized vocational qualifications and a job 'the TEC will determine how best to contribute to raising the achievement and practical skill levels of all young people. Working in partnership with the education service, the careers service, training providers and employers, the TEC can help smooth the transition from education to work' (Department of Employment 1989). In their work the TECs may either influence or take over the careers service (Farley 1990). This would be an important symbol of a systematic connection between secondary schools, FE, employers and the world of work. It would, too, be difficult for secondary schools not to concern themselves, across the whole picture of a student's achievement, in the preparation of what is described as 'careership' (CBI 1990).

TECs are regarded both as regulators of the local training market in the transition between education, training and employment and as the channel through which employers can influence the vocational education and training system. A Vocational Education and Training Task Force, reporting to the Confederation of British Industry (CBI 1990) emphasized that the connection between training policies and employer involvement would enable one of four targets to be met, namely that 'all education and training provision should be structured and designed to develop self-reliance, flexibility and broad competence as well as specific skills' (p. 19). The same report referred to the priority of creating 'a new culture in which the school leaving age ceases to be an end to education and in which the development of skills and knowledge continues throughout working life. A greater self-development ethic is needed which builds on entitlements and responsibilities' (CBI 1990: 21).

That each stage of education and training can build on what has gone before requires that the manager at each stage should know what is happening elsewhere. In the primary school, self-development means development which moves onward because the parent as well as the teacher can make use of the information and assessments provided by the school. At the secondary-school stage it becomes less a partnership between all three and more a matter for the individual student and his or her advisers, whether from inside the school or outside.

The emphasis, after the age of 16, is on the young adult, the trainer, the employer or the pre-higher education tutor. None can work well in isolation and for that reason it is reassuring that the CBI, in pressing its case for the TECs to be the local regulators of vocational training, stresses the importance of the young person's (and the adult worker's) 'personal file', building on the existing good practice of records of achievement in schools. In the same connection, the CBI urges that profiles should not only bridge the gap between education, training and work but should also 'be integrated into the learning process. Appropriate time, resources and training must be allowed to ensure that [the profiles] are completed accurately. It is important to market them to young people, teachers, parents and employers as well as to providers of further education and training' (CBI 1990:22).

In looking at training and education as parts of a whole process it is not surprising that TECs are encouraged to take responsibility not only for Youth Training Schemes and for Employment Training but also for non-advanced, work-related FE. This development underlines the need for the manager of education to be knowledgeable about the broad field of government initiatives for employment training.

Managing onward connections

There is money and faith behind the TECs. There is also a strong business-based drive for improved training. Together they can quickly achieve an interplay of information and planning between different parts of the education and training world. This is necessary too in the management of primary and secondary education. If such links are not built, schooling will suffer from being not only detached from the life-long vision of education and retraining which is foreseen by the CBI, the TECs and the NCVQ but also from appearing not to care about continuity, feed-through and quality assurance. This would deny the national curriculum one of its greatest strengths and would expose schools to blame for not playing a co-operative role in the mix of better education and training which is needed.

The messages for local managers are that there is a need to allow time to pass before the linked activities which revolve around the three major innovations of the 1980s (NCVQ, TVEI extension, TECs) reveal how much they can contribute to each other in terms of an essentially joint strategy. Regrettably, time may be their undoing, particularly as the diminished funding for TVEI extension work shrinks and as criticism grows about the lack of control in its financing by government departments. But there is at least some chance of cooperation, in contrast to the absence of an obligation to plan together between higher education, sixth forms in secondary schools and colleges of further as well as tertiary education. This omission attracts attention but little action (Maclure 1991; Ball 1991; Finegold *et al.* 1991).

Although institutions of higher education to some extent reshaped their admissions procedures before and after the Further & Higher Education Act 1992, they still appear to pay little attention to the effect which their policies have on schools and colleges. Credit must be given to the continued efficiency of the UCCA, to the successful launch of the PCAS and to the swift amalgamation of their efforts as the binary division disappeared. More is to be hoped, for there does need to be 'a truly comprehensive and integrated system of admissions to (full-time and sandwich) higher education' (Ball 1985:83):

Without some such system we shall always be guessing at the 'real field' – the true level of demand from those who are able to benefit from higher education and who wish to do so. But there is a more important issue. Just as the student award regulations are the 'hidden hand' of higher education planning, so also do our admissions arrangements determine more than just who studies where: they partly condition both the nature of our courses and the shape of sixth-form education.

Ball argues that the main engine in the shaping of higher education should be informed student demand, not manpower planning. However, one consequence of relying on patterns of student demand is that those in higher education 'rarely have to face directly the question of whether or not a candidate is suitable for higher education at all. And yet this is the prior question, decided, as often as not, without reference to admissions officers, by school teachers or parents or by the lack of confidence of marginal candidates themselves' (Ball 1985:86).

This seems to be an accurate description of the initial decisions about seeking entry into higher education. It is a long way from the 'careership' proposals of the CBI and a long way, too, from the systematic manner in which those parties argue who would wish to see TECs as the regulators of training and as the godfather of the careers service.

If schools respond in different ways to the requirement for guidance, special information and sometimes special effort which attends higher education entry as against guidance for entry into vocational education and training, is this because there are two cultures? Or is it a conscious decision on the part of managers to handle the processes differently because schools themselves differ in their habits of work?

Part of the answer lies in the need, when arrangements are new, to create a structure which allows preparation for, and feedback from, newly initiated operations. Plans are made as a whole and the analysis of failed innovations places particular emphasis on wholeness.

Connections between schools and the post-school system which have developed over many years lack simpleness of planning. Some parts of the connection are old and in need of review. The assumption that university matriculation still exercises any kind of influence on examinations at the age of 16 should be excised. The idea that GCSE, A level and AS level results are predictive also needs to be put to one side. At the same time it should be made clear that apart from false assumptions about matriculation, higher education should only have a small contribution to make to the range, standard and appositeness of 16+ and 18+ examination syllabuses and schemes of marking.

The lack of connection between schools and, when they were distinct from the universities, polytechnics is obvious: the latter played no formal part in examination boards. The same was true of institutes and colleges of higher education. Yet decisions about the significance, for entry into higher education, of school-level achievement in public examinations are made all the time – and it is odd that they seem to be made without reference to CNAA, BTEC or the NCVQ. As a result these bodies are not yet in a position to influence the preparation of individual groups of students for higher education. This is one of the results of there not being any systematic connection in the importance which government schemes attach to the flow of information between different spheres and levels of training, education and the use of skilled people. It brings a certain hollowness to the concern to guarantee total quality in continuous education.

There is no need to make a new case for the improvement of management connections with higher education. In the 1960s and 1970s the Standing Conference on University Entrance tried to deal with it on a large-scale basis but repeated efforts to bring about improvements of connection amounted to little. The hope for the future rests on the merging of the separately funded worlds of universities and polytechnics. As the binary divide recedes and vanishes a further revolution in creating links with schools will make the management of transition more rational.

Conclusion

It is the task of managers, across the phase gaps, to organize feedback from and into their own spheres of work. They need to make a regular picture available to the national originators of change and to those agencies who are responsible for change being organized in specific way. This is particularly true of the National Curriculum Council and the Schools Examination and Assessment Council. That picture should be one of shared progress, shared failing, of fitness of match or lack of match between policies and funding. The separate phases of education and training should be made visible to those who contribute to the process – teachers, employers, trainers and funders. This should be accompanied by a view from the beneficiaries and users of each part of education and training. In this way each partner can build up a capacity to contribute to the workings of an interlinked system. Schools alone cannot make guarantees about the quality of education. The whole range of contributors must join in the planning and control of quality. All partners must show a confirmable commitment to quality.

CHAPTER 7

Lessons from the past

Since the 1960s the impact of good management at school level has been increasingly clear. Despite this there have been long-standing assumptions that management is the same as administration. And administration was something which occurred in Whitehall or in LEAs.

The concerns of administration used to be the maintenance of law and regulation, the sustaining of working relationships with voluntary organizations and denominational bodies and the planning and maintenance of programmes across a range of responsibilities. These were concerned with budgets, building programmes and staffing. They were also concerned with curriculum development, advisory support and in-service education. Administration at local authority level also took responsibility for public consultation about major changes in school organization, for trade union relationships and for detailed arrangements relating to transport, admission procedures, school records, statistics and public relations.

How matters stood, even as recently as 1980, can be seen in a summary such as this (Brooksbank 1980:201):

Authorities are concerned to delegate powers, as far as is practical and efficient to do so. Inescapably, they must retain such things as overall financial control, a determination of the size of a school's teaching and ancillary staff, and major decisions about buildings, although many conclusions on these matters are reached only after an ebb and flow of consultation and representation. Equally, they wish to encourage local initiatives, and these are best taken by a partnership of lively governors and competent teachers.

This now seems a long way from the position taken in the Education (No. 2) Act 1986 and the Education (Schools) Act 1992. It is also a long way away from the local management of schools (LMS): local authorities, chief education officers and elected members of local councils now have little of the power of the early 1980s.

Despite the scale and depth of change little was done to prepare for new demands of management. Since the early 1960s there had been a movement for what had been described as organization development (OD) . There had been research and review carried out by the Organization for Economic Co-operation and Development (OECD) and by International Movements Towards Educational Change (IMTEC). The essentials were described as a series of common understandings (Dalin and Rust 1983:21–2):

First, OD is an activity which relies on concepts and research findings from the behavioural sciences, primarily from social psychology.

Second, the purpose is to improve the health and functioning of school organizations. In contrast to more conventional strategies for innovation, especially found in America, organization development is holistic or systemic in that it concentrates on the organization more than on the isolated individual or practice. However, the system is not here interpreted to be the broad political and administrative superstructure, but the school organization. . . .

Third, . . . it is a self-correcting, self-renewing process, undertaken by the members of an organization, although external support usually exists in the form of consultants or self-assessment instruments. . . .

Fourth, organization development involves a deliberate set of steps including self-assessment, diagnosis, problem-solving, planning and action phases. . . .

Fifth, it is a continuous or long term process rather than a one-shot exercise or a brief episode in the life of the school.

Sixth, it is usually evaluated in terms of its ability to enhance an organization's effectiveness and health as an organization rather than specific output criteria such as student achievement.

It was this last point which at the time led to some discomfort about OD. Not everyone was sure what a school's effectiveness or health amounted to. It was not conceived that these made up, in present-day terms, a system for securing and guaranteeing quality. By now, in contrast, the summary of the six points is very much what school management has to cover in the practical arrangement for giving assurances about, and for controlling, quality.

The fact that the requirements are those of central government rather than those initiated by individual schools makes a difference to the process of development. When Dalin and Rust were writing they pointed to a variety of stimuli for change: in the United States it had been competition with the Soviet Union. In Europe social democracy had, they said, tried to develop schools by passing social reform legislation. And it was thought that the movement in England and Wales in the late 1960s, towards the extension of teachers' centres was an attempt to create what was described as a focus for teacher renewal.

Management was scrutinized in the 1970s and 1980s as an instrument for innovation. Much of that lay in curriculum and pedagogy rather than in the large-scale organization of schools. It was not the administrative aspect, outlined in Brooksbank, which was in need of attention as much as the daily process of feeding change into a school through the conversion, retraining or updating of its teachers' skills and through the introduction of both new materials and new perspectives in the build-up of subject knowledge and human skills.

In this concentration of teaching and learning, school management pays less attention to three other categories of innovation listed in an OECD study, namely those relating to the objectives and functions of the school in its broader social and economic context, those concerned with the administration of the educational system and those which are mainly concerned with role definition and relationships (CERI 1973).

In the first of these categories, the impulse of schools to develop their community activities and the education of adults called for an approach which differed from the management of curriculum change. Confusion arose when heads were unclear whether they were developing a social rather than an instructional milieu. Confusion also arose when schools took over administrative functions which traditionally had been located in LEAs.

This movement of decentralization gathered pace in the late 1980s. Less money was left within the control of local authorities. They became less capable of providing central services on an economical basis (school transport, for instance) or on an equitable basis (such as evenly spread central library facilities or schemes of specialist instruction and the organization required in, for instance, music). In the decentralizing of money management, ambiguities also arose in connection with buildings (where were the dividing lines between repairs, maintenance and improvements?) and in personnel (did governors have a different responsibility for teachers in contrast to non-teachers?).

Schools thus slipped into the danger of carrying out a new range of management tasks without the benefit of fresh definitions. They could, with one part of their mind, cling to the idea of teacher autonomy. With another part they asked for the benefit of good management but without too much external pressure. In one study of primary schools, the 1918 *Handbook of Suggestions for the Consideration of Teachers* was quoted as making only one requirement of uniformity, 'the Board of Education desired to see in the teaching of public elementary schools . . . that each teacher shall think for himself, and work out by himself such methods of teaching as may use his powers to best advantage and best suited to the particular needs and conditions of the school' (Kogan 1973:145).

This statement was not only made but meant, said Kogan, 'When change has been positively mounted it has occurred through advisory teachers rather than inspectors, in-service training rather than managerially dominated systems' (Kogan 1973:145)

Because teachers' centres and the increase of in-service education in the late 1970s and 1980s occurred outside schools, there was some separation between the flow of curriculum development in the sense in which it was supported in schools by the work of advisers and advisory teachers and in the way it made its impact on individual teachers through regular courses of familiarization and in-service education. Heads and governors were not required to manage these two main influences although headteachers themselves were often directly involved in the committees and working parties which steered the programmes of teachers' centres. Governors were kept informed but as a decision of the headteachers rather than as a matter of right.

This changed when a specific part of each year's public expenditure at central government level was identified and earmarked for in-service education. At first LEAs made annual bids and had to ensure that money was passed to schools. The management of in-service work became more complicated when it was a matter of delegation to schools. The burden increased when it became clear that it was schools who would be held principally responsible in implementing the national curriculum, in taking the first steps in teacher appraisal and in managing their finances. At the same time the Training Grants Scheme was specifically excluded from money which was allocated to LMS. Added to this, the problem of teacher absence for in-service work and the difficulty of finding and affording substitutes meant that schools found participation in in-service education increasingly difficult (Williams 1991:189).

For managers to have information about what happens in earlier and later phases of education does not guarantee that they put that knowledge to good use. When those at the level of schools read about allegations of incompetence on the part of the earlier separate Universities Funding Council and about the individual difficulties of separate universities, they felt frustration about the apparent misuse of money in other sectors or believed that if other people got their sums wrong, they in schools should also have been excused. Schools at present can see that the same thing might happen to them – particularly when local decisions can be made about levels of pay and when local purse-holding is deliberately distanced from the machinery of national funding.

In the same way, information about how the National Curriculum Council (NCC) came down in favour of more information and factual knowledge in the history curriculum after months of comment and criticism led to a holding of breath as to what precisely would emerge in the shape of revised requirements. No one immediately set to in order to work out how a well-publicized national response in terms of content and expectation of achievement would actually turn out at each key stage. In other words, awareness that something was happening at national level did not provide workable lines along which local managers could shape their own efforts. Nevertheless, each change had to be translated into local activity and if that translation did not take place, managers ran the risk of national decisions being superseded by yet further alterations.

A further example of national information about which local managers were unable to act came with the expanding of the National Diploma level of BTEC in schools: when it was shown that there did not have to be an exclusive choice of BTEC and A levels and that to offer both at the same time was not only permissible but also helpful, the manager was able to make new local choices. Those new choices had to be afforded in terms of staff, accommodation, time, equipment and other items which needed a redisposition of money – but decisions about such items as these were already a normal part of management.

An extension of BTEC qualifications into schools, in the form of the one year First Diplomas, could not be supported solely by re-arranging internal resources. When the ban on schools in providing these was lifted, it was made clear that schools alone could not afford them. BTEC had to call on FE colleges to create closer working relationships with schools than most existing links provided – and the Council would only authorize a school to run a First Diploma course if it was satisfied that it could provide not only teachers with experience in working in business or in industry but also specialized accommodation and equipment.

Thus a local manager could make new arrangements about National Diploma work in a school but not about a First Diploma. An improved version of the Certificate of Pre-vocational Education (CPVE) was on the stocks but a manager's negotiation about it would have to take place with the City and Guilds of London Institute (CGLI). In addition to working out equivalences between Advanced level, a one-year BTEC diploma and one-year CPVE, the manager needed also to remember that the upper reaches of qualification under the National Council for Vocational Qualifications (NCVQ) would require another exercise in establishing equivalence and balance. If the NCVQ was too narrow in its concern with those skill-based qualifications which satisfied employers, the local manager could only wait and see what the final outcome would be between the force of BTEC (arguing for greater breadth and balance) and NCVQ. And in the end it would be national government which was expected to sort them out (*TES* 1990):

Parity of esteem depends on more than assertions about which NCVQ level equals an A Level. There is undoubtedly a growing consensus about the need for a radical rethink of the post-16 generation in both schools and FE colleges. But opinion has been hardening towards more coherence on curriculum and qualifications, less separation between academic and vocational, something more like a British Bac. It is not at all clear that stepping up the competition between schools and colleges, and between the territorially ambitious award bodies, will produce the broad choices in education and training that ought to be an entitlement post-16, just as much as the national curriculum is before that watershed.

The point at which the national curriculum begins to matter is the age of 5: assessment at each successive stage should in some way affect the ambitions and choices at each age. As the scheme of national assessment develops, the less crucial will earlier stages seem to become. Until then, having to provide a system of education which is nominally continuous but in terms of reality, disconnected and without knowing the full extent of its effects, is likely to lead to misunderstanding and tension.

Stress

The greater part of stress in education is described as arising from new pressures and, in particular, from new legislation. This ignores repeated steps which have been taken at several levels of management to reduce uncertainty. That task of alleviating anxiety is a matter for a whole school or college; it is, too, a matter which requires commitment at a high level if its damage is to be reduced.

The points at which stress and anxiety emerge can be mapped. Their occurrence can be predicted and it is helpful to have a guide such as that produced by the Education Service Advisory Committee (ESAC) of the Health and Safety Commission. The two most important messages emerging from that guide are that stress is a permanent aspect of life and is not peculiar to the education service. But if its harmful effects are ignored because it is thought that they are too generalised, too subjective or too difficult to tackle, then unnecessary ill-health will continue to occur. There is clearly no panacea but there are improvements which can be made in almost all work situations, and which all reflect good management. A more open and informed attitude to the problems of stress also allows more opportunities for individuals to emerge from the isolation of their own anxieties (ESAC 1990:26).

When the manager of any organization knows the worth of what he or she is doing it is easier to explain its purposes to other people and to seek their co-operation. Isolation – in the terms of ESAC – is reduced. But while 'worth' in a school or college is measured in terms of the advancement of learning and the personal development of the pupil or student, the awareness of what that amounts to comes only gradually. Evidence about it comes from a range of sources and that evidence is not uniform in the way in which it is presented. Nor does each type of evidence carry the same weight.

Information

What is easier to handle is information – and management information which is planned and delivered in predetermined packages should be particularly straightforward. But even that has difficulties.

Examples of confusion in defining and acquiring exactly the type of management information which is needed for specific tasks and policies emerged from a widely publicized aspect of management in further education in the 1980s. The Further Education Management Information System (FEMIS) had been launched with DES funding in 1982. It was designed for use in colleges and was based on the personal microcomputer. The broad aim was to assist colleges with the monitoring of their performance and to enable them to demonstrate to both LEAs and central government that they were cost effective. Four indicators were emphasized – staff student ratios, average class sizes, average student hours and average lecturer hours.

Difficulties about securing uniformity of approach to such seemingly uncomplicated measurements were experienced early in the trials of the system. The main problem was the underestimating of the planning and management which was necessary at the stage of implementing the system. Hopes were disappointed both among college managers and in LEAs.

Part of the trouble was that the information which colleges needed for their own purpose was on a scale different from that which was called for by local authorities and by the DES. When the system worked at its best it realized the highest hopes: 'The opportunity for college directors to purchase low-cost systems geared to institutional management, as well as to LEA or national data requirements, created a significant opportunity to improve strategic, tactical and operational management. Equally, many LEAs can now purchase systems for colleges and thus improve their own information base on the colleges' (Gibson and Wickham 1987:463).

The transition from traditional management techniques to those based on personal computers revealed the need not only for good early planning but also for high-level commitment in directing what was to be implemented and for what were described as decision support systems.

Despite the care which was taken, notably by the Further Education Staff College, to achieve success in FEMIS, a shared confidence in the accuracy of basic statistics between colleges, local authorities and the DES was not achieved. Hence an important tool of management whose common usefulness could be judged by the essential partners to collaboration failed to provide what had appeared to be promised – and one says 'appeared' because it may have been the wish of some college managers not to allow information by which their efficiency might be judged to become available to other parties. This is in contrast to that information which can be challenged and questioned which has to be made publicly available in support of quality assurance.

An aspect of this college view was revealed in one analysis of the advantages of introducing a management information system (MIS). It was conceded that the advantages within a college are clear (Williams 1987:490):

The increased awareness of the college environment which it offers the manager permits more forceful and effective action on his or her part. . . . However, coupled with this awareness of the benefits on offer must be a realisation that perceptions of management style, organization and staff development will be drastically altered. The impact is often profound, with the MIS acting as a catalyst for developing a milieu in which the quantitative and qualitative aspects of approaches to systematic review can be balanced and integrated.

If this is translated into terms of school management, the combination of quantitative and qualitative aspects might entail the organization and measurement of effective learning. But the information which was handled in FEMIS made up only the bones of college work and it seems likely that the initial difficulty experienced in FE about translating information into worthwhile knowledge about the improvement in learning would also be experienced at the primary or secondary levels.

Ideally, schemes of management information which are intended to help further and higher education should be of assistance to schools, both by pioneering new systems of analysing information and by making the resulting messages available to them. This could, for instance, have happened with two other FE developments – one related to the Educational Counselling and Credit Transfer Information System (ECCTIS) and the other to an initiative in the mid-1980s launched by the then Manpower Services Commission to provide a computer-assisted local labour market information system (CALLMIS). Had this been successful it would have been possible for managers of education and training at every level within a locality to identify major employment issues, to assess likely large-scale change in employment patterns and to identify educational links which might have to be developed or changed.

When is knowledge too remote?

The manager at school level could say that the plans and consequences of planning which emerge from employment strategies or from higher education are too remote to matter. But they cannot be too remote if a school – primary or secondary – is working to a curriculum blueprint which has been sought by successive governments and if we now accept that schools have only a limited choice in any broader expectations which society imposes upon them.

Eight such blueprints have been outlined in one cultural analysis. They point to universality of demand which range from those of socio-political and economic systems to those which embrace the importance of communication and technology and, further, which call for a balance of those requirements of society which are rational, moral, aesthetic and belief-centred (Lawton 1986).

As points of reference for the total curriculum of a school each of these falls within the usual definition of broad aims. Each requires the headteacher, the governors and the other teachers to know about approaches to learning which are wider than those of single subjects. Each also requires the managers and providers (whether as teachers, governors or the LEA) to be confident about the implications which emerge from the relevance to education of politics, economics, morality, technology and aesthetics. If they are confident, they can commit themselves to the importance of each of the eight aspects. If they are confident they can, too, justify that importance to parents and, at the secondary-school stage, to employers. Above all they will find ways of pursuing broad aims in their regular reviews of schools, in their planning and in their schemes of teaching.

This is a complex task in the midst of implementing other aspects of the national curriculum. Although that curriculum is often represented as diminishing teachers' choices and initiatives, it is important for heads and their colleagues to note how matters of culture which have many facets can be handled alongside a national concern that schools should be more readily comparable with each other and should be readily accountable, not least in their pupils' attainment levels. Lawton (1989) provides particularly useful guidance on this as a development on earlier work on cultural analysis.

One study of this issue was pessimistic. Carried out by Sneh Shah (1990) in an analysis of the place of equal opportunities in core and foundation subjects and working from a number of final and interim reports by NCC working parties, three key points were identified, relating to the ways in which equal opportunities were handled in definitions and statements about syllabus content, in criteria of assessment and in statements of non-statutory guidance.

Although a picture of NCC confusion emerged from this study it still held out the hope, if only by implication, that more rigorous thinking would achieve better results. As it stands, the NCC guidance to teachers is made worse by a random mix of explicit and unstated definitions. Hence, although the Council can claim that their guidance documents have contained some reference to equal opportunities and that guidelines from the Secretary of State have included reference to issues of gender and the needs of ethnic minority children there does appear, however, in the words of Shah (1990:315)

to be no consensus. In some instances the term equal opportunities refers to the attainments of girls, sometimes to gender differentiation in assessment, in some instances to both boys and girls, and occasionally to ethnic minority pupils. . . . There is a reference to social class disadvantages in the English report, but overall there is no clear target group. At the same time there are varying interpretations of equal opportunities or related aspects when other terms are used. Some of the subjects like science and history have attempted to be positive in the curriculum content so that the children attain the targets for the subjects, but also become better educated in terms of quality issues. The focus in the Mathematics report however is a reminder of the continued powerful opposition to equality, especially for black people. Even when the working party has produced its final report as for History, or made strong recommendations after wide consultation, as for modern foreign languages, the Secretary of State may well have a strong influence on the final version that becomes part of legislation.

When teachers have received each final version of guidance and ministerial requirement then, despite the connections which will have been included in that guidance between a specific subject and a broader concern (such as the encouragement of multicultural or anti-racist education), school managers will still be faced with a problem. Shah expresses this (1990:316):

The overall effect of the National Curriculum will be the reduction of spontaneous teaching. There is a real danger that the other perhaps even more important element, i.e. the hidden curriculum, may fade into insignificance. In the past if children were being particularly racist or sexist, the committed teachers would deal with that in the way they felt most appropriate, and with as much time as was necessary. With this loss of flexibility, an overall school policy, well implemented and monitored, is crucial.

Can an overall school policy which gives appropriate weight to equal opportunities, health education, political literacy, personal, social and moral education and the other emphases described in Lawton's analysis be planned, implemented and, in general terms, managed without a detailed understanding of what is needed to handle each issue? Can the managers make any precise allocation of time and other resources to planning and defining their operational steps in these amorphous areas? Can they reduce those steps to verifiable, traceable steps of quality control?

Conclusion

Management as local activity has taken time to distance itself from the field of administration which belonged, as recently as the 1980s, to varying tiers of government rather than to institutions.

The growth of management as a virtually separate discipline has been resisted. The organization and the development of institutions and systems sometimes took their roots from broad ideas about the ownership of education as an aspect of a larger community's life. At other times it was treated as a day-to-day activity, associated only with mundane needs.

The response of schools to the need to manage things for themselves has partly been linked with their development as organizations separate from central government and local authorities and partly with the preservation of teacher freedom. Inasmuch as teachers by tradition are more closely associated with the planning and delivery of the curricular components of education than with arguments about priorities and about the distribution of resources, curriculum development has been a prime element of professional management. Assistance was provided by traditional in-service education, by the activities of advisers and inspectors and, at one time, by activities which were sponsored or encouraged at teachers' professional centres. LMS has moved the central concern of school management away from curriculum development and nearer to the heart of pedagogy, teaching and assessment.

Management now requires a larger perspective than in the past: the school manager needs to know what is happening in higher education, in technical education and in the vocational sphere. Hence the world of other people's qualifications – and new schemes of qualification – must become familiar to the management team of schools, primary as well as secondary.

The need to become confident in one's knowledge about other phases and sectors of education can create stress. That can be ameliorated if the manager reduces uncertainty by turning to those sources of information – of every kind – which are essential for good organization and by ensuring that those who provide the information are reliable and responsive.

The management of information systems in education is still not free from their chequered past. Nor is management information yet available for every aspect of the variety of aim and blueprint which a school sets for itself. In particular, those who manage individual schools have not yet had much experience in making a practical connection between defining their aims and implementing them within the framework of the national curriculum and in terms of quality assurance.

CHAPTER 8

Managing the new

Management plans and schemes of quality assurance need time and care in being put together. To move quickly into the management of new policies in a school carries the advantage that an innovation can be explained to others, defended or modified by the decision only of the initiator himself. However, this carries the risk that what is being implemented may need to be later unravelled because of second thoughts and if the original putting together of a change costs effort and resentment, going back on it may create further difficulties of relationships.

The manager or the team must decide the pace. If its speed of planning is uniform with that of others, the school may prefer to be cautious. This in turn may make it difficult for the manager to evoke commitment and enthusiasm. On the other hand to be slower than other schools in developing schemes of quality assurance may bring credit for prudence. But this may also attract criticism from parents if they make their own comparisons about trends and innovations.

The options of speed or prudence are entirely open to the manager of a school in the immediate period after the introduction of the 1988 Education Reform Act. The programme of trials and different phasings for entry into local management meant that some schools were well to the fore and were able to demonstrate both the advantages and drawbacks of early thinking on the part of central and local government.

Second-phase schools had the advantage of longer preparation. Trial phases had revealed difficulties. These emerged from the separation of different schemes of preparation. In some instances governors, staff other than heads, those responsible for capital as distinct from revenue planning and those responsible, too, for maintaining the equitable treatment of personnel, all went through differing speeds of training and development. Second phase schools should have felt – but did not always do so – the benefits of a process of policy-making which was homogeneous.

Evidence of this could be seen week after week from 1989 onwards. The press gave the impression that governors were going through a series of complicated changes and that new puzzles and ambiguities about their powers were being constantly revealed. Week by week Joan Sallis and others gave advice and placed the description of what were regarded as new problems against the background of why powers were changing and why the best use should be made of the variety of forces, pressures and influences which supported governing bodies.

In the discussion about the exercise of governors' powers, the head-teacher was usually brought in but other teachers left out. Parents were often in the foreground of the picture but their relationship with tea-chers rather than with governors themselves was not often highlighted.

All in all, there was little to demonstrate that those who managed schools were working very closely together. In particular the impact of governors upon the curriculum and upon the pedagogic aims of schools was obscure, despite the claim that their power was consider-able. Thus (*TES* 1991a:14):

part-time governors are in no position to replace LEAs in the running of schools, says Ann Holt, director of the support group Action for Governors Information & Training (AGIT). Commenting on the recent claim by junior schools minister Michael Fallon that 'governors, not councils, now run our schools', Ann Holt writes 'My own experience as a governor, and as one who meets other governors, makes me less sure about the feasibility or desirability of Mr Fallon's ambitions. Many governors are uncertain about the level of responsibility being urged upon them and everywhere the spirit is willing but the flesh is weak when it comes to course funding. Governors are largely untrained volunteers doing what they can in their spare time. Some had no intention of meeting more than two hours, three times a year.

The limited nature of government response to the process of na-tional reform was explained by the relatively lower level of attention which was paid to curriculum than to mechanisms of money. Two forces were at work: the curriculum requirement of central government changed sufficiently often for critics to claim that important changes in original policy were repeatedly taking place. Also the day-to-day work of schools and the task of assessing pupils assumed a higher import-ance than the development of new curriculum. This preoccupation with assessment was regarded both as demoralizing and excessively demanding on teachers' time in 1989, 1990 and 1991. In the spring of 1990 particularly, trial runs of the assessment of 7-year-olds led to revelations about strain and frustration which led central government considerably to reduce its demands. This led to sharp antagonism to-wards the full launch of assessment at 7 in 1991. In July of that year the Prime Minister indicated that in future assessment at 7 would become simpler. In December it was confirmed that the assessment would be confined to paper and pencil tests taken by whole classes of children.

At the secondary-school stage, anxiety about assessment at the age of 14 and 16 years again led to an alteration in government require-ments. Conflict about assessment at Key Stage 4 and about equi-valence with GCSE ultimately led to the giving up of proposals for double testing.

Two further problems confronted the manager: was the national curriculum up to the age of 16 going to feed sensibly through to new policies which were emerging from the combination of general and vocational education from 16 to 19? Second, would assessments which had been made from the age of 11 up to 16 be reflected in the record of each student's achievement at the age of 16 plus?

In trying to find answers, managers – whether they were heads or governors – were caught between the need to make progress and to prepare for broad changes which had been widely publicized by central government and to prepare for the necessity that they should lead changes. Some changes were small but others significant – and all were being made virtually each month by Secretaries of State, by the National Curriculum Council (NCC) and by the School Examinations and Assessment Council (SEAC).

In picking their way through these priorities, local managers lacked the benefit of being able to rely on the NCC and SEAC working in harmony. At 16 plus the reforms in examinations which were proposed in 1991 added further complexity by implying the need for a new connection between SEAC and the National Council for Vocational Qualifications (NCVQ).

Although the need for one organization of policy-making for curriculum and examinations had been recognized as long ago as the mid-1960s (through the establishment of the Schools Council), it had been abandoned in the early 1980s in favour of centralized curriculum-making and a blanket acceptance that the assessment of individual pupils' achievement would lead to greater improvements in the system than the development of logically connected public examinations and national qualifications.

This development led, among some of the partners in the education system, to a sense of chaos (*TES* 1991b:12):

A combination of over-prescriptive legislation, a well-meaning but disastrously complicated assessment system and an indefensible system to use GCSE for the statutory end-of-stage assessment, produce here a conundrum. . . . Even by definition, Key Stage 4 is a sort of disaster area: the implicit message is that education comes to a full stop at 16 and is the antithesis of what we need.

Admittedly assessment at earlier ages was not approached as so all-enveloping a concern as at 16 but warnings about the national curriculum were serious. In terms, for instance, of the teaching of reading it was said that if children were not taught to read great books the result would be a wearing away of the national culture. In history, the NCC working party after consultation revised (December 1990) some of its earlier recommendations. It was criticized by the chairman of the Historical Association's education committee on the grounds that the whole syllabus had been created before the assessment system had been devised. He was quoted as saying that without more being known about assessment in history it was difficult to register the true significance of what was being proposed. He was also fearful that the increase of flexibility in the use of supplementary units (which were by and large non-British) would give greater weight to the largely British core. One press comment on this was that in the eyes of some it was all too late. The experts should have made stronger protests while the working group was still sitting. More broadly, a leader comment of the same date drew attention to the confusion which arose when the NCC reduced the curriculum workload and concentrated a single obligatory unit on twentieth-century British, European and world history in a particularly busy part of a secondary-school student's academic life. The whole point of a history curriculum might, as a result, be lost when what it *should* all have led up to, it was thought, was 'the modern historical underpinning of every future citizen's understanding of an economic social, cultural and political development' (*TES* 1991c:13).

The confusion created by the NCC in history compared with the decision by central government no longer to insist on a ten-subject curriculum up to the age of 16 (January 1991). If science, mathematics and English remained sacrosanct, compulsion on seven other subjects was removed. Pressure on time was, it was said, part of the reason for allowing greater flexibility and choice because pupils over the age of 14 would then be able to study three separate sciences, an extra modern language, classics or vocational subjects.

This might have been regarded as making the local manager's job more straightforward but as one set of pressures was removed others made themselves felt. The government's retreat did not mean, for instance, that pupils were free from compulsion to study some technology and a modern foreign language after 14 but that short courses, as the Secretary of State announced, and combined courses as well as syllabuses for qualification other than the GCSE would become available.

The easing of compulsion in one part of a school's obligations meant that those who managed curriculum balance, specific schemes of teaching and school policies of assessment at the primary as well as at the secondary levels grew uncertain about other issues. The place of art, music, history or geography became open to question. Any of these, it seemed, could be dropped after the age of 14. This diminished their status below that age.

Because some discretion about the curriculum had been restored to the manager, this might have meant that the task of timetabling and deciding priorities in staff appointments became easier. Instead, and linked with the Secretary of State's easing – at the same period – in the number of attainment targets in mathematics and science, the reduction in subject compulsions created an uneasy vagueness about where the boundaries of new management now lay. It became more difficult to decide what total quality might amount to if there were optional gaps in what was being provided. Fewer compulsory subjects and less assessment meant that each school's offering – represented to parents through school prospectuses and negotiated with governors and local authorities in compliance with previously agreed curriculum policies – became more open than had earlier seemed possible. It meant that heads had to discuss with governors and parents as well as with staff precisely how to make use of greater freedom.

This was not a freedom simply to return to the pre-Education Reform Act way of working. The prescriptions which had emerged in 1988 and from those conditions of service for teachers which had been introduced by the 1987 Teachers' Pay and Conditions Act had, despite criticisms and resistance, created some new certainties. These were by and large accepted by teachers, understood by governors and welcomed by parents. There was an awareness among people outside schools that schools could choose between a range of approaches to the curriculum (Lawton 1986) and there was an expectation that the chosen curriculum in, for instance, each primary school was one which would create the basis of a rational, moral and enquiring attitude to learning and to future experience. To some extent this made the definition of quality easier to adapt to the process of management planning. Traditional expectations and traditional assurances could again come to the fore.

The benefits of changes in law and regulation were less obvious in the curriculum of secondary schools. The need to build on that which had already been achieved at the primary stage appeared to be still undervalued. This was perhaps not surprising when – with government pressure to introduce some degree of pre-vocational work below the age of 16, together with the interest of employers receiving young adults at the age of 18 who were educated enough to make use of further training – the secondary school curriculum looked forward rather than back.

Whether they served the primary or the secondary sector schools could take their management responsibilities in two ways: they could plan with the expectation that a larger degree of local choice and discretion would be gradually restored to them or they could look upon their job as one of responding to differing levels of pressure from central government. As they went through their management tasks schools took soundings through their local groups, through professional associations, from in-service trainers and from advisers and inspectors. There was a temptation to regard the headteacher as being the major or the sole activator and this was supported, in the secondary sector, when a Manchester study suggested that most heads were too powerful and would not delegate responsibility. This, said the general secretary of the Secondary Heads Association, was slightly out of date. There were no doubt bad heads who could not delegate but things had moved forward very satisfactorily in recent years. It was suggested that a head who tried to do everything was on the way to an early grave (Torrington and Weightman 1991:6).

Did heads take in their stride counter-order and confusion in the implementing of the Education Reform Act? If so, were they helped by other people? Were these other people asked to advise only about matters of process and technicality? Did a manager's philosophy, over-all sense of aims and sense of priorities in the curriculum come from his or her inner resources? Who were the closest counsellors? Some light on the answers is cast by typical heads.

The source of value

A head who already had eleven years' experience moved to a post in which he had to confront two one-time grammar schools which had been converted into comprehensive single-sex comprehensive high schools. These, as he entered the headship, were coming together as a mixed voluntary-aided comprehensive high school. Using his earlier experience, he felt, when he moved in, that he needed to gauge where the new school should be in five years' time. His approach was to try out ideas, with which he had already been successful, on other people and to listen to what came back – particularly from governors and senior staff. As he listened to the answers he learned more than he could have done in other ways about the existing culture of the former two separate schools.

He had also to tackle the technical problems of bringing two cur-riculum systems into one entity. And he needed to judge what volun-tary-aided status meant to a newly combined school in what were then the 1980s.

It was easier for this head to talk about methods of producing unity than about the ideals behind it. There was openness of discussion with staff and parents. There were balanced and professional news-letters.

One essential was that the head had to make it clear to his col-leagues that he trusted them. There could be nothing which might be regarded as clandestine. There could be no secret hierarchy. Bosses still had to be bosses when the occasion required but that was under-stood easily and early. Suspicions were got out of the way. Staff and head settled down to discuss and plan the curriculum. 'Thinking for-ward' was their distinguishing mode of work. It was assisted when, in a period before 'Baker days', the local authority agreed to the school having its own in-service training days.

As planning progressed the four groups into which the staff were easily divided (because they had taught on four different sites) came together in their views. Once they recognized that their own groups' discussions were not very different from others, they began corporate-ly to own the curriculum of the new school.

The head who described this process pointed to two matters of im-portance: 'I wanted a systematic curriculum with the sharing of oppor-tunities fully understood by parents and staff, and with the pastoral organization of the school running smoothly alongside the curriculum scheme.' As he spoke he slipped into the description of what had been achieved, emphasizing that staff, increasingly, described themselves as a single body ('what *we* say clearly . . .', 'what *we* need to do next . . . .').

It may have been because the school was voluntary-aided that the head also wanted religious education to have an important place, not so much in shaping the school but in underlining the requirement that everyone should at least think about his or her religious belief. Nothing that the head could do would make religion pervade the life of the school but it had to be recognized, he believed, that religion does permeate some people's whole private lives. This had to be known, understood and respected.

Another pervasive, and important, influence for this head was technology. Here he knew that the school provided the only chance for its pupils to understand quite how much the newer technologies now mattered both in the life of work and in the daily organization of our private lives. Once, this head felt, it was simply education which was regarded as a universal blessing. It was the major enabler for social mobility and advancement. Nowadays, it was technology without which you would fail. In school – a view amplified by Eraut (1991) – information technology (IT) above all helped the pupils to see themselves. It could, for literate people, provide a more interesting presentation of fact and argument. For the person with special needs it could provide clarity of presentation. It meant, through IT, that quickly improved drafts could provide alternative ways to arrive at a near-excellent final version of what was being said. For those with special needs it meant that drafts were not something to be ashamed of. The mechanical process of elegant correction and rephrasing cut out the ugly, self-stultifying labouring of mistakes.

This head felt that the re-expression and development of ideas which IT made possible allowed every pupil the chance to have second thoughts. And in school subjects it was not those which depended on words alone which drew benefit from IT. The rapid recording or repetition of the circumstances of longitudinal experiments in science meant that in a day and a night, without any intervention from a pupil or a teacher, the replication of two terms' work could be completed.

A third view of what he wanted came from the same head telling himself that he wanted pupils in his school to have a vision of learning as an embodiment of self-improvement. No vision of self-improvement can be realized without a healthy degree of self-esteem. To achieve these joint ends, the school had to have a smoothly working tutorial review system and a thorough approach to records of achievement. Both had been implemented. Pupils reached the point where they could say that they realized that someone – namely their teachers and their tutors – knew them very well. This was welcomed by parents. They and the school together planned ahead in order to make it possible for pupils to feel that they, too, knew themselves better.

The head knew that he needed strengths. Two were particularly important but the first of these was not his to organize. He wanted his personal belief and his professional expertness to come out as a single attribute. It then had to be left to his governors and his staff colleagues to make such use as they could of any combination of qualities which he revealed. His own task was to make sure, no matter how it appeared to other people, that he constantly checked across from his private life of personal belief – and back again – to the professional, public and accountable life of a head.

This could be a highly self-centred, nervous process. It needed robustness of relationships as well as discussions and arguments which were free of pomposity. Good humour was needed – but the main message throughout the school's planning and implementation of change was that every party in the system had to trust everyone else. No other key to good morale was as important. Given trust as a first condition, the changes which followed each stage of review, assessment and evaluation came more easily – even if it did mean that some criticisms had first to be voiced and discussed (JM Dobson conversation, 1990).

A second head placed equal stress on the importance of trust in the promotion of good morale. After two headships in Inner London he sought to keep his provincial school as one which was good at caring for its pupils as well as one which was well organized in providing sought-after subjects on top of the core curriculum.

The combination of these two aims could be managed, he felt, by giving every member of staff, including himself, a tutorial group to look after during the whole length of a pupil's high school life. Within those groups he wanted to make sure that pupils who had special needs were not individually identified. Each had to be in the mainstream, each had to be approached in and through a group of mainstream pupils.

The organization of this was not at first easily accepted by every member of staff. It began to prove its value when the members of pupils' own groups helped each other and came not always to rely on the initiative or instruction of the teacher-tutor. Although this active altruism was said to wane in the final year at school when each pupil had a wide range of other preoccupations, the strength, the compactness and the self-reliance of student groups only occasionally had to be challenged by teachers. From time to time discipline required some distance, briefly, to be drawn between the adult and the student but managers deliberately kept such periods short, in order not to dissipate the strength of the group.

Both headmasters recognized the personal sources of their ideals. Both acknowledged the lessons they had learned from mentors early in their careers and each accepted that as time elapses heads appoint other teachers who have something of their own style about them. A management team takes time to build up. Some of its members undergo a change of attitude as the team goes about its ordinary work. But what emerges is a team of people who do not simply acquiesce with the head. When the team trusts itself it builds up a view not simply about the one school and what needs to be done in small detail but also about the pressures and demands of society as a whole.

Confidence on the part of the head is necessary if the senior team – and it always appears to be a group of three, four or five teachers – is to disagree, to question and to criticize him or her direct. Once that confidence had been achieved, it was felt that the school would benefit if every pupil were given a three grade assessment (acceptable, unacceptable, exceptional). This was not to be a matter of mark-books and tests but a freely managed regular assessment which depended first on the subject-teacher but which took in the view of everyone who had dealings with each individual pupil. Teachers in their subjects and teachers in their year groups reviewed these assessments; all reached the head and his deputies. Formative enquiry and discussion was then carried out between teachers and pupils. From time to time, and not only when yearly reports were sent home, parents were involved. They knew as did their children when things were going well and when they were not. And above all pupils were the first to acknowledge the moment when they moved from acceptable to unacceptable standards.

The school did not take a very romantic view of these broad assessments: teachers knew when sanctions had to be applied but they were also aware that pupils realized the power of reward.

This vision of justice, sought and organized in a simple day-to-day manner, sprang from the head's experience, as he described it, of Division 10 in the Inner London Education Authority. Acton and Shepherd's Bush, he said, were a long way from Islington but it had not needed the history and memory of Risinghill and William Tyndale to make headteachers alert to the damaging way in which matters of discipline, race, criminality and parental disquiet could be brought together into presentations of hot and not always accurate news. He distrusted the media. Instead, he felt, it was important that inside the school, inside the pupil and inside the minds of parents, a belief in justice and the importance of education and self-esteem should be genuinely stimulated and sustained. School uniform, a build-up of service to charities, a development of sponsored activities by pupils to raise money for the school itself – each of these was part of the armoury of management. Self-help meant that, for instance, libraries and resource centres within the school could be equipped, furnished and maintained in an unvandalized condition.

Staff were separated less and less from pupils; they used the same library and the same resource centres. Being together in this way did not mean that either party treated the other with excessive informality but it did mean that teachers knew pupils well. In particular the care system flourished, not least because the head had learned the benefit of a full support team in school in his previous authority (psychologist, social worker, counsellor and welfare officer) and had struggled successfully with his new employers for one school-based counsellor. He had swum against the tide at a time when schools to which specific counsellor appointments had previously been made had used a counsellor's vacancy, at a time of teaching staff reductions, for other purposes. The employers felt that designated counsellors had outlasted their usefulness. But the head in question did succeed in winning this point. Nor had his management team, he felt, been complete until that bridging appointment had been made (I.M. Weir, conversation, 1990).

Using the past

Part of the equipment of a good manager is the experience and the bank of memories which he or she carries from one school, one area, one education authority to another. It takes at least two terms even to become familiar with a new job but, after that, few management changes can be put off for more than a year. Each alert head looks for problems but not for fault-finding. Ideally each knows the strengths and disadvantages of small as well as large schools. And it is the variety of a head's management experience which provides a sense of realism.

Ideals and a vision of education's unrealized potential have to go hand in hand with pragmatism. Satisfactory staff relationships cannot be achieved simply by issuing instructions. But heads do nevertheless need to say what has to be changed from time to time – and should see the need for change before their colleagues. To insist on this would cancel out the mature, trustful, open and continually self-reviewing benefit of a good management team. And above all, if the head, inside the school, is seen as someone who has a calm and consistent view of the rapidly changing priorities of school management, there is a chance that parents will come to the same view and will feel the same trust. This is particularly important when the head has to be seen as one among many who play their part in a community. However many communities a school serves, the head must represent a prime interest and involvement.

This aspect of a head's management is better understood now than it was thirty years ago. The difficulty of a head was then highlighted when Leila Berg described the crisis which led to the closing of Risinghill Comprehensive School. She quoted an education lecturer, 'if Risinghill were a country place, the natural conditions of rural life would throw the teacher into the community, but in London social conditions do not do this; unless you see it as a need, you would go along quite happily thinking the community is not part of your job' (Berg 1968:273).

Community is part of the job but it needs good management (paying teachers, costing the use of premises, the division of time other than that which is needed to provide the national curriculum) as well as a personally felt sense of value. The position of the head as manager and the position of the manager as leader needs to be thought out – and the head is likely to be more isolated in organizing a school's community role than in most of its other activities.

Leading by example is not enough – nor was it at the time of Risinghill. Michael Duane, its head, then said (Berg 1968:283–4):

I am under no illusion about the size of the task faced by this staff. Some problems we have in common with other schools e.g.

(a) Shortage of normally qualified and experienced Staff and high turnover of Staff, though our pupil/Staff ratio is the best in London.
(b) A school population of widely varying abilities and with very mixed ethnic and cultural backgrounds.

Some problems we suffer with other schools though perhaps to a more intense degree:

(c) A complex site that is difficult to administer and to supervise.
(d) An open site with playgrounds and classrooms often in full view of the outside world and where every misdemeanour is likely to become the subject of exaggerated rumour in the locality.
(e) An immediate environment in which, during the past years, three murders have actually taken place, where prostitution, larceny and violence are commonplace in the lives of many of the children and where the hangings that take place at Pentonville Prison periodically create deep disquiet in the minds of all our children.
(f) A locality where a large number of the parents are antagonistic to the values and purposes represented by the school.
(g) A dearth of children with high levels of ability . . . and a plenitude of children in the lowest levels . . . with a corresponding difficulty of providing a full educational programme for both.

I am also in no doubt about the amount of devoted hard work that has gone on during the last four years. No headmaster could have wished for more.

The head alone cannot overcome resistances and antagonisms which lie outside school. Sometimes there is a uniformity of antagonism based on shared rumour and widespread disrepute. If that is the case, the head of a school is no different from the head of any other unloved institution. Isolation, the call for a lonely struggle against hostile critics, will not help. W. H. Whyte (1956) appealed for the leader not to lose his identity inside his organization. But Whyte's critics pointed out that his call

for the individual to fight a lonely battle against conformity was never going to get very far. Individuals already did and still do. But the capacity to change realities is partly dependent on the availability of alternative methods of behaviour and structure. For organizational participants in normal circumstances, such alternatives are inevitably restricted by their experience and the tendency to take what exists as natural, though constraining (Thompson and McHugh 1990).

This represents a limiting view of initiative. Certainly previous experience shapes present and future conduct but the good teacher or the good manager will not be contented simply with repeating what he or she has already been through without questioning the constraints of the organization which seems to stand in the way. It is the putting together of thoughts about previous experiences and the emergence of new and hybrid ideas which enlivens a manager's approach.

Learning from experience is not, then, a straightforward repeating of what has gone before. Nor is it the selecting and putting together of parts of apparently diverse lessons from the past. There has to be another ingredient – the spark and the quick glimpse of something new. That spark can set light to further proposals, ideas and chances in the manager's mind.

Personal ideas, however, cannot – any more than can experience, intuition and vision – provide a reliable base for quality assurance. Acceptance by parents of the personal standards of heads and other managers has to be buttressed by activities which are verifiable and which are planned outside the framework of personal preferences and skills.

This is so because a limited accountability in terms only of satisfying employers in local authorities or inspectors of schools has given way to openness and to the multiplication of participators who claim a say in the running of education. School-based choices about curriculum and curricular goals have given way to external requirements and to a greater measure of centralized uniformity. The shifts of responsibility are sufficient to justify the claim that the education service being managed at the end of the twentieth century is different from that which was characterized by teacher-based choice, classroom autonomy, voluntary consensus and a supposedly new liberalism forty years earlier.

The fall of Risinghill in 1965 was as much a precursor of change as was William Tyndale in 1976. The connections between the establishment of the Assessment of Performance Unit (APU) in 1974, the establishment of the Taylor Committee to study the management and government of schools in 1975 and the publication of the Black Papers from 1969 to 1977 have been charted. Even in 1981 it could be claimed that those who held a 'strongly anti-progressive, pro-standards line had been enjoying increasing credibility and increasingly strident support from most of the popular press' (Dale *et al.* 1981:307).

What Dale *et al.* described as an atmosphere of growing disenchantment with the achievement of the education system as a whole and with some segments of the teaching profession in particular was made worse when troubles in schools increased sympathy for attacks from the right wing. These undermined 'the dominant educational ideology and the legitimacy of the teachers' authority both at classroom and national levels' (Dale *et al.* 1981:307).

The dominance of teachers meant, in the 1960s, that the management of education was in virtually powerless hands at the DES. The same was almost true of LEAs – men of goodwill who had, as Vernon Bogdanor described it, a concern to improve the service 'and whose reflective judgments remained untainted by the intrusion of party ideology' (in Dale *et al.* 1981:308).

This changed when there was explicit recognition of the place of party politics in the shaping of education. This was accompanied by a late acknowledgement that it was difficult or impossible to direct education into new pathways while teachers and their unions retained their power. At the same time unusual changes were taking place in the late 1970s and in the 1980s because of the drop in pupil numbers and because an increasing number of interested parties were identifying themselves as appropriate new participants in its management (Bogdanor 1979).

Although the surprise which seemed to greet these changes now seems misplaced, they represented significant alterations in the way heads and others were to manage education. Changed circumstances began to alter the criteria which were used for the selection and appointment of heads. Laws and Dennison (1990) have traced the history of change in this connection between 1965 and 1982. Changed circumstances also mattered to Waters (1979: 47) who described outstanding schools as places which were run by heads 'with flair, wisdom, energy and that sense of knowing how things ought to be' but who emphasized, too, that these qualities needed to be partnered with an ability in organization and management in a wide variety of fields.

The increasing importance of a senior participant's ability in management and organization led to the conversion of traditional heads from being people of experience and goodwill (and who had a sense of how things ought to be) into planners and implementers. At the same time it gave a signal to aspiring heads that a commitment to the improvement of education had to be accompanied by a capacity to marshal minds and money.

Certainties about new education were few: little was known about differences of quality. There were few evaluations of successful innovation which matched, for instance, the clarity of Warburton and Southgate (1969) in their work on the initial teaching alphabet. After sorting out their unequivocal conclusion from those which were divergent they ended their work with a statement which underlined how managers as well as researchers need to be ready periodically to go over old ground (Warburton and Southgate 1969: 284):

It would be unfortunate if the mainly favourable tone of this report was taken to imply that the use of the initial teaching alphabet for beginning reading with infants was the final and only solution. The experiments of the past six years have demonstrated that in many cases the usual ways in which children have been taught to read can be improved. We should continue to investigate how children learn to read and the most effective media, methods, materials and procedures for helping them.

A comparable straightforwardness put an end to false hopes about the efficiency of the Nuffield/Schools Council scheme for teaching French to children in primary schools. Few managers, at any level of

making decisions about budgets, training programmes or school organization, could ignore Clare Burstall's final word in her report of 1974:
'Now that the results of the evaluation are finally available . . . . it
is hard to resist the conclusion that the weight of evidence has combined with the balance of opinion to tip the scales against a possible
expansion of the teaching of French in primary schools' (p. 246).

Sources of clarity

Heads can create their own clarity if they organize their time in such a
way as to digest and weigh reports, views and experiences from sources either outside the school or inside the staffroom. They can give
themselves time to reflect and to simplify. But the surveys and researches reported by Laws and Dennison showed that while there is
admittedly an increasing demand for a primary-school head's time to
meet the requirements of legislation, the heightened expectations of
governors and parents and the demand for ever-better presentations
and public relations, they nevertheless devote the bulk of their time to
brief, fragmented and highly intensive tasks. Observations reported by
Davies quoted in Laws and Dennison (1990:275) showed that 'on
average 60% of all activities were less than nine minutes in duration,
while only 7% lasted beyond an hour'. The largest sustained activity
by heads in primary schools is said to be teaching. In a study by Hall
secondary heads were, however, said to devote only 14 per cent of
their time to teaching, with 10 per cent given over to 'ceremonial', 10
per cent to educational policy and curriculum matters, 33 per cent to
'operations and administrative management', 22 per cent to human
management (staff and pupils) and 10 per cent to external management
(Hall quoted in Laws and Dennison (1990:276)).

There may be several reasons, concede Laws and Dennison
(1990:276), why primary heads appear

so attracted to doing many things themselves. Others, and particularly the teachers, may seem too busy with their classes for the head to ask them to share
this part of the school work-load, there is a shortage of clerical support, the
heads want to be seen as in charge of everything as far as possible, and so on.
More generously, the head accepts a role which involves many menial chores
and tasks as a means of encouraging continuity and high level performance
from staff and pupils.

Although information about the roles of heads is argued as being
incomplete, particularly if new bases are needed for management training, there seems little doubt that their willingness to help the performance of their colleagues by taking on more of the low-level chores of
school life can be misdirected. In response to increasing demands for
expert self-awareness and self-evaluation in meeting the demands of
the new curriculum, the new organization of school government and
the new involvement of parents, a head's disposable time could be bet-

ter spent in grappling at his or her own level with those organizational, philosophic and marketing questions which lie behind the giving of a professional account of a school. All these should add up, too, to guaranteeing the provision of quality.

In making time to provide reflection the head not only has to be clear about the relative priority of helping out, taking on chores and providing workaday leadership but also has to have confidence in the extent to which his or her colleagues expect leadership.

To think about this in terms of the relative roles of heads and other teachers is in the words of Campbell (1985:154–7) insubstantial and dated. His preference for examining collegiality and for finding its stumbling blocks in the conditions in which primary-school teachers have to work seems more appropriate when real schools come to mind. Staffrooms, for instance, are used during break-times, before and after school and during the lunch hour. Their furnishing is seldom above the spartan level and the main focus of activity is made up of jars of instant coffee, electric kettles, a sink and a draining board. Two teachers can just about find the room and comparative peace to talk together about the arrangements for the next lesson and next week. The atmosphere is good-humoured, with a strong sense of relief that adults can for a few moments get together without thinking of what is to be done next with twenty or thirty demanding, stimulating and occasionally frustrating children.

They are not places for quiet reflection, they are not clubrooms in which plots and schemes can be laid nor do they have useful collections of books, journals and other aids to professional thinking. They are centres of friendship where relationships which are light-hearted combine with the serious business of running a school on corporate lines. That they are empty other than at times when children are out of their classrooms or outside the school premises is a constant reminder that primary-school teachers do not have time in the working day to do other than teach. The 1987 changes in conditions of service did not alter that. Those changes created a comparatively small number of hours in the year when planning and the exchange of ideas could be conducted other than in the helter-skelter of a school day. 'Baker days' provided a very limited number of whole days for corporate preparation. And, very exceptionally, a school's staff might be marginally increased in such a way as to allow time for a curriculum leader to do some leading or for the mentors of new teachers to provide their counsel.

Neither time nor space assist the head in reaching colleagues easily or regularly. The smaller the school, the better is the chance of more frequent informal interchange. But small schools are often those in which the head has to spend – and not simply as a matter of choice – a good deal of time teaching.

A detached head, who acts with detachment, coolly weighing matters up, allowing the mind to soak up ideas and to put them together in new ways, is not a primary-school image. He or she may choose to accept the load of small and troublesome issues and there may be no one else to take over certain tasks. To clear the decks needs a double effort: the machinery of school organization has to be kept rolling, the crises and questions which start outside the school have to be dealt with. At the same time documents have to be read, thinned down and explained to colleagues, usually with a footnote to mention that there is more documentation that the head will protect them from.

Reading, thinning out and explaining the demands of NCC, SEAC, local authorities and governors takes more time than a head can find during a school day. It has to be seen to after the children and staff have left. It has to take up private time – and at home. This is the first source of isolation. The manager does not have the opportunity gregariously to share and sort out ideas with staff colleagues. The manager, whatever style of approach is adopted by outsiders who seek a collegial response, does not have an immediacy of contact with colleagues at the first, important stage when, after the preliminary reading of basic documents, thoughts are being formed about interpretation and response.

This isolation may be damaging to the manager. Those who deny it will often be the same people who provide in-service training, conferences and seminars and who read or write articles in the educational press. At worst the effect of their work is to produce a half-formed readiness for what is new, together with a half-understood response. The gingerbread should not be robbed of its gilt and yet this is what happens whenever hot news about impending changes turns into the cold gruel of daily management. The manager who does read the latest circular, the latest information pack, the latest draft of organizational requirements in the privacy of the weekend at home has already gone through the experience either of having an appetite whetted by prior knowledge or of a palate blunted by a flavour which is already old.

Few managers admit that boredom is a threat to the job but equally few would deny that being part of a pilot scheme or of being part of a trial run of new development can carry with it some air of excitement. This, in England and Wales, was very evident in the early stages of Nuffield schemes for new approaches to mathematics, science and modern languages. In the period from 1963 to the late 1970s, headteachers and other teachers enjoyed the *frisson* of being first, of lacking confidence but at the same time enjoying the mixture of sharing their nervousness with other people. But as Nuffield schemes and Schools Council innovations petered out, so did the network of those study groups, clubs and coteries which the pilot schemes of well-known curriculum developments deliberately fostered.

If the manager lacks the chance to engage in a fully collegial approach, if he or she can only find or make time for the essential step of ingesting or thinking new ideas in an atmosphere of enforced professional seclusion, does this obscure his or her clarity of mind? If the subject-matter of management was a set of imperishable truths, the answer would be no. But management is a mixture of knowledge, skill and judgement. It is made up of tact and impatience, it is sometimes marred by self-certainty and is attended by the occasional shaft of diffidence and fear. To be a good manager requires one to handle this array in such a way that education is fed and fostered – education which is provided by teachers, encouraged by parents, watched over by governors, expected to be accountable to central and local government and capable of satisfying everyone that high quality is delivered.

Because management is made up of virtually constant negotiation and adjustment it can only flourish in the context of other people. It cannot see how good or bad it is in reaching its objectives unless it engages with them for most of the manager's time. Some time must be found for first thoughts and to allow flashes of private insight. That apart, there have to be limits to the manager's isolation.

The argument that those who teach – and one would add those who manage teaching – cannot be expected to go it alone was pursued by Clive Beck (1990). If teachers were to improve, he emphasized that other groups and institutions in society would have to play their part. His plea is powerful (Beck 1990:49):

teachers must become 'intellectuals' to a greater extent than they typically are at present . . . they should have greater awareness of the interconnected theory that bears on both the content and method of their teaching. And this awareness should not be merely as a result of receiving more ideas from others (although that is important); teachers should not, any more than students, be the objects of a pure 'banking' education. Teachers must be intellectuals in the sense that they are engaged in constant co-operative inquiry into the content and method of schooling, an inquiry in which their own experiences and thoughts provide major input.

Beck goes on to stress that teachers must become more politically aware and involved, that they should adopt a thoroughly interactive role with those whom they teach and that they 'must be growing in social, moral and spiritual characteristics' (1990:50).

These elements of teacher growth cannot be forced. Instead, it is argued that they must be 'impelled towards them not out of fear and guilt but because of a positive desire to build a better life for students, themselves and other members of society. To a large extent they must come ''naturally'' ' (Beck 1990:50).

Large-scale expectations may depend for their realization on changes in society and its value patterns. But those who are already teaching should be given a lead by heads and by governors. Each group needs to see for itself the importance of indirect and hard-to-define influences. Each needs to find time to discover what exactly such issues as intellectualism, world consciousness, political awareness and moral values mean to their professional lives.

Some help in the process of internalizing these ideas will nowadays come from national curriculum guidance. Of Beck's nine groups of moral topics, for instance, (1990:148) virtually all have some coverage either in specific subject guidance or in recommendations about non-statutory cross-curriculum themes and activities.

This source of support can be used by a head in the management of the curriculum provided that there is some sharing with teacher colleagues. Absolute word-for-word matching of ideals and practices cannot be expected nor should the manager slavishly seek that. If, however, a head cannot show a personal commitment towards specific but nevertheless broad values, no amount of organizational skill will compensate. And the test for the manager is not only whether there is this personal commitment but also whether it can be communicated.

Managing the natural process of teaching

Because teachers often cannot answer the question of why they teach as they do and because they refer to statements such as that they just know what to do or have a feeling or sense about what to do, it has been suggested that what guides teachers in making sense of their work and what commits them to action is a mixture of 'personal knowledge, tacit knowledge, routine knowledge . . . when conscious thought is not permitted the time to percolate and inform practice' (Simons and Elliott 1989). It is also pointed out that

the danger of 'hurrying' and teaching 'more' is that time for gathering information and reflecting on practice and the implicit and explicit theories that guide it can evaporate easily in the busyness of increasing demands. . . . This 'teaching as breathing' at first sounds appealing, almost natural. After all how many artists have time to explain what they are doing while, or even after, they are doing it. Upon reflection we realise that teachers do not paint on canvases; their work is not done in isolation. Children do not hold still, nor are the consequences of effort always immediately apparent (Simons and Elliott 1989:106).

Reflection is the manager's ally. If everything is taken on the wing, some planning, certainly, can be carried out. But the quality of activity which then follows and the way in which that activity is judged (either as an event in itself or through the assessment of the child's learning which emerges from it) still needs patient examination. Holly (in Simons and Elliott 1989) reminds us that Dewey in 1916 quoted, as the opposites of conscious enquiry and thoughtful action, the twin phenomena of routine and capricious behaviour. Both the latter are more concerned with present action than future consequences. Since working out the consequences is the most important result of the process of reflection, the exclusive adoption of either routine or capricious behaviour is not valuable.

What is the mid-point of the argument that some teachers do not want to reflect, others can never find the time for reflection and others feel it unnecessary? Light was thrown on this, in the context of secondary school departments, by Earley and Fletcher-Campbell (1989). Apart from the singleness of subjects and the number of staff who are involved, their findings could, without stretching, apply to leadership of primary schools. For instance, heads of department seemed to take an unselfconscious view of leadership and of their management style. Headteachers were aware of differences of both style and strength among departmental heads and accepted those differences, possibly because the contexts in which each worked were different.

Heads differ in style and approach but at both school and department level one essential for successful management lies in keeping staff informed and in giving reasons for decision. Prior consultation and participative decision-making has not always been regarded as a right but teachers' involvement should be regarded as a professional entitlement. It is not something to be bestowed whimsically by a benevolent manager (Earley and Fletcher-Campbell 1989:203).

If teachers dislike the pseudo-democracy of being consulted after decisions have been taken, if they are irritated by being consulted over matters of little consequence and if they are satisfied that senior staff have the right to make decisions without staff consultation, they nevertheless expect to be consulted about major issues. Added to this

indecisiveness and slow decision-making were seen as undesirable qualities in school leaders, and teachers liked to see an outcome from the consultative process. There is a need, therefore, for those in leadership positions to create *genuine* opportunities for participation and yet be prepared, on occasions, to make decisions with little or no consultation. A lot will depend on the issue and the level of commitment that is required (Earley and Fletcher-Campbell 1989:202).

Commitment to the assessment of pupils is the requirement of the 1988 Education Reform Act which most directly touches teachers. That directness of involvement was signalled by each teacher at the first stage of assessment receiving from central government late in 1989 and early in 1990 packs of materials, descriptions of policy, examples of assessment and timetables. Assessment became the field in which there were the largest number of changes and retractions in government policy. The manager's task was to remain up to date with the changes, to encourage a confident understanding of the purpose and methods of assessment and to make sense of the ambiguity which surrounded questions of parental and governors' access to the assessments.

In this issue there was little philosophy to unravel. There were technicalities to handle and, above all, the management of time was important while heads and their deputies led their colleagues through new patterns of requirement.

In contrast, the national curriculum was not a matter in which government sought to address teachers individually and directly. Working party interim reports, Secretary of State reactions, draft materials and final publications were all sent direct to schools but, unlike the organization of assessment, the mapping out of the curriculum and its proper support through staffing, books and other resources, time and leadership were a matter for heads and curriculum leaders. There was little reason, certainly in primary schools, to identify some teachers only with some subjects. The core subjects of mathematics, English and science (and in Welsh-speaking schools, Welsh) were shared responsibilities and, in primary schools, much of the rest of the national curriculum was also a collaborative responsibility. History, geography, technology, music, religious education, art and physical education were not dealt with in separate departments.

Because they were neither entirely new nor so complicated, the requirements of the national curriculum settled down more quickly than those of assessment. Heads, deputies and curriculum leaders shared rather than led each school's preparations. Localized planning for the use of common resources between schools (and in some instances the sharing of teaching staff) made demands principally on heads, who were involved both on their own account and in response to LEA initiatives.

Separate from curriculum and assessment, a third element in the 1988 Act, although it affects teaching staff only indirectly, still has the potential to affect the whole future of a school. This is the reform of admissions policies and the introduction of open enrolment. Parental wishes and the filling of every desk in the school (as it has been described) takes priority over matters of efficiency and economy. No longer are local authorities cast in the role of protectors of unpopular, run-down schools. No longer can parents' wishes be set aside. In the organization of enrolment it is the headteacher who principally has to make decisions along which governors are guided. Technicalities about the relevant standard number of places in the school are decided between the head and the local authority.

Some aspects of open enrolment go back to the 1980 Education Act. Through the 1988 Act, however, it can affect the future of a school because it bears on competition for the school. More pupils mean more money for the school. More money means more staff. More staff may mean a broader curriculum.

It is at this point that individual teachers become involved in the policy. However hard a head or a governing body may try to remain outside the arena of competition, the insistence of parent interests and community awareness and the effect on even the price of houses in a local estate agent's listings will continue to make sure that parents believe that clever children, as measured in the national assessment, are produced by good schools and by good teachers. Whatever the subtlety which is brought into arguments about the quality of teaching, those classes and groups within a school which, regardless of individual children's difficulties and disadvantages, regularly register high attainments will enhance the name of the school.

This view is hedged about with reservations – and indeed few parents who know both their children's capacities and their teachers' helpfulness will expect schools to be measured entirely in this way. But schools now inevitably become more tense about a failing teacher or a teacher with personal problems or problems of health who may not be able to concentrate on a pupil's assessable skills. Teachers will help each other, and heads and senior teachers will continue to provide their traditional extra assistance, but in addition to a school being run happily it now matters that other verifiable indicators of performance which form the basis of outside judgement are also taken fully into account.

Judgements about the comparative quality of schools are a consequence of open enrolment and need good management. Two other changes brought about by the 1988 Act make it important that other aspects of policy are also managed in as full and collegial a manner as possible. These are the delegation of financial authority to schools and the rules about the appointment, suspension and dismissal of staff.

A school's annual budget share has to be managed by the governing body. The governing body delegates the task of making broad recommendations and the task of day-to-day management to the head. The policy itself has to be handled by the head as fully in collaboration as possible with all other members of staff – non-teaching as well as teaching. Only by using as much knowledge and experience as resides in the whole school can both the broad issues of school management and the minutiae of its efficient operation be appropriately financed.

The head has to examine the balance between expenditure on maintaining the fabric of the school and its daily servicing and expenditures on unavoidable commitments as against the occasional opportunity for one-off changes. The head, the deputy and the school secretary have to put together the information which can lead to first comparisons on the basis of the Guidelines for the Review and Internal Development of Schools (GRIDS). Whether GRIDS themselves are used or another comparable scheme of self-review, choices slowly emerge about what should be strengthened, retained or phased out over the next four years. The points of choice have to be put to other people and it takes patient consultation before everyone can agree about the management plan for a school in which social, academic, moral and community developments all have their place. Alongside these developments the plan also has to cater for the projection of a school image which is honest and intelligible and for making and fulfilling promises about quality.

The whole process of review makes considerable demands (Bell 1988:231):

the aim is to produce internal school development rather than to provide a mechanism for external accountability. It demands the identification of a co-ordinator who should ensure that consultation with staff is genuine and that they feel involved; explain processes clearly from the outset; help teachers draw up a realistic timetable and ensure that deadlines are met; provide advice and keep a check on what is happening at each stage; contact people outside the school who might be brought in to help; try to ensure that the review and the development are rigorous and systematic; and make some evaluation of the effectiveness of the GRIDS method after about twelve months.

A GRIDS-type review fits smoothly into the pattern of formulating, implementing and evaluating a school development plan as defined in the DES Circular 7/88. That circular laid the duty on governors and headteachers of developing and carrying out a plan for the school – a plan which took account of the full range of their responsibilities under the 1988 Act. Of the eight possible components of such a plan, a scheme of staff development to make sure that the other seven can be implemented has high importance. The other seven emerge in one formulation (Gilbert 1990: 36–7) as a statement of curriculum objectives, a review of current provision, changes and priorities in the next immediate year, strategies for implementing those changes, a statement on the use of resources, a plan for monitoring and evaluation and a statement of development priorities for the coming three or four years.

If staff development is part of a management plan which in turn is controlled by governors this means that governors' powers are still further increased. The local authority remains as the employer but all appointments are made by governors. It is the governors, too, who manage the teaching and ancillary staff. This means that in addition to staff appointments governors are involved in the responsibility for staff dismissal and for the distribution of incentive allowances.

They do not, unless they are particularly unwise, take action on staff appointments or dismissals without guidance from the head. But because the way in which the 1988 Act was drafted appears to give them overriding powers, other teachers and the ancillary staff of any school are bound to ask for consultation about any staffing changes. Unlike the other four main changes in the 1988 Act (national curriculum, assessment, open enrolment and local financial delegation) the alteration of power in the control of staff calls for a high degree of collegiality between the managers and the managed.

While, in this fifth major change, assistant teachers and ancillary staff have firm advice, support and representation from their trade unions, it is difficult to see who can help them with the sixth innovation, namely the possibility of a school's opting for grant maintained status (GMS). Certainly articles in the press and in professional journals did not, for the first 100 aspirants for GMS, provide a clear picture of the position of the head, let alone the position of other teachers. It is a political matter, weighed between a school's governors and its parents. The latter can certainly be encouraged by statements made by the head. But there is no literature other than in guidance papers produced by, for instance, the National Union of Teachers and the National Association of Headteachers, to show how far a head should consult other members of staff.

Because the choice of opting out is largely represented to parents, former pupils and the local community as a means of securing a better financial arrangement from the DES than has been possible with the local authority, it is sometimes argued that it is not ethos or education but funding which alone lies at the heart of the decision. But this is not a satisfactory reason for leaving teachers out of the management of any attempt to opt out. Nor is it a weighted argument to suggest that when teachers find that their school may be blackballed in future schemes of co-operation with other local schools they might not notice if in fact they had felt little practical benefit from any co-operation in the past.

Teachers, too, are assumed by some of the proponents of opting out not to care whether the school, with a changed status, has to buy in the traditional services of local advisers, librarians or in-service training. Even if these are not services whose impact is deeply felt by teachers and by ancillary staff nevertheless they can enrich the school when they are provided as additional services and they can, if they are absent, narrow a school's horizons.

Does the same exclusion of teachers apply to the Act's seventh and final change, namely the enhancement of governors' powers? Articles of government were altered in such a way as to increase the range of governors' overall responsibilities. The role of the head has not been ostensibly diminished but, in the words of Maclure (1988:140–1):

there is scope for an over-zealous governing body to get at cross-purposes with an over-zealous head. The secret of a successful school will, as always, lie in the effective co-operation between professional leadership (the head and his/her staff), the lay government (the governors) and the local authority and its advisers. The Articles of Government purport to clarify this relationship, but often this clarification takes the form of more ambiguities and blurred distinctions. The power of the governors in relation to the ethos of the school will rest in their ability to call for reports and explanations – the ability to make clear their approval and their criticisms of particular aspects of the school, as they are aware of its reputation and character. Whether this power is enough to justify the description of the governors as the body under whose direction the school operates, is a moot point.

It is this balance of power with governors which perhaps most intensely tests the management capacity of a head in relation to other teachers, but at the same time the power of teachers themselves to convert policies which are handed down from above into classroom practice by means of adaptation, domestication or subversion should not be overlooked (Shipman 1990:156–7).

Governors and staff

The ideal which has been referred to more than once in earlier chapters is that heads, other teachers, governors, parents and non-teaching staff should combine their efforts in some form of corporate management. This is nearer realization than it was in the late 1980s if only because the practice and principles of GRIDS, together with further movements towards total self-evaluation, have removed some of each party's defensiveness. But behind the ideal, the practical difficulties are still significant. Joan Sallis (1988:170) summed up some of the common problems before the 1988 Act began to bite:

Governors say headteachers are defensive. Head teachers say governors don't show any interest – or in the very rare case show too much. Headteachers say governors come to school on special occasions but don't seem disposed to become involved more routinely in school affairs. Governors say they don't know how to advance beyond the ceremonial involvement to something more real. Heads say governors are obsessed with lockers and lavatories and show no interest in the curriculum. Governors say they are afraid of a rebuff if they venture too near territorial waters. They stay with the paving stones and the plumbing because they understand them, and because they don't constitute a challenge to anybody.

Both the 1986 Education (No. 2) Act and the 1988 Act changed the attitudes of governors as well as their ways of working. Many more parents became governors, governing bodies changed in their size and balance of membership and they were given at least a formal opportunity to exercise greater control over the conduct of a school. As things stand, they are required to balance their own views, the local authority's policy, the head's guidance and the imperatives of the national curriculum in their school's curriculum statement. They are given the opportunity to involve the local chief officer of police in their curriculum planning and they must make an explicit decision about the place of sex education in the curriculum. They have some power over the length of the school day, they are an avenue for parental complaint and they have wider powers than in the past over matters of school discipline and in the appointment and dismissal of teachers.

Of these, the involvement of governors in the curriculum relies heavily on the guidance and initiative of the head. Here above all he or she has to organize as far as possible a staff consensus, to present it to the governors and to explain any requests for modification back to the staff – and then if necessary to carry out the modification. Complicated though this can be, nevertheless when firm-minded heads, firm-minded teaching staff and firm-minded governors learn how far to go, where to negotiate and when to stop negotiating the ground for curriculum debate and subject planning itself becomes more certain.

Less familiar to teaching staff are the details of financial management. Many governing bodies appear to have at least one member who has some skill in financial planning and most governors are prepared to be sympathetic towards financial proposals from heads who show that they are competent. That combination, too, is sufficient for staff members who do not wish – or who are unable – to engage in detailed arguments about resources.

Because financial management is a major part of the school/

governor relationship, it is particularly important that the head should handle affairs with a mixture of care, adroitness and vision. Again, there is heavy reliance on the deputy or deputies, on one or two other experienced or senior staff and on the capacity of one or more of the governors not only to understand, to discuss and if necessary to change first ideas without bloodshed but also to explain the professional side to their lay colleagues.

An incompetent head is one who fails to master the task of reconciling a management plan with a financial plan, who fails to communicate and to ensure enough understanding for the financial plan with his or her teacher colleagues and who is unable to engage with governors at a level where there is both trust and understanding. There may be cases where all the fault lies on the side of the head, and indeed in the earliest days of financial delegation many governors were said to have resigned because they could not find enough time to master the intricate responsibilities of new government and because a path through those intricacies had not been mapped by the head.

In contrast to the position of governors, the position of parents in coping with an incompetent head is confined to their power to complain. They are likely always to complain less about bad financial management than about pupil assessments. To complain individually is not as successful as to complain within a unified forum. That forum, also established by the 1986 Education (No. 2) Act, is the annual parents' meeting (APM). Even the earliest study of its effectiveness stressed the view that it should improve the degree of accountability. In reporting a national conference in February 1988, Earley (1988: 64–5) reported:

As for the future of annual governors' reports and APMs, most participants agreed they provided an opportunity for governors, teachers and parents to work together. Lessons had been learned from the first round of these activities, especially about accountability and communication between the governing body and parents. There was now a need to ensure both activities were seen by parents as having a purpose. . . . The APM and the report provided an opportunity for governors to explain, justify and evaluate what they had been doing, especially with regard to the quality of education offered. Parents' main interest was seen as the opportunity to influence the quality of their children's education . . . the view was expressed that the APM should be seen as the climax to a continuous relationship between various parties and an opportunity for them to come together and ask questions about what had happened over the course of the previous 12 months.

Conclusion

The reforms of the 1986 and 1988 Education Acts cannot be handled through any single pattern of management.

The head is still the leader and acts as chief executive from the viewpoint of governors – partly being told what to do, partly being expected to put forward alternatives of policy and plans for action, partly being used as their principal adviser and partly as the intermediary and negotiator with the other parties.

For parents too the head is the leader. Past reputation, either in the same school or elsewhere, matters because it is slow to change and because laymen's views change equally slowly. Many of the changes of the 1986 and 1988 Acts are new enough for heads to be given the benefit of parents' earlier trust.

In the eyes of the employing local authority the position of the head as leader-cum-manager depends on how much he or she can manage without the authority's assistance and on how correct his or her activities are in terms of fitting into national and local patterns of responsibility. Otherwise, from the viewpoint of the local authority the head is treated as acting independently. Collegiality in management matters if its absence leads to signs of misunderstanding and discontent on the part of other staff, governors or parents. The style and method of management matter less than the question of whether the headteacher can collaborate with other schools and is prepared to make adjustments and concessions in the way the school is run in order to allow better pooling of time, staff or other resources.

It can certainly happen that a head might at the same time be expected to manage the school democratically by the staff, deferentially by the governors, assertively by the local authority and pliantly by parents. Filling these four different expectations has to be consciously entered into. Not to be aware of the differences of demand and not to pay heed to them would amount to disregarding the purposes and moral cost of adapting to change. A manager's lack of awareness of how he or she should bend in the wind is a sign of poor intelligence or insensitivity.

On the other hand, to be too knowing about one's shifts of stance can amount to cynicism. Between the two lies balanced self-awareness. This entails personal views and values, a judgement about the degree of respect in which one holds the view of other people and a sense of whether something is being sacrificed or enhanced as a result of making adjustments. Some adjustments can amount to a loss of steadfastness, others can lead to values becoming curtained or shadowed in such a way that they are no longer clear to other people. Other adjustments may be so serious as to amount to jettisoning a carefully worked-out position.

The head does not always have the time to ponder the price of those personal and professional adjustments which have to be made in the regular course of management. One reason which can be given for this is the claim that a head is simply a functionary and that his or her views and judgements have to be variable for the sake of other people. This may not do justice to the proper degree of personal and professional self-regard which is expected of a head. If positions and viewpoints are too easily set aside they might be regarded by other people as not having, even in the first place, amounted to much.

But jettisoning a view can go beyond personal damage to the manager. To write off the ideas and conclusions which one has reached in order to allow an accommodation with other people's expectations may mean getting rid of a conclusion which the manager had reached after listening to and observing other people's experience. In other words, in addition to explicit consultation and the pursuit of a visible consensus on any matter, the manager carries within his or her subconsciousness the sediment of many terms and years of other people's wisdom. To disregard that is to show disrespect for those who are colleagues, those whom the head is leading and without whose support he or she cannot manage.

When the manager faces in four directions – fellow-staff, parents, governors and local authority – the first need is to remember which type of management is being exercised at any one moment.

The second need is to be equally well prepared in six areas of management – the curriculum, the social organization of the school, the efficiency of assessment and the efficient feedback of assessment's findings, staff dispositions and changes, financial priorities and the triple task of giving account to governors, parents and the local authority. Equal success in all six requires mastery by the head of the detailed requirements of those matters which are covered by regulation (curriculum, assessment, staffing, finance, accountability) and a well-formed, carefully agreed practical philosophy about social organization, the school's values and its ethos. Each area of responsibility requires good preparation and hard work in sharing, adjusting and reaching agreed policies and practices.

The third need is to remember that while the 1988 Act changed many aspects of management from the point of view of the insider, it changed few things from the point of view of the parents, the employer or the public. To the outside world what was happening was a tightening-up of some matters, a clearing out of unexamined clutter and the creation of a sense of accountability. The purpose of the legislation was to get the education services to deliver what parents, the community and taxpayer wanted. This means that the manager has to keep his or her activities tightly geared to the reactions of teachers, governors, employers, parents and of that part of the community to whom education matters. It also means that the manager receives no plaudits for doing what ought already to have been done since.

Ideally, good management in education is a discreet matter but one in which nevertheless training can be offered. Its concealed and overt sides reflect the balance of personal belief and professional judgement on the one hand and publicly assessed activities on the other. The latter have been as well represented in in-service training courses since the 1988 Act. But personal belief and professional judgement have not received the same attention.

Alan Coulson provided a summary of the balance of views taken about headship potential in the field of management in Clarkson (1988). He included in his review a summary of eight characteristics which were consistently associated with successful school management and, in summing up, he pointed the way forward very clearly (Clarkson 1988:273):

In schools, changes in legislation, organization and curriculum tend to attract considerable attention when they are first introduced. Yet changes which at first seem major or dramatic often fade in significance as parts of them are assimilated into school operation or attention is diverted to newer concerns. Regardless of the changes the near future may bring, the central importance of the head as an exemplar of personal and professional qualities will remain. Since these qualities are fundamentally expressions of values, attitudes and feelings *within the persons*, traditional in-service training approaches which concentrate on conveying new knowledge, imparting particular skills or prescribing certain patterns of behaviour are insufficient for headship development. To be successful, future education for headship will need to pay greater attention to the prime importance of the development and growth of heads *as persons*; it must therefore embrace consideration of their values and assumptions, their feelings and their intentions, and their relationships with others as much as their professional knowledge and teaching skills.

Some aspects of training and some courses of advanced qualification can meet this need.

CHAPTER 9

New training for new management

The quality of children's learning is assumed to improve when education is managed well. If aims and objectives are clear, if resources which assist the reaching of those aims are properly distributed and if other matters which bear on relationships, self-evaluation, assessment, planning and reporting are thought out and carefully put into operation, pupils will be better educated.

To achieve this, information has to be shared between several participants. The importance given to better education and training differs from country to country. In a comparison carried out by the National Economic Development Council and the Manpower Services Commission (1984:85) it was said that

the concern for a sound basic education is voiced strongly in all the three countries [USA, Japan and the then Federal Republic of Germany] as it is in the UK, but nowhere more so than in the US. Americans think they have lost more ground than others and are now making great efforts to catch up. Competency testing in high schools is rapidly gaining ground. A recent study . . . suggests that German basic education leads to better examination performance than does the British; and Japanese schools have always insisted on high achievement in basic subjects. If there is a lesson to be learnt it is that success has been related to demonstrated achievement in a core of subjects . . . a qualification requiring a minimum level of achievement and minimum level of performance being set against specified standards. It would appear that the objectives of many of the current measures of educational reform in the UK bring us nearer to the actions of our competitors.

The three other countries were said to have better systems of information – information used by communities, by employers and by individuals. The consequence for the United Kingdom of the relative lack of public information is that 'individuals are poorly placed when taking decisions which will affect their own futures' (NEDC/MSC 1984:89). But while it is relatively straightforward to find what courses are available 'it is much more difficult to discover what has actually happened, and is likely to happen, to people who have chosen one course of study rather than another. . . . The message from our competitors is that effectiveness is based upon (but not limited to) hard information about performance. That information arises from what individuals and organizations collectively define and act upon. The system has to be transparent' (NEDC/MSC 1984: 89).

The report called for the better organization of training and education between employers, trade unions and individuals. Any faults
which had to be corrected lay with weaknesses of management in not
providing forums in which every interested party could combine its efforts.

Five years after the NEDC/MSC report Training and Enterprise
Councils (TECs) were launched, with an emphasis on the need to provide a meeting-ground for several interests: 'Each TEC will shape its
own agenda to reflect the special economic and social needs of the
area. It will serve as a forum for business and community leaders to
identify problems, set priorities, define strategies for change and divert
resources accordingly' (Department of Employment 1989). The introduction of TECs was critical of the past because matters had not been
managed collaboratively: 'We stand at the crossroads. In one direction
lie the behaviour and attitudes, the short term planning and the easy
options which have so bedevilled our performance in the past' (Department of Employment 1989:19).

The criticisms were not specific: British people were not well
enough trained in comparison with people from some other countries,
their training did not take sufficient account of what employers
wanted, there was too little emphasis on the connection between the
launching of new enterprises and the training of people in readiness
for and in order to follow the consequences of those launches – and
the absence of collaborative management in the past had led to poorly
organized training.

Opponents of the idea that the management of education and training can benefit from the lessons of business and industry found it
ironic that the messages which were put out in the two documents
criticized weaknesses in the world of employers rather than of educators.

Another approach which was more closely connected with general
education in schools than with vocational training and employment
training came from the Audit Commission (1989). In looking at the
way in which schools and colleges were managed after the 1988 Act,
the Commission pointed out that LEAs would have a less directive
role but would still have to monitor the services of schools and colleges. This monitoring was needed in order to guarantee to the electors
in a local authority that an appropriate service was being provided.
Monitoring meant assessment and the Audit Commission report was
concerned with the local services of advisers and inspectors and with
how schools and colleges were managed. It pointed out that not all the
monitoring carried out by an LEA required the application of professional educational judgement. 'Information can be collected by recording routine statistics; the professional judgements called for in
considering financial probity or the condition of buildings are not educational. But part of the necessary information can be gathered only by
professional observation and requires the application of educational

judgement before it can be used to assist in the formulation of recommendations for action' (Audit Commission 1989:7). Although not everyone will agree that the condition of, for instance, educational buildings can be adequately judged without an educational view, the main point which the Commission was making was that information was the key to the assessment of quality in education. Examination results were limited, national testing and assessment would provide 'a wider-based source of information' (Audit Commission 1989:7) but again this information would not reveal how much was attributable to the school and how much to the home. Above all, it was necessary, in the search for quality, for LEAs to have their own direct observation of teaching and learning: 'it is important to know whether improvements are needed in the organization of teaching, in the provision of equipment and materials, in the quality of teaching of one or more teachers or in some quite different area' (Audit Commission 1989:8).

In its recommendations the report noted that while some kind of internal evaluation is part of good management practice for all organizations there was nevertheless an absence of external moderation of those evaluations. The internal measures which were often used (with a notable slant towards secondary schools) were examination results, tests of literacy and numeracy, attendance patterns, pupils' records of achievement, curriculum information and national testing and assessments. Other measures came from budgetary information and, for FE colleges, the reports of vocational examining bodies, the views of the then Training Agency advisers and FE efficiency indicators.

The messages about the importance of using and sharing information were the same as those which emerged from the international comparisons of the NEDC and from the explanations of the work of TECs. They are all linked with parts of educational activity which fall within a typical institutional plan and are now largely covered in the requirements for the publication of comparative information laid down in the Education (Schools) Act 1992.

Because an institutional plan has to guarantee quality at a level which is sought by parents and employers, the information on which it is based has to be that which they value. Not all information will be regarded as of equal weight and therefore a truly total assessment is unattainable. For example, HMI reports, which are consistently self-limiting in their commentaries, make it clear that they cannot, except in national surveys, go beyond specifics. In such surveys, however, such as that of 100 primary schools implementing the national curriculum, the conclusion was that as long ago as autumn 1989 'the best work seen in year 1 classes fully met, and went beyond, the requirements of the National Curriculum attainment targets and programmes of study in the core subjects' (HMI 1990). This reassurance about quality looked at management (HMI 1990:14):

The leadership exercised by heads is of crucial importance in successful implementation. Effective heads have realistic but challenging expectations of the

degree and rate of change that are manageable by staff; involve their colleagues in school-wide curricular planning and decision-making; delegate genuine responsibilities to subject co-ordinators; see staff development as one of
their major responsibilities; and target resources of time, materials and personnel to areas of agreed priority.

Managing quality in this example is based on the assumption that
long-term and medium-term planning of all subjects is important, that
the analysis and modification of the use of time have to be repeated
from year to year (if not from term to term) and that targets and statements of attainment should feature in schools' schemes of work 'and
provide a valuable focus for the planning and transaction of classwork
by individual teachers' (HMI 1990:14). The importance of programmes of study, too, is recognized, as also is the place of non-statutory guidance in the carrying out of review and further planning. Most
important of all, to ensure that a school's management plan makes a
difference at the level of classroom management, there has to be an assessment of the extent to which the quality of individual children's
work is affected by an individual teacher's classroom management and
by his or her adoption of the relevant part of the school plan.

That plan must rest, in the first place, on an audit, and in its advice
to governors, heads and teachers (DES 1989e) the School Development Plans Project (SDPP) gave some ideas about how a school would
undertake that. There had to be a clear decision about how to compile
the relevant information and evidence and how to select certain areas
for audit while others were postponed until later years. The project
pointed out that an audit

is easier if it is carefully planned and responsibility for particular aspects is
shared out. For example

● a curriculum leader in a small primary school leads a small group to
  scrutinise a selection of pupils' work from different year groups to
  examine progression and continuity and their relation to the National
  Curriculum
● a department in a secondary school reviews its curricular provision;
  assesses the implications of the National Curriculum for that subject;
  analyses policies and practice on pupil assessment; analyses examination/
  test results; reviews pupils' written work to check on progression and
  continuity
● a team considers relations with parents and the wider community
● the head, a deputy or a senior teacher leads a working party on topics
  such as cross-curricular issues, curriculum provision as a whole, pupil
  attendance, school documentation
● the staff development or INSET co-ordinator leads a working party to
  review staff development, INSET provision and dissemination, teacher
  appraisal, care of probationer teachers (DES 1989e:8).

This breadth of preparing for and following up a development plan
should then, suggests the Project Team, be broken down into detailed
action plans with specific targets for the following year. Examples are

given of the working documents which should emerge from this process, in keeping with a school's priority. The examples are: 'revising and improving the whole curriculum for a particular year group, taking account of the programmes of study and attainment targets of the National Curriculum; developing a whole-school assessment policy, including marking and recording; piloting a scheme for staff development and appraisal' (DES 1989e:11).

This represents a clear way of connecting a school plan and the daily practices of its teachers. The same report also, when it turns its attention to taking stock, extends itself to pupils. In particular, the collation of brief reports which can make up an evaluation at the end of each planning cycle should enable the head with both colleagues and governors to create a bridge between good management and good learning.

If the work of the SDPP is taken alongside that of another team on school management, the School Management Task Force (DES 1990a), the benefit emerges of seeing how detailed proposals for management and review penetrate deep into the daily work of the school and how that detail can be set in the larger context of characteristics (thirteen in number) of effective schools (DES 1990a: 5–6), set against six management tasks which are regarded as having high priority following the 1988 Act.

These are concerned with the local management of schools (LMS), national curriculum and assessment, appraisal and staff development, working with governors, strategic planning and monitoring and evaluation. A common pattern of response is suggested: 'Action is needed in four complementary areas, planned as a single programme: training opportunities, management information, practical advice and assistance and management tools and techniques' (DES 1990a:12).

The targets set by the School Management Task Force are realistic as part of large-scale management, and the detailed approach of the SDPP is likely to be more immediately valuable to schools. Both provide guidance on the management of quality. Both take us much nearer the heart of connecting management to learning than the broader approaches of NEDC/MSC and the TECs. The views of the Audit Commission and of HMI provide further depth of guidance.

Each of the six noted different aspects of management and observed differences in importance and difficulty in each aspect. They did not describe how managers would, separately from publicly shared measurements, make their judgements. They did not, for instance, examine how a head looks at the development of fellow-staff after the time of first appointment.

Staff development

Schools choose teachers to carry out a specific duty, to teach specific subjects and to contribute to the school at large. Heads take care to let those who are interviewed for new posts know what sort of school it is, what it believes in, how it relates to its community and how it is planned that it should develop and improve. Few teachers are appointed for only one of the three tasks and even if their hands are full with teaching or with a senior teacher's responsibilities or a large clutch of pastoral duties in their early days, they will know from the head what kind of organization they are joining.

If a teacher at the time of appointment has agreed to play a part in the larger framework and in the long-term plan for a school, the head will after a time weigh up the capacity of the new colleague to add his or her contribution to the larger task. A staff development interview often reveals that the teacher, once settled in, wants to do more in order to extend the interest and the responsibility of teaching. If everything goes well, the teacher grows. It is part of the job of the head to make sure that the skills and gifts of teachers are allowed to develop. And if it is part of the head's job to assist in that process, it should be part of the teacher's professional equipment to respond to stimuli and opportunities to do more (J. M. Worrall, conversation, 1990).

Heads as they appoint new staff have the chance to turn the long-term realization of a school's plan into a shared reality, but the same commitment can also be won from those teachers who are at a school when a new head arrives.

Frameworks of commitment have to be built and maintained with care. Once everyone knows what the framework is, most will contribute readily to the development of the school inside that frame. One or two will be unable to play a part, because of illness, personal distress or a preoccupation with unavoidable non-professional matters. These are the teachers who, with one exception, will be understood and helped by the head and by other teachers. The exception is the teacher who dissipates other people's goodwill by edging further into a personally disorganized life or by losing any real sense of what is required of a teacher.

By explaining the framework of a school's aims, by giving opportunities for growth, by bringing separate contributions together and by, as far as possible, helping the colleague who needs help, a head can both lead and serve as an equal in collegial management. The head can then also decide whether the plan which exists in his or her mind is being realized. If not, should heads settle for less than the whole of their ideal or keep on pressing their colleagues?

Good sense says that they should go as far as they can but return from time to time to those parts of the plan which have not at first been realized. This will not always satisfy governors, parents, the LEA – or the church or religious order if it happens to be a voluntary-aided school. Nor can an incomplete job description fulfil such requirements of good planning as those laid down by the two post-1988 Act teams on management (DES 1989e, 1990a).

Those two special projects are not likely to help the providers of training in management to avoid the pitfalls which were noted by the National Development Centre for School Management Training in 1987 (Wallace and Hall 1989). There were seven weaknesses in most of specially provided courses which from April of that year transferred from being funded by the TVEI-related In-service Training (TRIST) scheme – which had been managed by the Manpower Services Commission – to the LEA Training Grants Scheme (LEATGS).

Management training was designated by the DES at that time as a national priority area of work and received a relatively high level of financial support. Despite being picked out in this way there were still failures and difficulties. It is significant that one which was encountered more than once was a 'lack of follow-up support after the course and a lack of procedures for evaluating impact on participants' performance as opposed to the quality of the training experience' (Wallace and Hall 1989:165). Linked with this latter point, it was also reported that when it came to an evaluation of training courses 'higher education providers revealed that their concern was very largely with improving the quality of their courses rather than assessing their effectiveness upon participants' management practice in school' (Wallace and Hall 1989:172). Later, the point was made that the 'development of systematic support for managers in schools has become heavily orientated towards the immediate needs generated by education reforms at the expense of that longer term development of heads and senior staff' (Wallace and Hall 1989:173).

Extended development of heads and others has in the past amounted to little more than the agglomeration of courses relating to specific short-term issues. This approach is not the key to finding how managers can develop the combination of visionary gift and pragmatic skill.

Heads who are asked where that combination took its origin in their individual histories make it clear that it did not come from training. Nor is there much evidence pointing to their general education as the origin of their vision and managerial skill. The experience of working with gifted teachers and heads in their early career, the sense that they have in some cases been given the benefit of working closely with other wise and successful teachers – particularly inside a religious order – the fact that they in some cases went away from teaching and, having had time to reflect in quite unrelated work, then saw that teaching was an obligation which they should meet – these are among the backgrounds which heads are prepared to reveal. They are hesitant about calling their sense of vocation as being in any way visionary. They prefer to think in terms of gift, skill, interest, satisfaction. Above all they regard as their major drive the obligation to help children and young people to grow (E.G. Howard, conversation, 1990; C. G. Teuten, conversation, 1990).

If managers say that they gain their vision and their pragmatic skill informally and from diverse sources, if they see their own development as something which took many years and came from a wide range of contexts, it is unlikely that a short-term substitute can be found which will fit into either the narrow limits of brief in-service training courses, year-long secondments or part-time study in higher education.

In helping in their colleagues' professional development heads see this difficulty. To overcome it some look upon their own experience and try to offer its essential characteristics to others. One head may decide that the opportunity to understand other systems of education is a considerable stimulant for thought and professional reflection. Another may see that a powerful and confident experience in one field – such as music – brings contacts and perspectives which remain useful. Another will feel that a range of different experiences – not all directly connected with teaching – gives a depth of understanding and sympathy with other people. The examples are not numberless nor are the responses. In terms of giving teachers more chances to learn and to develop it comes down to releasing them for as long as they can with some financial help, some doubling-up of teaching and a well-organized use of locally managed funds. Placed in a formal framework, it becomes a matter of staff development. Less formally it amounts to providing trained and experienced adults with the opportunity professionally to expand (G.E. Jones, conversation, 1990).

Providing opportunities runs through two aspects of management: unless colleagues are given the opportunity to understand the world outside education, unless they have the opportunity to look around and to come to some new conclusions of their own about what they are doing, the head will say that he or she is failing. It is not defined how an opportunity should be used, nor can the head or the teacher know at the outset whether any development or new insight will emerge. The head has to take the chance and to trust that an opportunity will in the end turn out to have been well handled.

A second example of the importance of giving opportunities to other people comes from the type of head who, in pursuing the argument that good management of a school should lead to good learning by the child, watches pupils for signs that they do in some way match hopes about independence of mind, wholeness and honesty. Management here is aimed at giving pupils the opportunity to develop these characteristics. How they emerge or whether they will always be visible and measurable is a matter of doubt.

Although a head's trust both in colleagues and in the capacity of pupils to use what teachers offer is an essential part of management, the uncertainty involved is, to some managers, frustrating. But a head must in the end tolerate something less than the hoped-for whole being achieved.

Along with trust, patience is a characteristic needed by potential managers. Those who feel that patience, trust and a capacity to put up with uncertainty are gifts rather than skills – and gifts which not all adults share – will doubt whether these personal dispositions can be amenable to training. If they are, they are likely to be shaped by management training which emphasizes the importance of personal factors as well as those which touch on performance indicators. Thus, the good manager needs the energy as well as the interest to transmit to others an understanding of obscure but still important requirements and regulations. Because they cover a wide range of responsibilities – about assessment, financial management, curriculum balance and accountability – the manager provides a better service to his or her partners if a single interpretation is provided and if disparate demands can be connected by a common thread.

To pursue with equal clarity the ideas which are associated with both the technicalities and the broad aims of management calls for reflectiveness. The manager who can understand each issue clearly can develop a repertoire of managerial qualities.

Self-development

A typical school policy statement about staff development will include definitions such as 'it is essential that we continue to grow in professional stature and experience, backed by the support of a comprehensive programme of in-service opportunities designed to help all of us to meet the growing demands with confidence, a sense of purpose and, as can be the case, an increased personal job satisfaction' (Hewton 1988:88). The progress made towards that increase allows 'individual staff to commit themselves to their own professional development and makes it possible for management to accept responsibility for implementation' (Hewton 1988:89).

Implementation includes establishing a structure and a sharing of responsibility between the head, other senior members of staff and individual teachers who carry out the tasks involved in identifying staff development needs, with formulating a programme and with evaluating its implementation.

In this last stage self evaluation is included and in a commentary on the White Paper on teaching quality (DES 1983a), John Elliott's characterization of three levels of professional development through self-evaluation was quoted as an argument against assuming that government policies of dealing out more doses of in-service education would improve teaching quality (Slater 1985). From a combination of three levels of professional development – unreflective self-evaluation based on practical knowledge, self-evaluation as practical deliberation and self-evaluation as action research – it was assumed that teaching quality would most noticeably be improved through deliberation and action research. 'A more thorough understanding of how teachers can evolve new ways of working as they move from tacit knowledge to practical principles will also contribute to making in-service education more effective.' But more in-service education may miss the point, because 'day-to-day demands on the teachers will sometimes lead to gaps developing between what teachers say they are doing and what they are actually doing' (Slater 1985:51). To avoid this confusion teachers need time for reflection and deliberation. It is they who must first work out whether there is a gap between theory and their own activities.

The subsequent connection between a teacher's self-evaluation and the head's view of performance is a normal, if delicate, part of internal management. The view from outside the school on the other hand, is more direct. The Scottish Education Department's (SED) survey of parents' views on school education reported, in the particular study of teachers and headteachers, a wide range of parent opinion (SED 1989). Of teachers, four examples, at random, covered approachability, humour and sensitivity (SED 1989:8):

If you don't have a sense of humour and can't laugh with the weans, you'd crack up more easily. Some teachers take everything a mite too serious.

They're quite strict. They have to be or the bairns would knock a rise oot o'them. But the bairns aren't feart like they used to be.

A good teacher is one who inspires confidence in the children and who can pick up problems early on before they get serious, and can bring the kids on.

She's been a wizard. She never blames Andrea for not being able to do it. She tries to find a way through and because she's patient and understanding she gets there. She's been magic!

Comments of this type in one sense only reinforce the point that the quality of a school's management is judged by the quality of treatment which the child receives in the classroom. The Scottish summary of what it is that parents value in teachers and what makes a poor (as well as a good) teacher (SED 1989:7–11) is in some ways an up-to-date version of parts of *Enquiry 1* (Schools Council 1968). It bears out the straightforwardness of parent comments, too, in its report of how they regard headteachers, good and bad, as in these examples (SED 1989:7–11):

The parents used to have their own meeting room. Now this head has pulled it back and parents have to meet in the playground.

He should be sent on a PR course. He just can't deal with parents and adults because he's so used to talking down to students all day.

The school is a different place. Friendly and welcoming. I would never have gone there before. Its down to the new heidie.

We have a great headmaster. I guarantee he knows every child in the school . . . and their parents and who they're related to . . . where they live.

Few if any of the matters on which these parents commented would have been the subject of any explicit policy statement in a school.

Style, manner, sensitivity, humour, trust – all these remain undefined but essential parts both of good teaching and of the good management of public relations. They are under the control of individual teachers. As personal traits and gifts, as the fruits of experience or as the outcome of maturity they remain essentially a private matter, not amenable to management training but open to approaches which might be based on good practice in counselling or on well-handled programmes about the development of interpersonal skills.

Parents see teachers and headteachers as the shapers of quality and effectiveness in any school. Their views have a reality which management must treat seriously, but to bring the worlds of common sense, theory and research together brings its own difficulties. When a commentary on Michael Rutter's *Fifteen Thousand Hours* was formulated by Tizard and others (1980) it acknowledged in the first place that in the report an impressive base of data supported 'an architecture in which many common sense perceptions about schools were co-ordinated' (Tizard *et al.* 1980:11). But one criticism made later in the same commentary drew attention to what was thought to be missing 'above all, two things: one of them a sense of history, both a broad and more local framework within which the achievement of these schools can be placed and evaluated; the other a sense of the actual texture of the schools themselves' (Tizard *et al.* 1980:13).

The texture of a school may be made up of old-fashioned and perhaps idealized certainties as far as parents are concerned. Teachers on the other hand may nowadays feel certain only about where they stand in the curriculum. They feel less certain about how the outside world will look upon attainments and assessments once the whole post-1988 process is open to public question.

It is the head's task to meet from among the more traditional views held by parents those which are still relevant to modern schooling and to affect, as far as possible, the way in which they look upon change. The head, too, is the only leader who is in a position to handle professional uncertainties and tentative first steps in a process of professional enquiry. For example, in looking at the way in which primary-school teachers respond to new ideas in environmental study and mathematics, Briault and West (1990:20) pointed out that teachers

came to understand environmental studies more fully by engaging in such work [i.e. action learning], became more confident about investigative approaches in mathematics by undertaking problem-solving activities in a supportive, non-threatening climate. Such approaches take time but . . . such shared activity helps to create a climate in which individuals may change themselves. Many innovations have more to do with changes in the value systems of the individuals concerned than with the acquisition of wholly new skills. Changing existing values is the key which opens the door of change.

Briault and West went on to comment that the headteachers in two of their studies gave a good deal of attention to the process through which individual teachers can change themselves. 'It takes time for staff to say openly "Can we say what we really feel?" Openness in discussion, the acceptance of the searching question and the admission of uncertainty are all signs of the process of change proceeding at an appropriate rate for the individuals concerned' (Briault and West 1990:20).

Moving on to parental understandings of change, Briault and West concede that parents will in some situations hold traditional views on matters of classroom practice. They add: 'In any case, there is always a degree of uncertainty about outcomes at the beginnings of a new in-itiative, when alternatives are imprecisely mapped out and staff are to be engaged in a process of critical reflection. This uncertainty is prone to be interpreted as "woolliness" by parents who prefer to trade in certitude' (Briault and West 1990:21).

As the views of parents as consumers become increasingly import-ant so the need for sensitivity towards their views becomes sharper. This underlines 'the usefulness of collaborative approaches to school improvement and the ultimate goal of implanting inquiry as an on-going process in the school. These are major targets of organizational development and will thus take time and resources to achieve. Those schools which have moved in this direction will find their responses to the National Curriculum much more easily managed' (Briault and West 1990:21). This sentiment appeared to be accurately echoed in the terms of reference of the enquiry into primary school methods which were announced by the Secretary of State in December 1991.

In summing up what they learned from their primary and middle school case studies, Briault and West (1990:99) came back to the pur-poses of good management:

The objective of management, in whatever sphere, is to improve the product and to meet the customer's requirements. In simple terms, school management is for the children. Many of our studies and our own commentaries have in fact made little mention of children. . . . But it is perhaps salutary to remind ourselves that the object of the enterprise is to provide every pupil with the best learning experiences. These . . . necessarily relate to the physical, social, intellectual and aesthetic environments in which they take place. Each of these aspects of the learning environment will now be even more fully under the control of the school than it has ever been before and this is the challenge to leadership and management in every school. The price of failure is boredom. The reward of success is lively and interested pupils.

In-service education

Reflecting the connection between good teaching and its management and good learning, institutional statements about the principles of in-service work include, as an example, 'The ultimate aim of all in-ser-vice education for teachers is the improvement of pupil/student learning through the development of teachers as reflective, autono-mous professionals who have not only developed a range of skills but also a broad knowledge of understanding of subject content and of the conceptual framework of teaching and learning.' (Polytechnic South West 1989:13). In extension of this, in-service education and training at its best is responsive both to teachers as individuals and to teachers as they function in their workplace. To be successful it has to be the 'product of continuing negotiation between those planning and delivering the course and those for whom it is intended' (Polytechnic South West 1989:13).

Just as in-service education does not work if it has not been tailored to match the stage or condition of the teacher who is to benefit from it, so the manager cannot manage unless the method and style of management are acceptable and unless its purposes have been first unravelled and then knitted together after consultation between the manager and the manager's colleagues.

This was noted as long ago as 1975 (Hughes) when it was pointed out that the administrator had to present an *acceptable* change, 'for today only acceptable schemes are operable. In all parts of the world this is a task which is likely to prove a formidable and exciting challenge to the educational administrator in the years ahead' (Hughes *et al.* 1985: 19, quoting Morris).

Acceptable training

Just as change has to be acceptable if there is to be success in implementing it, so training for management has to be acceptable.

The search for training which fits this description in the management of education is hindered in two ways: it has long been an area for tension between theorists and practitioners and it has from time to time been exposed to management models from fields where practice and purpose are very different from those of education.

The first has been very clearly described by Meredydd Hughes (Hughes *et al.* 1985:3–33). Recalling the emergence in the mid-1950s of the 'New Movement' in educational administration in the United States and Canada, he refers to the intense romance with theory, 'Sceptical practitioners were assured in the oft-quoted words of Dewey . . . that 'theory is in the end the most practical of all things'. It involved nothing less than a new paradigm and a new approach to the relationship of theory and practice in educational management' (Hughes *et al.* 1985:10). But even in the early days of the New Movement there were critics. Halpin is quoted: 'There are scientists, and administrators too, who consistently soar in the clouds. They forget that theory must be rooted in the actual world of experience.' Halpin later complained that theoretical modes were too rational, too tidy, too aseptic and that those who were responsible for school systems felt that there was an omission of 'much of the palpable stuff which quickens his pulse in his daily job' (Hughes *et al.* 1985: 32).

Although the New Movement faded in its significance, because it ignored parts of the practical experience of educational management which practitioners themselves regarded as important, what was left was still a recognition that education management is a field of application which allows fruitful connections to be made between theory and practice. Again Hughes has clearly described the influences, movements and inputs which have questioned monolith models and which have drawn a distinction between the more and the less valuable insights of the practitioner.

The form in which, however, the tension still emerges in the in-service education of teachers and in such training as is provided for education management in the period after the 1988 Education Reform Act is that of a preoccupation with the separate skills and tasks of management. Know-how is all important – and it is quite typical for a deputy head following an advanced part-time degree in education management to sigh with relief at the start of a module about, for instance, the management of assessment and to say that this was precisely what his head – with an eye mainly on the short term – hoped he would get out of the course.

One reason for seeking immediacy of value in management training is the absence of time in which to treat matters thoughtfully. Despite the concern for promoting reflectiveness among teachers, their in-service opportunities have to compete with a week-by-week preoccupation with in-school organization – modifying the management plan, feeding information back into the cycle of formative teaching and testing and balancing the books in order to cover one more curriculum or non-curriculum speciality. The practising education manager (or the potential senior manager who hopes to grow into that role through further professional education) may have, in other words, more to occupy the mind than was true in, for instance, the early 1980s.

At that time there was a more or less continuing concern with curriculum review. There was a still young involvement in national pupil assessment and there were the beginnings of more power being given to, and accountability expected from, governors. The pace of in-service education had already quickened. But management still lay, in Britain, more with LEAs than with heads or governors because in schools – primary, secondary or special – daily management was still at some distance from the control of finance, from the decision about a school's total allocation of teaching staff, from the establishment of policies and schemes of priority in the school's curriculum and organization and from the presentation of the whole picture of aims, methods and performance to parents and to other members of the local community.

The late start on training

New demands on management led to some confusion as to whether there were in existence models which were still of value. And, after the 1988 Education Reform Act, one question was whether that reform had led to a new education service in England and Wales. If so, did managers have access to the type of training which would guarantee their quality?

If one looks at the diversity of approaches to the development of education management in the past four decades, it seems that there are two or three which will meet new needs. That diversity, particularly in the field of structural models, has been traced (Hughes *et al.* 1985:21) from concepts of structural relativism (which took the place of the idea that there was but one right model of organization, on the basis of a firm hierarchical structure) through structures of which some were mechanistic and others organic and into the realm of 'contingency' models (structures of management which alter according to the issues with which they have to deal). In this connection Hughes has described some work by Lawrence and Lorsch (Hughes *et al.* 1985:21):

They identified and produced measures of distinct organizational sub-environments, matching each sub-environment to an appropriate sub-unit structure. 'Goodness of fit' became the important issue. The more turbulent and uncertain the environment, the greater the tendency for a high level performance to be associated with high differentiation among sub-units, coupled with effective integration achieved by means of shared information, flexible procedures and open decision-making.

One application of the theory of the contingency approach (Hughes *et al.* 1985:21) led to the view that belief systems and ideologies associated with religions deserved study. Although this might be reinforced by the suggestion, earlier in this chapter, that vision and the ideals fostered by a head can shape the total approach to school management, it is the contingency model and its capacity to take account of turbulence which seem to fit the description of several management approaches in this final decade of the century. But is turbulence the right word? What principally affects the environment of management is not so much turbulence as the wave upon wave of not very closely related demands and pressures from public and governmental sources. More apposite might be models of 'loose coupling', ascribed to March and Olsen (Hughes *et al.* 1985: 22) and of 'organised anarchies', as approached by Cohen and March (Hughes *et al.* 1985:23). Of these, the first (loose coupling) is typified as signifying that 'the parts of an organization are in *some* relationship to each other, but that the linkage is limited, uncertain and weak, and certainly much looser than the tight hierarchical control of bureaucratic theory' (Hughes *et al.* 1985: 22).

One conclusion about loose coupling was that it 'helps to maintain the facade that formal structures are really working when they are not' (Hughes *et al.* 1985:3). Taken to an extreme, this looseness led to 'organised anarchy'. 'In such an organization the goals are inconsistent and ill-defined, the technology for achieving them is unclear to the members, and those involved in decision-making vary unpredictably. Thus problems, solutions and decision-makers are not systematically related to each other' (Hughes *et al.* 1985:23).

Those management approaches which are presented in in-service education occasionally fall into the category of those which describe organized anarchy. More often they pursue the model of loose-linked internal connections within a management structure, together with a strong belief that the structures of management are contingent upon the problems with which they have to deal.

This mixture of anarchy, looseness-of-link and contingency encourages the discrete offering of management skills which will help the student to cope with the four or five separable outcomes of the legislative changes of the late 1980s. This discreteness does not encourage a unity of view about the way in which vision, total purpose and the management of whole-school quality assurance can be developed.

Skills of the manager as student

If the content of in-service work does not encourage the formulation of a unified way of approaching the purposes, implementation and evaluation of effective management, does the process of continued professional education promote a wholeness of view on its own?

In the case of short-term and occasional courses the answer is no. Under the wide distribution of in-service funding, decisions will be local about which courses should be organized and sought from other people (from local authority advisers, educational consultants or higher education) and which courses the teachers of the school or group of schools which holds the purse-strings should be asked or encouraged to attend. They will aim at bringing new knowledge and skill into a more or less parochial setting.

In longer courses, notably those which lead to postgraduate qualifications, not only is the view longer but the intellectual breadth is also wider. The student is expected to acquire knowledge and has also to prove a capacity for wide reading and understanding, an up-to-date awareness of the state of both debate and development in educational ideas, a capacity to criticize in a constructive way and an overall capacity to link those skills with collecting and analysing data and with the planning of projects.

If these approaches are common to courses of study which advanced degree students follow regardless of the content (for some will be specializing, for instance, in the field of special educational needs, others in the arts and humanities, others in mathematics and science) it is because it is regarded as essential that the same grasp of knowledge and the same development of intellectual-cum-practical skill should typify all holders of a second degree in the field of education.

This is appropriate for those who pursue such a higher degree in education management. Whether they are already leaders or aspire to more senior positions or are any part of those steadily developing collegial teams which are necessary to manage the diversity of educational change, then breadth of knowledge, a political awareness of the wider field of debate, the capacity to stand back, criticize and to argue to an acceptable and workable end, all these are essential parts of the professional's equipment.

This alone does not automatically encourage a singleness of view about management's purposes. The process of approaching one end along four or five different avenues may be intellectually unifying but discrete definitions of course control, particularly in modularized courses, can lead to gaps.

A modular course in education management can cover broad issues such as the management of change as well as narrower questions of the management of time and money, the management of curriculum development, of assessment and review, of the handling of relationships both inside and outside schools and colleges and of the management of staff development policies and practices which make and sustain effective institutions.

On a taught part-time course with thirty hours of teaching for each module, messages about both the breadth of management's responsibilities and the quality of mind which it requires can to some extent be repeated. Teaching and particularly a scheme of one-to-one tutoring and counselling has to encourage a response from each student which testifies to that student's commitment to thorough enquiry, hard thinking, self-scrutiny and honesty of purpose, all set within a context of the daily practicalities of management.

Little if anything beyond these qualities can be asked of any teacher or manager. Well-structured courses prevent the sense of singleness of purpose from being dissipated. Modularization alone carries a risk. The absence of a sequential pattern of modules – for students may choose to pick and mix – can be regarded as the loss of the chance to develop one idea and one field of knowledge from another. There may also be the loss of a chance to provide consistent and developmental counselling for the student.

The success of module-based part-time advanced degree work depends very much on the connection of studies between differing realms of subjects and differing fields of organization. That relationship can be affected if the scale or seriousness of a student's compulsory assignments (knowledge of the literature, a capacity for critique and argument, ability to design a project and to collect and analyse data) is in any way diminished.

Rudduck (1991:138) draws attention to the weakness of some private, classroom-focused styles of practitioner enquiry: 'What it ignores are the wider social and political frameworks, beyond the classroom and the school, that shape the parameters of education in ways that teachers, with their eyes drawn to the minutiae of their own practice, too often fail to see. The distinctive feature of teacher enquiry, the individual struggling to understand the events and interactions of his or her own classroom, may not be a powerful force for change'. But later, in answer to critics of the 'soft approach' Rudduck (1991:139) responds: 'Such research, they say, can run the risk of addressing trivial questions, lacks cumulative power and offers no collective, radical challenge – but on the other hand reflective, classroom-focused research is a way of building excitement, confidence and insight – and these are important foundations for career-long personal and professional development.'

This long-term view of the benefit of in-service work takes us back, in management, to the two major hindrances. One, the theory/practice tension, has been referred to already. The second, the inappropriateness of models from other fields, touches on the significance of teacher-led, classroom-based or school-focused enquiry and action research. If the data and the questions to the answering of which the analysis of data leads are trivial, parochial or unrelated to larger issues, does this lock education management inside its own cell? Is what is small scale and open to observation by only one teacher capable of demonstrating a broader relevance?

If the answer is no, there may be a case for dismissing the attempt to apply to education management some of the models which are drawn from business and industry. If the answer is yes, is that to be taken as part of Rudduck's message which says that small scale studies are not trivial if they nevertheless provide excitement, confidence and insight? Or is it that inside all organizations there are, continuously, small discoveries to be made in order to improve what is being done – and that schools do not differ from other organizations?

The double answer – schools are different from but they are also the same as other organizations – was confirmed when Handy and Aitken (1986:34) asked whether, in their essentials, schools were just like other organizations. 'If they are, then it becomes appropriate to learn from those organizations and to apply the theories and findings of organizational research to the running of schools. Schools, however, and schoolteachers have instinctively felt that they were different, not unique, and have needed their own set of theories and precepts.' Both views are right (Handy and Aitken 1986:34):

In that they are collections of individuals brought together for a purpose, schools are subject to all the problems, limitations and excitements that are inherent in getting people to work together, wherever they do it. But schools are not businesses – it might be simpler if they were – and many of the organizational concepts were hammered out and tested in business organizations. It is important, therefore, to be clear about the differences as well as the similarities so that one can know what to query as well as what to accept in the concepts.

Later, as though echoing their regret that schools are not businesses, Handy and Aitken (1986:45) sum up the question about differences:

Schools are obviously different – and more complex. A school is not a business, but it is important for a school to work out what kind of a business it is in order to make the complexity manageable. . . .

A school has to decide what kind of organization it is (a factory, a work community, a market-place?), who its customers are, what they want and how that is to be delivered and measured. If the students are *workers*, for instance, not raw material, then it makes sense to ask what products they ought to be producing and for whom; it is possible to work back from this to a process for delivering those products. There is no reason at all why an organization should not be serving a *range* of markets with a *range* of products as long as this is deliberate and not accidental.

This, as an essential part of preparing a strategy of quality assurance, emphasizes for Handy and Aitken (1986:45–6) the point:

assumptions about the way things should be run and organised have a major effect on the way people see themselves, the way they behave, think and react. Even if the assumptions are unwitting or unconscious and have been around as long as the scenery, they are still potent. Anyone who is charged with running classes, sections of schools or whole schools needs to be aware of what those assumptions are and of their effects.

This definition of the importance of a unity of view in management and of the importance of sharing interest and concern allows the significance of the classroom and of the small-scale, almost invisible base of experience of the individual teacher to take its place alongside larger aspects of policy and of governmental requirement in the total framework of a school's management.

The size and complexity of that framework are dictated by the interplay of national policies on education, local authority implementations, HMI monitorings, whole school policies, practices in evaluation and individual teacher input. Many industries and businesses have the same range of control, freedom, accountability, autonomy and interrelatedness. Other public services, notably the health service, have a comparable complexity even if they appear to have fewer levels of authority and discretions of autonomy. But no business or any other public service other than education has – as have maintained schools and colleges – to engage with every family, child and parent in the land for a long, important and compulsory period of years.

Education and its management can learn lessons not only from the examples of individual industries but also from the movements which have stimulated the evolution of quality circles (Nissan), employee involvement (Ford) and participative management. These have been subsumed under a quality of work life (QWL) movement which in turn has been defined as a managerial effort . . . 'to involve workers in management decision-making, to systematically empower workers in management decision-making . . . . particularly as groups' (Thompson and McHugh 1990:208).

Associated with the advocacy and development of teamwork and flexibility in management within industry is the 'just-in-time' (JIT) system. While this is basically concerned with 'ensuring that the exact quantity and quality of raw materials, parts and sub-assemblies are delivered 'just-in-time' for the next stage of production . . . [it] is not merely an inventory system. To work properly it requires flexible labour utilisation and harmonising of tacit skills, close managerial involvement. . . . It feeds into the overall process of continuous improvement' (Thompson and McHugh 1990:203).

The relevance of these messages to any form of management, in education or elsewhere, is easy to see. Equally important are two more statements, first (Thompson and McHugh 1990:362):

A further reason for not regarding the worlds of today and tomorrow as wholly sealed off from one another is that there is much to learn from the existing practice of *employees*. . . . There is a massive 'hidden history of the workplace' which needs to be recognised and uncovered. That history is based on the self-organization of workers trying to resist and transform work relations. . . . Old-style movements for workers' control are no longer feasible in a world of transnationals and global production and semi-skilled labour. But there remains a wealth of untapped experience and knowledge in employees' informal job-controls and patterns of organization.

In time teachers will learn from their European Community counterparts and from their newer international colleagues elsewhere how they might organize their work differently. Management will move at the same pace, absorbing as proactively as possible those contributions to continued improvement which, regardless of their source, focus on quality assurance. The lessons are varied. Many of the items of management, quoted here from Landry already have a relevance to the management of that assurance (Thompson and McHugh 1990:365):

There is a vital distinction to be made between 'management' and those people who hold managerial positions, and 'management' as an assortment of integrative functions which are necessary in any complex organization – planning, harmonising related processes, ensuring appropriate flows of information, matching resources to production needs, marketing, financial control and linking output to demand.

Conclusion

Good education is the product of good management. There are ample claims that reflection, proactive planning and a defensible allocation of resources lead to improvements in teaching and learning.

Management is described in terms of change more often than in terms of standstill or consolidation. Change is perceived in different ways by heads, other teachers, governors and parents. A considerable part of the manager's task is to reconcile and be reconciled with other people. Lest this become too amorphous an activity, managers concentrate on discrete parts of the job – on improving the flow of information, on establishing practicable schemes of staff development and on self-evaluation.

Encouraging a manager to use and to enrich his or her own personal resources of belief and experience is not often a part of management training. Nor does coping with uncertainty and living with mistakes often appear in the programme of a manager's preparation. But taking the fact into account that schools have a history and a texture, the manager's armoury of awareness has to be constantly reviewed and expanded.

Some courses of management training reveal an unwillingness or incapacity of trainers to assess whether their courses affect the later professional behaviour of managers. And because education is thought by some people to be unique, its very isolation seems to justify the fact that its management should not be evaluated on lines comparable to the management of business, industry or other spheres of large-scale public work. But this is not tenable at a time when the voice of the consumer and the making of comparisons between education and other enterprises grows more insistent. Approaches to management and training have to be sought which concentrate on meeting these demands.

CHAPTER 10

Responding to alternatives

If the effect of any particular style of a school's management could be assessed in terms of the speed of individual pupil's development, managers would have verifiable evidence of their success or failure. In the absence of that direct evidence, it is necessary for managers to be self-critical.

In asking questions about itself a management team must avoid a morale-damaging appearance of excessive self-doubt. Any process of self-examination must not be so public as to lead others to think that something is wrong when, in fact, everything is satisfactory, but at the same time self-scrutiny must not be so discreet as to appear secretive.

The style of self-evaluation will be determined between the head, senior teachers, the chair of the governing body and one or two parent governors. In deciding which approach to adopt the first essential is to define the style or approach which the school has used so far. Has it been based on consensus? Has it placed importance on the establishment of priorities? Has it been open enough to explain and allow questions, criticisms and debate about its policies?

Genuine self-examination can only be conducted in connection with decisions which have been explicit, recorded and which have had a starting date. If a policy has not been written down and circulated to teachers, governors and parents, it cannot be claimed to be a policy. If it had no fixed starting date, no review will know where to start in looking for its effects.

In making matters explicit, managers must make sure that a range of policies is identified which is thought to contribute to the consensus-based view which the school takes of itself. In the same way an explicit list of priorities of implementing and measuring new action has to be checked in order to confirm that the management has lived up to its own aims. A list of items has to be deliberately presented to other partners in management in order to elicit response, questioning and possibly criticism. Each of these has to be checked. Has each stage been completed? Can management show that it has kept its promise of accountability?

If all the answers are positive, the process of self-review can start. Initially the judgement about whether the school kept to the line which management set out for itself has to be one on which the head alone can adjudicate. Later it will be shared and at that stage there has to be a check to ensure that any subjectivism was not misdirected. The checking has to be properly organized. Trust alone will not suffice because in the words of Jennifer Nias (Glatter *et al.* 1988:143)

trust . . . depends upon the predictability of personal and institutional behaviour and of technical competence, and upon awareness of school goals. . . . There is bound to be conflict over the aims of education. . . . To claim that this conflict can be resolved by mutual trust rather than by 'formal procedures' is to be guilty of circularity. It is also to ignore the part played in the establishment of trust by forms of organization. In a world which is 'crooked as corkscrews', accountability must be expressed in part through formal order. . . . Formal procedures facilitate the growth of trust and help ensure it survives.

When those formal procedures make it clear how the school's management comes out in its first scrutiny, the head must put up alternatives, whether to go on as the school has in the past or to change its approach. If everyone who has been a part of a consensus of management feels that his or her involvement has been real and if the managers can be shown to have acted upon the reactions and feedback of those who have been included in the consensus, the choice lies between going on with the same procedures or improving them. If parents, for instance, have been regularly consulted but have not contributed very much, do they need encouragement? Or should their importance as consultees be diminished? If teachers have failed to respond significantly, should management reduce the frequency or the immediacy with which it seeks their views?

Whatever questions are asked and whatever response they receive those responsible for management must have alternatives for the future in order to avoid complacency. They must be clear too about examining only that which has been genuinely shared with others, that which had definition (and a timetable) and that from which a verifiable effect was expected. If it cannot meet these conditions, management must admit that its work is not based on explicit policy-making nor on sharing the practical implementation of its intentions. It must, if this is true, admit that it has not lived up to its claim of being based on consensus. The choice is then of whether to go on as a hierarchical or a bureaucratic or an autocratic machine. Above all management must describe and explain – in published detail and to a timed programme for future implementation and review – how exactly it intends to change its ways.

Changes of style

There are three ways in which managers can change their style. They might opt for dictation but to tell teachers, governors and parents how they should react requires a dependence on non-existent sanctions. What could the head and the senior teachers do if an instruction was ignored? Nothing, unless the core management group felt that its own position was so weak that it had to coerce those who did not agree with it.

As an alternative should the head withdraw from the machinery of consensus? The law permits a head to opt out of school government but in terms of day-to-day management any withdrawal from the search for consensus might be regarded as a sign of a too ready acquiescence with other people's views. Withdrawal can be taken to mean that the headteacher and his or her immediately accessible power group can be denuded of influence.

The third choice is for management to introduce a step-by-step pattern of response. This involves approaching first the parents, then the teachers and finally the governors in a pattern of consultation which is separate at each stage. Teachers and governors might always act in concert but a sequential pattern of consultation would deny consultees the defence that they felt that they always had to defer to the wishes of other people. They could not claim that they always, as a matter of solidarity, had to follow the views and interests of parents. Nor could parents refuse to express a view on the grounds that they felt that they should not upset the position of governors and teachers.

But if it is not practicable to pursue a separate and perhaps confidential expression of views, in a closely-knit school managers have, as a further alternative to operating without a consensus, the chance of presenting less than the whole of any particular issue for decision at any one time. In other words, consulters should not seek consent for the whole of a draft policy concerning, for example, personal and social education. They should start instead with the question of whether there should be differences of approach between the sexes. Nor, in the same way, would they ask for consent to a curriculum policy about the whole of environmental education. Instead they would ask about its connection with history alone before involving biology, the other sciences and geography.

Debates about single questions may at each stage give a lop-sided picture but they might be more real than debate about over-broad issues and in that way can provide consensus management with a firmer base.

Time-scales

While the search for consensus can be varied in its approaches – particularly in the choice between meeting contentious issues head on or breaking them down into smaller and more easily handled areas of debate – it is unlikely that management will often have the choice of doing anything other than to pursue broad agreement and commitment. If to hasten the search for broad agreements leads to superficiality of debate, managers must decide whether they can vary their time-scales in the making of policy.

School management plans have to be reviewed every year but the purpose of review is often assumed to be the making of adjustments rather than the providing of opportunities for radical rewriting. Nevertheless a year-to-year review can lose sight of the longer vision of where the school is going. Without that long view a school can be moved in a slightly different direction by every new regulation or by every shift of community or parental opinion. On the other hand, an unchangingly long view of school policy renders parents and governors powerless. Each opinion which they express is neutralized by a vision of long-term ends. In order to achieve the right balance two decisions are needed, one about the frequency and depth of review and the other about its purposes. In its policy about the assessment of pupils, for instance, management needs to review its plans and practices each year. In contrast, its policy for teacher appraisal management can, after a short period of annual review, function well with a triennial or quadrennial policy cycle. Policy about curriculum content, too, can be reviewed at irregular intervals while, in contrast, a policy about the development and support of the curriculum will, in one form or another, need to come up every year.

Cross-curricular activities and themes and the non-statutory aspects of the national curriculum need to be reviewed at intervals no longer than two years apart because these can easily fall out of sight or be assumed to succeed without too much explicit care. In the same way, the connection between a school's pastoral and social organization and the national curriculum needs annual review, as does the feed-through from earlier and into later phases of education.

Alongside the review of policy concerning teacher appraisal every three or four years, staff development policies and schemes need to be examined frequently. But while the outcomes of these need to be noted each year, the management of staff development and the management of staff appraisal should be able to proceed at different paces.

In addition to varying the frequency of the review of different parts of their total plan managers need to estimate how quickly changes which are already in hand are affecting their school. If, for instance, a primary school feels that ideas about career and vocational education are unlikely to affect it with urgency it can set itself a rather longer time-scale in which to look at this long-range concern. The same is also true of other large questions. For example, how does an individual school look at subject specialization? Should it find the resources for additional subjects? Should it help pupils and their families to be ready for a type of schooling which at the age of 14 combines vocational and general education? Is a school ready to establish policies about parents complementing school education? When specialist teachers are in short supply and when in-service opportunities for teachers are inadequate should the school encourage distance learning for pupils and teachers?

There are still broader issues. If, despite the best efforts of the Na-

tional Curriculum Council (NCC) and the Schools Examination and
Assessment Council (SEAC), compartmentalization becomes stronger,
will ideas about the unity of learning lose ground? If so, how will a
primary school compensate for any loss of belief in the transferability
of skill and knowledge? Would it then be time for a school to think
again about its broad aims of producing educated people?

There can be some common elements in the approach to these
questions. For instance, in the sphere of careers work the CBI/Voca-
tional Education and Training Task Force (CBI 1990) proposed that
Training and Enterprise Councils (TECs) should allocate money to
employers and managing agents in order to pay colleges and others to
provide courses for individual students who pursued 'appropriate nationally recognised qualifications as part of an agreed individual Action Plan'. Linked with this the TECs would ensure that 'the
employers and providers involved offer quality training by meeting the
requirements of Approved Training Organisation status' and would
make sure that each student's 'market choices were well-informed
through developing advice and guidance systems based on individual
Action Plans, Records of Achievement and appropriate vocational
counselling' (CBI 1990:43).

Because all parties had long agreed that 16–19 education and training needed thorough reform, a proposal for the unification of records
of achievement which were originally separate was not unexpected. It
was insisted that young people at the age of 16 should have a record
for use by employers – a record which did not include every detail of
assessment at the primary- and secondary-school stage but which did
merge with a system which provided year-to-year and stage-to-stage
assessments in the core subjects. There was also the need to record attainments in the pupil's foundation subjects between the ages of 11
and 14 and between 14 and 16. The total connection between assessment, the process of recording achievement and motivation was assumed to bring self-evident benefits (Broadfoot *et al.* 1991:79).

Against this background, the detail of recording attainments in primary schools will be confined almost entirely to their own use. To
play their part in building up a record of achievement which it is
hoped that employers will use when young adults enter work or further
training is so broad a process that primary schools can justifiably be
doubtful about their own role. They have to be prepared to organize
what is virtually an abstract about each pupil's attainment in order to
provide a selectively summative report at the age of 10. This, together
with such information as is locally useful at the entry into the next
stage, provides a platform on which the secondary school can build its
total record for the employer or trainer. At a time when employment at
16 is no longer the norm, the habit of providing a record which covers
the whole of schooling and not its last four years alone has to be an
important part of management's responsibilities – in primary as well
as in secondary schools. Curriculum-related assessment offers the

possibility of continuous appraisal which spans a pupil's entire school career (Harding and Beech 1991:156).

Ideally, one could hope that trainers, vocational educators, sixth forms, tertiary colleges, FE and higher education would in due course encourage the development of records which covered the whole span of education. Rather than compile a narrowly-drawn, phase-by-phase record of a pupil's entrances and exits at each level of schooling the usefulness of a comprehensive record of academic attainments, personal capabilities and standard qualifications should stimulate the pupil, the student and the family to expect the providers of education to offer clear evidence of continuity and progress.

Vocational education

In securing continuity planners do not always distinguish between technical and vocational education. To bring in training blurs the picture further. The purpose of primary school in contrast is to provide general education and it is largely at the secondary stage that the vocational relevance of general education is recognized.

The process of bringing the two together reaches down into the 14–16 year old period of secondary schools. It is possible at school to pursue qualifications of the Business and Technician Education Council (BTEC). The bringing together of vocational and general education was stimulated in the late 1960s with the establishment of early tertiary colleges in which sixth forms and FE colleges combined. The movement of collaborative work down the age range was slow mainly because of the insistence that only public examinations related first to university requirements (GCE), and then exclusively to secondary schools (CSE and GCSE) could be permitted in schools.

Despite the breakthrough of tertiary colleges there is still little permeation between a general and a vocational curriculum into schooling as a whole. We are still some way away from the full development of interconnecting academic and vocational pathways advocated by Smithers (1991). This may change under the influence of the national curriculum: NCC documents about individual subjects which were published between 1989 and 1991 made it clear that at Key Stage 4 the school curriculum was intended to show not only its internal interconnectedness but also its relationship with an understanding of issues in the world at large. That understanding could not avoid questions about employment, vocation and training. And although nothing was explicitly said about bridging the school/FE gap there was nothing to prevent it.

At the level of the primary school managers cannot rely on the assistance of the national curriculum. In order to make sense of the internal connectedness between parts of the curriculum they first have to verify that parents do expect their children's schooling, at all ages, to have an effect on how they turn out and how they earn their living. Although literacy and mathematics have always been invested with the idea of usefulness managers now need to plan their schools' handling of the curriculum in a manner which shows that the humanities, the arts, religious education and physical education are also useful. Managers need to become familiar with activities, programmes and writing which are associated with the quality-of-working-life movement. Those who manage schools must keep abreast with the changing use which future working life will make of their pupils' knowledge, skills, personal characteristics and traits.

Specialization

The first call on the teaching resources of a school are the needs of the national curriculum. On top of that managers have to recognize that some arrangements will always be out of the ordinary in that they have to be related to the specific needs of individual pupils.

Teachers are ready to offer all that they can to children who are disabled or whose capacity for learning is impaired. Although teachers may be less certain where they stand with very able, gifted or highly creative pupils, managers have to ensure that the needs of these, too, are looked after. They will use a categorization on the lines of a six-point list (Jones and Southgate 1989:8): teachers' value systems encompass the principles that 'children should be treated as they might become rather than as they are and that all pupils should be equally valued'. They should expect 'that all their students have it in them to walk a step or two with genius'. In any school 'the staff unitedly should stand for the successful education of the whole person, should contribute to the development of mature adults for whom education is a lifelong process and they should be ready to judge their success by their students' subsequent love of education'. Staff, too, should encourage self-discipline, a lively activity to breed lively minds, good health and a sense of interdependence and community.

An even-handed way of thinking about giftedness and equality is tilted in a different direction in a report of a study to identify able children in one county. This suggested that 'gifted education' was still an important growth point 'which could improve the outcomes of education for this particular group of pupils and, at the same time, give valuable insights into how to cater properly for the whole range of ability and disability in our classes' (Jones and Southgate 1989:164).

Managers cannot fit everything into the fixed resources of the ordinary school. When they look to the future, should they plan wholeheartedly for special assistance not only for the child whose learning is handicapped by disability but also for the creative child and the prodigy? If so, one approach which needs a broad organization of interest and assistance is that which is centred on mentoring.

Shaughnessy (1989) summed up aspects of its management: the demands on the mentor differ when the person being helped possesses creative as against academic gifts; differences lie not only in the creative process in which the person who is helped is actually involved but also in personalities; the selection and then the support given to the mentor needs care; it needs the understanding of governors and the local authority; it needs a clearly stated policy with which teachers and parents can sympathize and above all it needs a detailed preparation of the relationship between the person who is being helped and the mentor.

In order to organize these requirements managers have to make certain social and ethical issues clear. They must stimulate discussion and work towards unambiguous agreement among teachers, governors and parents on the basis that every child has to be educated in the way that is best for him or her individually. This imperative cannot be concealed behind statements about wholeness and about an undivided society. When the results of individual pupil assessment become known, parents and the world outside school will already have hold of half the story. It is necessary for managers to look ahead and to ensure that the impression does not exist that a school is one which does not care or where, in defence of equality, it is said that it does not know the difference between the bright and the dull.

Schools acknowledge differences between pupils, and HMI, when discussing curriculum (1980:20) said:

If it is to be effective the school curriculum must allow for differences. It must contribute to children's present well-being, whatever the age and stage of growth and development they have reached, and to their ability to take advantage of the opportunities available to them. Disadvantaged or handicapped pupils or pupils from ethnic minorities may have learning difficulties which require special help, and any children may need extra support at some time or other. Much of the time and concern schools devote to the personal welfare and 'pastoral care' of their pupils is supportive of the curriculum. . . . As pupils grow older and their abilities and interests become still more diversified, account has to be taken of their differing aspirations beyond school.

These aspirations lead to differences in schooling. One view (Passow 1989:68), favouring what is described as a global curriculum, insists that a differentiated curriculum is

a necessity for all youngsters if we are to have a 'more enlightened citizenry' but it has particular importance for the gifted. Their unusual potential for intellectual initiative, creativity, critical thinking, social responsibility and empathy combined with their potential for the exercise of leadership makes it especially imperative that we create a curriculum which will nurture in them the caring, concern, compassion and commitment so that they will use their unusual gifts and talents to grapple with society's myriad problems as well as their own self-fulfillment.

In this link between giftedness and social duty managers can make explicit the obligations which are laid on educated people. Passow, in addition to looking forward to the life of gifted pupils after formal education had ended, argued that world studies had been neglected. He underlined parts of the curriculum which needed special attention: 'Important aspects of the global curriculum should include peace education, inter-cultural studies, the development of thinking and valuing capacities, world problems of hunger, poverty and injustice, the ethical and moral dimensions of problems, the changing nature of knowledge, future studies, real problem-solving and communication across the world in a system of networking.' Educated people – and perhaps highly educated people in particular – owe a duty to pay attention to these concerns. Those who manage their education must look well ahead in order to provide equal education for pupils of all levels of ability, to nurture special gifts at the same time as counteracting handicap, to take those parts of the curriculum which are complementary to the core to the point of well-planned allocations of extra time and staffing. Despite the already heavy loading of the management system these tasks are unavoidable.

Additional subjects

Educated people are expected to understand a wider range of issues as communications grow faster and as the immediacy of world awareness increases, but when managers compare the priority of those parts of the curriculum which are issues-based and those which are fully covered by established subjects, they need a clear understanding of how to distribute their resources.

It is impossible to add a mainstream subject to a school's curriculum without everyone understanding whether it involves additional expenditure of time and money. Managers cannot add subjects on the basis of goodwill, or of relying on teachers who do not have either some experience or some training in the speciality in question. Lessons about this were learned in, for instance, the unsuccessful attempt to teach French to 8-year-olds.

The National Foundation for Educational Research (NFER) evaluation of the attempt revealed that there were many issues to be addressed apart from the linguistic capacity of teachers (Burstall 1974). A properly managed introduction of an additional subject meant that materials, the environmental support provided by the school and the commitment of someone more than the head had to be brought into play.

This message is still valid, although in the 1990s there are more people who have to be satisfied that things are being properly done. The energy which a manager can devote to any extension of a school's activities has to be set against a background of questions about whether he or she is using time wisely. Parents are easily dissatisfied if they feel that the basics are not being attended to: does the primary school ensure that children can read well? Is the school's discipline good ? Every question subdivides: are the children free from a stigma of being uncontrolled and unreliable toughs? Are they free of the fear of bullying?

If a head cannot satisfy parents that he or she is doing the utmost they are likely to lose trust. A great deal of time is therefore devoted to giving assurances about quality in these basic terms. Once it can be certain about its success with fundamental matters and the school can show that it is to be trusted, there is a chance that parents will more readily fall in with its larger ambitions. Unless, however, managers can find time and money from their self-managed resources to carry out their promises they will be neither followed nor trusted. The world outside a school may be full of the rhetoric about expanding education. Inside each school the first task is to provide for today and to avoid giving hostages to scepticism.

Additional pathways

Not all the additional strategies which a primary school wishes to adopt will be a matter of additional money. Each year's planning and costing, each annual review of purposes and resources will reveal that something is left over. The amount can vary widely (Audit Commission 1991:10–12). In setting their priorities on how it should be spent the managers of schools have a range of choice which could certainly extend to the possibility of bringing into the primary school the start of an activity, course or scheme which has not traditionally been possible. It may make it possible to bring into a primary school such activities – careers, the beginning of vocational education, high specialization and additional subjects – as have been regarded until recently as solely a secondary-school matter.

Primary schools have by tradition been excluded from providing more than one route towards a given goal. In secondary schools there have on occasion been attempts to provide more than one way through to the qualifications or status which are available to young adults. Education is provided in a series of steps – narrower at the young age and broader as pupils get nearer to the age of 18 and to the stages of FE and higher education.

In the step-by-step approach to education and training schools need helpers. How choices are made rests with the advice and influence of the family, with the professional voice of teachers and tutors together with some assistance from an external agent in the shape of careers counselling. There is little long-term planning: choices are not made quickly and sometimes it seems that the very opportunity to make a choice is well concealed. This might be opened up if there was action early in a pupil's primary-school life which could prepare him or her for a dual approach at the secondary stage.

Such attempts as were made to broaden choices in the 1970s and 1980s were not always successful. In preparation for entry into a new tertiary system at post-16 the attempt was made in at least one local authority to establish a twin-track curriculum from the age of 14 to 16. It was rejected by teachers and parents because it reminded them of an earlier system of secondary school selection, when secondary technical schools competed with grammar schools for able pupils at the age of 13. The vocational stigma in time weakened the secondary technical schools and it is therefore not surprising that even a tinge of vocational education was, in secondary schools, a matter of suspicion until TVEI was initiated. Even at that stage, the concern of many parents and teachers was that the chance to take a full range of O levels or the then CSE subjects should not be lost. And in the second half of some TVEI courses there was a comparable preoccupation with A level.

Little has changed: it would be difficult to introduce a pre-vocational element into primary education. It would carry with it the risk that it would be interpreted as a selective judgement. Even so, if dual education and training from the age of 14 are to become strong – and even stronger after 16 – the managers of schools should, in the first decade of the national curriculum and national assessment, be on the look out for chances of neutralizing the negative aspect of differences between vocational and general education. They should build up a picture of how to help young people to realize their twin potentials and how to get them to see that achieving both is part of their own responsibility. For this purpose the introduction of enterprise education in primary schools should be welcomed.

Parents complementing schools

In combining education and training at an early age and in providing for its continuity several people can help the pupil or the young adult. Continuity is unlike transition from pre-school to primary school. At that stage of a child's learning several aspects of parent–school liaison are well documented. In contrast, the connection upwards in age to post-16 education and training seems not to work effectively except with well-motivated pupils from interested families. And even when, in terms of behaviour and discipline, the importance of parental responsibility is emphasized (such as in the Elton Report (DES 1989a)), policies appear to stop short of a school–parent contract. The most is not always made of good motivation and collaboration.

Since the 1986 Education Act the position of parents as consumers has developed as has their role of being the people who can call schools to account. Parents take their place in one of the several communities which are connected with schools. They are in some cases organized by bodies such as the National Confederation of Parent–Teacher Associations who believe that children need the help and support of their parents if they are going to develop their full potential at school, that parent interest can best be nurtured through active home-school associations, that those associations provide parents and teachers with the opportunity to develop trust and confidence and that parents need a say in national policy-making (Sayer and Williams 1989:113).

Broad definitions of the importance of parental involvement are useful, such as that of Docking (1990:122). 'Home and school need to work together so that each understands the other's perspective and adopts practices which support those of the other in working towards the solution of the problem. The initiative, however, has to be taken by the school.'

Beyond these broad approaches, can schools manage a more pointed relationship? (Cullingford 1985: 54–6) noted the development of parents acting as reading tutors, as partners in paired reading and as participants in precision teaching. He pointed out that projects which involve parents can cover pre-school, primary, special and secondary education and can assist with overcoming the difficulties of children for whom English is not their native language as well as those of children who suffer moderate and severe learning difficulties.

The position of parents must not be jeopardized by allowing schools and their teachers to appear to be too private. Some parents are happy to stand back and watch their children progressing smoothly (Wolfendale 1990: 35)

while other parents, despite massive interest and proximity to them of their children's school, remain intimidated and ignorant of the vast number of hidden agendas of the school and as a system of education and as a multi-level, multi-purpose social institution. So the assumption that parental participation in children's education will of itself bring about educational enhancement begs the question – parental involvement for what purpose?

Trevor Bryans (Wolfendale 1990:43) goes further. He notes the history of the internal convenor or co-ordinator in organizing a school's liaison programme but, in the primary school setting, prefers an approach through a 'key worker':

For most pupils the key worker would probably be the child's own class teacher, but not in all cases, for some children retain a lasting attachment to particular teachers with whom strong home–school ties have been formed in the past. For other pupils, a welfare assistant or support teacher may be the best key worker in the sense that good and positive links have been established and that there is no reason to change that arrangement. The key worker concept goes much further than the remit of a single responsible liaison teacher. . . . Every teacher in the school would then be a key worker for a number of children, some of whom may not be in his or her own class.

To organize key connections from within the school requires faith in the capacity and value of parents. Are they the natural educators? The term in itself is some way away from the position of the qualified teacher. However, if managers do not probe the variety of differences between the positive attitudes which parents show towards their children at school (over-protective, seriously concerned, officious or fully supportive) they may be accused of leaving relationships too much to chance. Teachers can adopt a range of differing attitudes towards their children. This can lead to parents feeling the school has a confused view about the notion of complementarity between themselves and teachers.

One task of the manager is to encourage teachers to trust the strengths of parents. Parents must be treated with equality and a school has to manage its affairs in such a way that there is no in-built preference for those parents who are friendly and articulate at the expense of those whose sense of intimidation leads them to express an awkward hostility. Nor should heads regard it as far-fetched to be quite explicit about the school's openness to those who are diffident about their language. Prejudice has to be avoided, not least towards parents and families who are not at home with standard English. Thus Honey (1990:70):

The extension of educatedness, from being the property of a small elite, to something available to everyone who can take advantage of the mass education system, has thus not only helped elevate one accent – (Received Pronunciation) – to the highest prestige position, but has also helped devalue those accents which have the least perceived connection with literary forms of communication which are esteemed more highly by the most educated people than are the more colloquial communication styles which form the basis of everyday living.

Diffidence about language is only one example among several aspects which can deter the parent from being confident. The Scottish Education Department's survey of parents' views (SED 1989) described the dilemma which is faced by managers: 'Most parents feel unqualified to make judgements about teaching and were happy to leave this to the professionals.' However, 39 per cent of parents interviewed said they thought that they should have some say in how their child was taught. Moreover, 56 per cent of parents of secondary pupils thought they should have a say in what was taught (SED 1989:21):

Parents very commonly expressed concern about changes in teaching and curriculum that they did not understand and a 'hands off attitude' by the school. Parents could suffer the frustrating experience of the child getting no help at school and yet being told not to help at home because it would be confusing for her/him. 'If they can't give the extra help at school she'll just have to be learnt the way I was learnt.'

This parent then finds that the way she learned means nothing to her child. Schools teach things differently (SED 1989:21):

Many parents wished to be able to supervise or help their child especially in primary, and it was in relation to new maths that the greatest difficulty arose. It was an experience that was often frustrating for the parent who wished to work along with, and support, their child through the school: 'It damages your relationship with her. You feel foolish and she gets upset because I can't understand'.

If parents do not seem to function easily as natural educators, it rests with those who manage secondary as well as primary schools to examine how far they can go. The importance of the parent in school has become a commonplace since the mid-1960s. It has still further to develop not simply in terms of the school rendering an account to its users and customers but also in putting to full use a unique and supportive bond.

Distance learning

If parents cannot be educated by the school into a confident extension of their family role, help may be available from adult educators, community educators, certain social workers and some paramedical staff. These four categories do not have regular contact with all parents and indeed their commitment to assisting parents to help their children is limited by the exigencies of other responsibilities.

There are other constantly accessible sources of education – particularly those radio and television programmes which involve mothers with their very young children in listening to a story, newspaper and magazine articles about parenthood, courses in secondary education about parenting, the work of family centres, day nurseries or nursery schools, classes or units. All these can communicate some part of the message about the school/parent bridge but they are concerned with parents – and usually the mother – mainly or only with the youngest children. The message does not penetrate the full depth of parental support. The task of teaching fathers where they come in and the involvement of parents in supporting the education of older children was, when children who lived in geographical isolation had to be helped by a combination of correspondence courses and parental supervision, almost wholly the task of the Parents National Education Union (PNEU), together with such advisers, peripatetic teachers and specialist inspectors as local authorities could provide. To meet the more general needs of the present day and regardless of locality there are few concerted schemes other than those which are voluntary and which are encouraged or promoted by the Campaign for the Advancement of State Education.

While managers should treat parents – fathers as well as mothers – as far as possible as partners with the school, their capacity to monitor the school's work and sometimes to hinder it cannot be overlooked. These roles conflict with their capacity to act as para-professional aides, pre-school educators or as sole providers of consistent support (Meighan 1989:105).

The 'parent as problem' needs more attention than most schools can spontaneously provide. To win over the parent who is dissatisfied the manager has to make sure that he or she is helped to be well informed about the way the school operates and about its aims. If dissatisfaction persists despite the parent demonstrating a strong interest in the education of his or her children and a high motivation for their success, managers are not bound to succeed unless they themselves examine what they mean by a 'good' parent. They also have to examine whether they are managing the school in a manner which is beyond criticism and complaint. This should lead them to organize matters in such a way that parents accept and support the school's view while at the same time accepting their own role as prime educators. Schools and their managers need to make sure that both teachers and parents understand the reality of parent-supported education, and although that reality does not confine itself to the earliest ages of a child's schooling, the best-documented examples of parent concern do come from that phase (Meighan 1989:110):

Most of the first wave of parents . . . were motivated by desperation because their children were so unhappy at school, or achieving little, or both. A second group of parents who are able to articulate their views on the harmful effects of schooling and are well-informed about research on the hidden curriculum of mass education have increased from a small minority to a large grouping within Education Otherwise. These parents decide to remain the prime educators and to continue the work they have begun in the first five years with a home-based educational programme.

While the PNEU model can assist parents who are determinedly part of the home-education movement, other services are also at their elbow in the form of targeted programmes through the Open University and Open College. In time too, the Open School will provide support in the form of distance learning to parents of secondary-school children, children with special needs and children whose secondary education has been interrupted.

Although the managers of schools may sometimes seem neither fully to sympathize with nor to know how to help parents to have access to distance learning, it is in the best interests of a school to seek and provide help.

There will still be some families who opt out, permanently or from time to time. The fact that these may wish at irregular intervals to opt back into the maintained school system should not be regarded as creating an insuperable difficulty. Meighan (1989:111) sees this as an entry point to one form of flexi-schooling:

Many families decide to opt into the education system at various stages and then out again according to their needs as they define them. Education officials have sometimes expressed exasperation and asked families to make up their minds whether they are for school or against, to which the reply has been that they are neither for nor against schools but in favour of education in whatever form worked for a particular child at a particular time. These parents operate a form of flexischooling already but one limited to large blocks of time in one place or another rather than a flexible use of locations.

If managers decide to regard parents as prime educators then they need to be clear about the way in which teaching staff should look at the position of parents as intervenors, critics, assistants or full-time bearers of responsibilities. The management of schools can cope with parents exercising their ideas briefly and in disparate ways. But a long-term and unpredictable exercise of all these legitimate activities on the part of parents requires tolerance, understanding and a readiness on the part of teachers to provide the intellectual cohesion between the positions in which they and their pupils' parents place each other.

That cohesion would best come from training but while there is encouragement for parents to become well-informed activists there is no training to help schools to accommodate or make the most of parents, particularly if they act in widely diverse roles. The position is summarized by Meighan (1989: 104):

One surprise is that competing visions of education can co-exist in home-based education. It may seem odd to argue that staunch rivals such as the Black Paper writers, the deschooling writers and the progressives are not necessarily at odds at all. The complexities of modern life are such that inflexible people, fitted only for a simpler world, are at risk. In some situations it is necessary to be able to cope with authoritarian behaviour either by taking a lead or by taking instructions. At other times we need to co-operate with others and behave democratically. Sometimes we need to be self-directing, take decisions for ourselves and act autonomously. It follows that an effective education requires experience of all these approaches and an awareness of when each is appropriate.

Distance education for new collaborators

Those who manage schools are not themselves trained to provide a variety of forms of support, information and stimulus either for their professional colleagues or for their lay allies, whether those are governors, parents, committed members of the local community or employers. They may turn to other sources for that range of support. Commonly they will expect to find it in adult education, and in particular training courses for governors after the 1986 Act made much use of adult-to-adult teaching skills. Adult education is often a part of local strategies of community education and these in turn mean that adult education is linked to social action.

Social action in the shape of being a good parent, a good governor or an active encourager of community life represents few problems for the adult educator. Adult pupils will keep their learning on their chosen track but, while student attendance and student interest are irrefutable indicators of the perceived efficacy of adult education programmes, not all parents or governors can come together in regular classes. They can be held together by occasional meetings and by association through formal groupings (parent–school associations, governors' associations) but often they will be isolated. This means that the only time when they do come together (parents' evening, govern-ors' meetings) will be in a form at which the dominant part is taken up by a chairman or head. In less formal settings, those who should play a part in the collegial management of a school can learn how to enter into discussion and can gain that confidence which springs from a shared awareness about key issues.

The isolated adult is in one sense the ideal target for distance learn-ing. By correspondence, by the use of video and audio-tapes and by relatively infrequent tutoring on the model of the Open University he or she can soak up a range of messages about which decisions are im-portant. A parent can be helped both to absorb and to question the values which are attached to decisions about ideas which are as diverse as discipline, homework, goal-setting or the mapping of either a school's or an individual pupil's future. But benefit cannot always be drawn from the individuality of the adult learner. One-to-one tutoring is not always possible and the benefit of the alternative, namely small group work, with the necessity of a convergent, common denominator view has to form part of a larger approach to informal learning.

The manager who sees that distance learning is a good way of help-ing lay people to be aware and alert about the changing demands which are made on their participation has to remember that no single message can with equal value inform the consciousness of every col-league, whether professional or lay. Divergence of view and of priority must be encouraged. It was said, for instance, of the Open Tech (Na-tional Institute for Careers Education and Counselling 1985) that al-though there was a great deal of experience in operating tutorial systems in open learning, there was new ground to be broken and novel schemes to be used: 'There are as many ways of collaborating as there are versions of open learning. . . . Diversity is necessary . . . to see which open learning approaches succeed, which are cost-effec-tive, which embed themselves in existing practices or transform tradi-tional modes of training.'

A school can influence the community education organizer and, through the organizer, influence the style and range of adult education which is provided in its locality. Ideally, a joint strategy will be de-veloped in which the staff development of professional colleagues and the broadening of lay people's knowledge and understanding will complement each other. This is not an easy strategy to build but the problem and a solution were described by Smith and Kelly (1987:173). In a discussion about making a coherent staff development policy in higher education, it was emphasized that while distance education em-phasized the need for particular aspects of training

these are not generically different from mainstream teaching; they merely show a change of emphasis arising from organizational differences in distance education. Staff development . . . is far broader than 'teacher training'. If it is to meet the needs of the individual . . . it must recognise the varied array of teaching–learning organizations which now exist. . . . Many of them relate to defined categories of students and require slightly different methods from those which we understand as mainstream teaching. However, they are all, in reality, points on the same continuum.

In a more specific analysis of the sharing of contributions made by distance learners to community activity attention has been drawn to the necessity for the content of the material of distance learning and the processes used in study to be relevant to the learner (Hodgson *et al.* 1987). In defining what is meant in particular by interactive learning material the importance of three approaches is emphasized, namely getting learners to 'examine their own experiences, values and resources, to organize these to make decisions and to take appropriate action'. Pointing out that in the Open University approach, material has to be seen to be relevant either to a stage in the student's life or to his or her role in the community, seven types of material are referred to – concerned with parenting, health, consumer choice, energy conservation, governing schools, unemployment and racism. Of these topics it was said that only two, racism and school governors, were concerned with facilitating change and development with the community rather than with the individual.

Distance learning cannot always provide tailor-made individual training but it can reach a more personal level than some aspects of conventional education because the planning and management of the latter place great emphasis on 'hierarchical management, and there is lower tolerance of collegial, politicised and anarchic modes of academic management' (Rumble 1986:227). The tasks of organizing a school or college and organizing a system of teaching and learning on the open principle are dissimilar. The informal but closely targeted approach which is called for in distance education means that managers must seek, if they can, consensus before action. They need, too, to learn as much as they can from existing practices of open learning and distance education and in particular from noting how contexts and purposes differ. The lessons of the Open University throw light on the progress of the Open College of the Arts, on the complexities of the Open College and on the promise of the Open School. While not all the relatively innovatory lessons of these are equally well publicized, heads and governors should make sure that they are kept up to date by those who locally arrange their community education.

In particular they need to broaden the mix of institutional and personal education. To help one's local school, to help one's child and to help oneself is more in keeping with purposes and style of today than to allow the school itself to set limits on the mobility and capacity for the voluntary helpers' self-improvement. The approach should be the same as that recommended by Michael Young (1988:11–12) in meeting the new needs of those who are employed:

An educated workforce for the new age will need something quite different. In the new era people will not be limited by the habits and timetables they have for centuries been drilled into at school and in their ordinary workplaces. They will be less the creatures of the greater and the lesser bureaucracies and more their own men and women, still working but to unfold more of their own span of capacities, their own ability to create, their own sense of beauty, their own sympathy for each other than any society has ever before tolerated. In this new era the new people will need education more than ever; the signposts are already there to indicate its direction.

In pursuing these ideals of an educated workforce the governors of a school may wish to go outside the bounds of the national curriculum. They may wish to diversify the tracks of education, to add subjects, to arrange early specialization, to pay attention to the special needs of giftedness as well as of handicap and to turn to other sources of education – for pupils as well as for adults. Two hurdles stand in the way of a school – and governors themselves may be seen as part of the problem. An editorial in the *Times Educational Supplement* (1991d:19) described one difficulty in terms of the frenetic round 'of staff, resources and building problems . . . augmented by angry or distressed parents and over-enthusiastic or under-enthusiastic governors. Then there is the apparently endless stream of documents and demands from local and central government. These leave little room for any conceits the school may have about aims of its own.' On the same day the second problem, of constriction and limitation, made its mark when it appeared that government decision would allow the national curriculum to treat all arts (music, art, dance, drama) as optional.

The hindrances which arise from both situations are familiar: either life is too busy for long-term planning or the long-term plan is wrong. In 1989 HMI published a second edition of *The Curriculum from 5 to 16* (DES 1989b). This included a summary of responses to the original publication in 1985. The central tenets remained: curriculum had to be characterized by breadth, balance, differentiation, progression and continuity. The responses showed that there was more than one way of providing breadth and that there was a general agreement on the need for balance. But relevance met with a divided response: was it to be a matter of the pupil's perception of self-determination or of negotiation in order that there might be a match between curriculum and individual pupils' expectations, attitudes and interests? In the same way, views about differentiation were not uniform. Some welcomed it, others felt that problems were not resolved in the effort to meet different learning needs within a common curriculum. In contrast, there was general agreement about the need for the curriculum to allow both progression and continuity.

These responses came from LEAs, professional associations or national bodies, institutions of teacher training and schools. The indication of differences of opinion was important but became lost to sight when the Education Reform Bill was published in the autumn of 1987. Nevertheless HMI noted that there was a broad acceptance of the original framework for curriculum analysis and planning. They believed, too, that it was clear 'that there is broad agreement within the education service that the design and evaluation of the school curriculum at national, local education authority and school levels need to be underpinned by a rationale' (DES 1989b:63).

The central section of that rationale needs to be kept in focus. For the manager it is perhaps the only comprehensive guide about the role of central government in the national curriculum, about local decisions relating to that curriculum and about local choices of how to approach cross-curriculum work in such a way as to educate the whole person (DES 1989b:63–4):

the curriculum at national, local education authority and school levels has to serve a variety of functions. It has to contribute to the fullest development of individual pupils' capacities, personal qualities and attitudes to their development of, and commitment to, a set of personal values. It has to play its part in initiating pupils into the complex culture of our multi-racial society, including the ideas, beliefs, human actions and the natural, social and economic forces which have shaped and continue to shape it. It has to prepare them for an informed and active involvement in family, social and civic life. It has to provide them with the knowledge and skills required to meet the demands of work and the economy. In fulfilling these functions it has to reconcile two seemingly contrary requirements: to cater as far as possible for the uniqueness of individual development by allowing for differences in abilities, aspirations and other characteristics, and also to provide a common educational foundation which contributes both to the continuity of the social and cultural order as well as to the possibility of changing it constructively.

That HMI themselves were responsible for this firm and comprehensive statement is an example of the sensible alliance which, since the early 1980s, the Inspectorate had maintained between its services to professionalism and to bureaucracy – a balance which was well summed up by Lawton and Gordon (1987) but which is now limited by the Education (Schools) Act, 1992.

National curriculum and the education of the whole person

The education of the whole person on the lines of the HMI statement is not contradicted by the national curriculum. Managers need to know about the links which the NCC has described and about the way in which connections can be made across a number of gaps in the curriculum. Also in order to decide how far a school's policy for total education is succeeding, managers can benefit from familiarity with the aims which are specified in particular in NCC curriculum guidance documents which cover cross-curricular themes. One such theme is to do with careers education: at about the age of 11 (Key Stage 2) the aims in careers education and guidance are made up of the capacity to review personal experiences as a basis for setting new targets, the ability to recognize and respond constructively to discrimination against certain social groups and a capacity to understand how work involves a variety of related tasks, undertaken by people with different roles.

The practical value of the guidance in this example (NCC 1990b) is that it draws attention to other parts of the curriculum from which light will be thrown. For the first of the aims in this example (the capacity to review personal experiences) the field of personal and social development is expected to cross-refer. In the second aim (responding to discrimination) art, economic and industrial understanding, citizenship, health education and environmental education are all expected to make a contribution. For the third aim (of understanding how work involves other related tasks) the curricular contexts which are suggested are those of PE, art, music, economic and industrial understanding as well as education for citizenship. In the four other developmental aims – for Key Stage 2 – more or less the same range of curricular inputs from other directions is expected to be of value. For the seven aims in careers education and guidance at Key Stage 3 a contribution is again expected from economic and industrial understanding, education for citizenship, health education, environmental education and the arts. For the nine aims associated with Key Stage 4 (at about the age of 16) modern languages are added as a possible cross-curricular contributor in the aim of exploring the international perspective of work.

The definition of aims and the NCC's identification of steps and stages should make it possible for heads and their professional colleagues, governors, parents and, in the example of careers education, employers to be clear about the opportunities and sources of opportunity offered to each pupil and young person. Cross-curricular planning is offered a framework. How it is used remains with school managers to decide.

In a second of the five cross-curricular themes – education for citizenship – the guidance document (NCC 1990c) recognizes that different schools will be at different stages in implementing their cross-curricular arrangements. Five steps are outlined for implementation of a programme of education for each of the four key levels. The steps are those of discussing the school's objectives, identifying possible ways of teaching education for citizenship, analysing the readiness of the school, deciding the policy and planning the implementation. In contrast to the procedures outlined in connection with careers education, the emphasis this time rests on making a judgement about where a school thinks it stands as well as about the other subjects which are to be brought into play.

The NCC identification of possible ways of teaching citizenship are realistic and practical in their connection with the normal range of a primary school's activities and approaches (for Key Stages 1 and 2). For Key Stages 3 and 4 the choice is more closely but not exclusively related to subjects. Hence, for secondary schools up to the age of 16 a range of approaches is suggested for teaching citizenship, including allowing it to permeate several parts of the whole curriculum, treating it as part of the personal and social education programme, as part of a pastoral/tutorial programme or as something which can be handled if it makes use of 'planned blocks of activities, e.g. police weeks, charity days'. Further alternatives are to treat citizenship as a separately timetabled subject, through specific national curriculum subjects or through religious education and additional subjects such as social sciences and classics (NCC 1990c:17).

Although the structure for this guidance on citizenship is looser than that which is offered for careers education, the NCC still lays out check points and definitions of what to expect from each approach. No management team or governing body would expect step-by-step development or development which can be easily measured in the skills of citizenship. The result is that the NCC's suggested structure for citizenship seems more detailed than it need be. In careers education on the other hand the importance of the ages of 16, 17 and 18 – with their degree of urgency in preparing the young adult – makes the reason for a more tightly-structured approach more obvious.

In a third cross-curricular theme a different approach may be adopted. This is in health education (NCC 1990d). For each of its key stages nine areas of study are outlined, with relative changes in the depth and detail of study at different ages and stages.

In contrast to careers education and citizenship, the guidance on health education places a very heavy burden on a curriculum planner and on a school manager. The repeated categorization of nine approaches is supplemented by an indication of the contribution made by health education to the whole curriculum (which in itself is different from involving a one-way form of assistance from other subjects). A curriculum map is then presented which shows how attainment targets in English, mathematics, science and technology relate to health education's nine points of coverage, together with anticipated connections in a comparable form from art, geography, history, modern foreign languages, music, physical education and religious education.

The health education approach probably overloads itself as a manageable contribution to total education by its insistence not only on a wide and specific range of subject connections but also on bridgings into named additional subjects or programmes, but from these examples of a curriculum approach to 'whole education' managers must choose those which they can handle. Because one is constrained for time (careers education), because another is less amenable to the measurement of outcome (citizenship) and because another is put forward as an all-enveloping strategy (health education), managers should not permit themselves to skip or dismiss a well-structured approach to those parts of teaching and learning which contribute to wholeness. But at the same time they must make sensible judgements about the value of curriculum guidance which to some people's view might seem to be a matter of propaganda rather than of education.

One example lies in the fourth of the NCC's cross-curricular themes, namely in the outline for education in economic and industrial understanding (NCC 1990e). Case studies are clearly set out for each of the Key Stages, six economic concepts are discussed, two approaches to business enterprise, four approaches to industry and the world of work, a further four to consumer affairs and a final four dedicated to the interplay of government, the economy and society. Because – unlike health education, citizenship and careers education – the teaching of economic and industrial understanding is, for many schools, new (particularly at Key Stages 1 and 2), managers need help in linking it with the established curriculum of their school. The NCC's guidance makes a brief reference to connections between economic and industrial understanding and national curriculum subjects (NCC 1990e:46–7) but it is difficult to pick out criteria by which to judge whether attainment levels are satisfactory other than by reference to performance indicators in the management of an action plan (NCC 1991:9).

Providing a 'whole education' is not, despite the NCC's readiness to give good advice, a matter of sewing together – alongside the main curriculum (or even permeating it) – a collection of additional opportunities in which pupil competence and attainment can be assessed. If this were all that could be handled, there would be little chance that a manager could be satisfied that the system for which he or she is responsible is indeed building up a whole person – unless it is that schools are to continue to be looked upon as underpinners. You cannot be an educated person, in other words, without the basics of schooling, but the actual recognition of being an educated person comes later, after breadth of experience and reflection. As things stand, schools provide knowledge and some understanding. But they do not deeply stimulate or question the life-competence of the student.

If a manager takes a larger view and wishes to go beyond the idea of the school as an institution to provide the underpinning of education, he or she must overcome the general scepticism about the label of 'educated people'. This is difficult, particularly when national schemes of assessment have been put into operation. The head and the other managers have to sustain their faith in the virtues both of a centralized system and of personal direct knowledge of – and involvement in – the growth of individual pupils.

Those who use education can take one of the two views: parents, friends and the families of those who are passing through our schools ask for the production of educated, tolerant, energetic people. Employers on the other hand are, still, more likely to trust summative statements of assessment, examination grades and the recording of standards which are set against criteria relevant to the needs of their own business or industry – despite the enlightened view of the CBI (1990). It might be more profitable if they adopted the argument, at least, of the Careers and Occupational Information Centre (1990:13):

'If knowledge and understanding is necessary in order to perform, there is no need to assess it separately because a performance will be unsatisfactory without it. Assessing a performance implicitly assesses the underpinning knowledge and understanding.'

These and other signposts are available for the guidance of managers when they combine the provision of the national curriculum and a broad education. Although their audiences may not always believe that the two can be combined there is time both to persuade the doubters and also to manage the system efficiently. How long that time will be was assessed by the Audit Commission in 1986. It called for urgent action by managers in secondary education, for example, in a list of problems which included falling pupil numbers, standards and quality, education's relevance to employment and adult life and the declining level of support from central government for local education services (Audit Commission 1986:6–9). The message was aimed at central and local government and underlined the Commission's impression that the time for reform was limited because change would have to go ahead while secondary pupil numbers were particularly low. The period of opportunity for reform, the Commission felt, would end in the early 1990s.

As it happened, the Education (No. 2) Act of 1986, the Teachers' Pay and Conditions Act 1987 and the Education Reform Act 1988 substantially altered the focus for management action. A broad view and large-scale action were still required, but it became more urgent in day-to-day management to see how responsibilities could be broken down and distributed in ways which were more local than the Audit Commission had foreseen.

Despite the parcelling-out of management tasks on the basis of placing answerability as close as possible to the point at which direct action with pupils, teachers and parents takes place, the responsibility of heads, their senior colleagues and the governors of schools for even the basic parts of the national curriculum remains very large. And where errors are being made it may not be until the turn of the century that their significance will be known.

Conclusion

Management has to carry out a continuous and honest self-review. It has to prove itself trustworthy. It has to decide who comes first when consultations are carried out and when consensus is sought. It has to decide on the frequency of its planning and review cycles. Above all it must put into some order the extra demands which are made on schools. Because of this variety of pressures, managers need to be clear about which problem they are tackling at each stage. And they need, too, to be able to gauge the strength and value of their critics and allies. They need to make sure that both aspiration and criticism are well informed.

Some extra pressures come from the ideals of heads and their staff, from governors and from parents. Other pressures come from competition between schools and from the steady increase in the number of issues in which education has to engage.

In creating their own priorities education managers need to be able to count on others keeping themselves up to date. But they themselves have to be aware of the current state, term by term, of the feelings of parents and employers. They need to be able to gauge, in particular, when it is that a school is being asked to do more in the area of verifiable and short-term achievement and when its services are being invoked on a broader basis. There has to be a well-judged balance between short- and long-term activity. There has to be a sensitive reading of what it is that society will make, in the next decade, of those who were educated ten years earlier. Larger still, the manager has to think about what the learner will contribute to that society, and whether it rests with a school to provide the basis for a social and human contribution to other people's lives as well as the basis for employable skills.

Management has less time than in the past to look back and to learn from its errors. Perhaps it did not use the time for reflection when it was indeed available. By now, however, the most urgent task is not so much to learn from the past as to manage today's issues at the same time as predicting how to avoid mistakes in the future.

CHAPTER 11

New demands on management

Managers have to include in their development plans more than could be foreseen in the Education Reform Act alone. Mistakes were made in the early stages of implementation; corrections have had to be inserted in institutional plans. New demands have arisen which also need to be included in the revisions of plans. As an example of large-scale change, it is innovations such as AS levels and the speed of developing a modularized curriculum which make their demands on sizeable secondary schools. But, in the context of the 1988 Act, all schools, whatever their size, have to devise ways of dealing with cross-curricular themes and all schools need time to reflect before changes are put in hand.

The management of smaller schools has to make time for reflection in the same way as it has to carve out time for evaluation and self-review. In understanding what is new, governors, teachers and parents need to be both led and retrained. In the approach to what is new efforts are put to better effect if they are combined and if there can be some use of experts.

In the continuous job of making management better, schools need to look at past mistakes, to find substitutes for those who from LEAs in previous times guided them through new intricacies of organization, to decide which vision they are trying to put into effect and to know how well they are doing.

Errors

Errors of management which are made at government level arise from misjudgements about the complexity of reforms, about how much time is needed to prepare for them, about the amount of retraining and additional training which they call for, about their intelligibility and, in the long run, about their effects.

Some misjudgements can be put right during the process of reform. Demands can be rendered less complicated, easier schedules can be devised which while sticking to the original dates for implementation can still reduce the number of steps. In contrast, misjudgements about the type, quality, frequency and length of training cannot be put right until enough is known about implementation for the initiators of change and their agents to know that something has gone wrong. Was it ignorance, maladroitness or lack of foresight on the part of managers which was responsible?

About training in procedures which are entirely new or which are infrequently practised broad predictions can be made as to how much time and effort are needed. To be accurate in assessing whether the right amount of training has been provided calls for the adding up of items, finding the trainers, devising methods of self-training and putting a price and a time allocation on the total. Some errors can be detected at intermediate stages and put right in passing. Others have a cumulative effect and can only be rectified after the final evaluation of the training scheme, package or programme.

Errors of intelligibility may be corrected by improvements in presentation and popularization. But more often it will be arguments about clarity of purpose, the meaning of one change in the context of larger issues of education or public policy, the urgency of the need for reform or the honesty of its motives which will be thought to be unclear.

Judgement about the effects of change will, at government level, be a long process. Effects are not easily agreed or measured. Side issues can be confused with the definition of main purposes. If, for instance, the aim of the changes in education in the 1990s was to make the country economically more successful, would a future government look to the management of education when it wished to find the cause of success or failure? Or is it more likely that a government which wants to know the truth will be forced to examine the network of policies about interest rates, industrial training, the comparative strength of currencies and all policies of public expenditure rather than simply those of education?

Against this background, local managers are unlikely to be confident that they know how their success will be judged. Legislation and the parliamentary arguments to support it look at long-term national ends. Locally, managers have to decide whether success is to be measured in terms of their school's popularity, its cash flow, the satisfaction of its parents or its reliability in handling the connections with earlier and later education.

In this list popularity is as much to do with the performance of other schools as with their proximity. Cash flow can in the short term be adversely affected by there being staff dispositions which take time to unravel and by buildings which are in poor shape. In contrast, parent satisfaction is the immediate and continuing concern of school management. Pupil assessments, discipline, reputation and reliability combine within a package of policies and practices which have to be manned, monitored and either confirmed or altered year by year. These take their place, too, on the list of obligations which management must meet not only for the satisfaction of parents but also for the sake of enabling a school to be a reliable receiver or sender-on. Hence, managers must satisfy professional as well as laymen's expectations.

One cannot connect better education with better management in an easily verifiable, causal sense. In contrast, education which is judged to be flawed is attributed to bad teaching and bad local management. Whether the source of criticism is a single dissatisfied parent or the parent body, the local community or individual interests within it, inspectors, those who conduct comparative reviews of attainment or those who scrutinize the efficient use of money – from any of these sources, local managers still have to recognize that specific praise and blame will be aimed at them rather than at county hall, town hall, Whitehall or Westminster.

When managers seek reasons for a decline in a school's popularity, for a shaky financial position, for a lack of trust demonstrated by other schools or for dissatisfaction on the part of parents or employers, they are entitled to weigh strong against weak arguments and informed criticism against gossip. In the end they must separate excuses about other people's criticisms from legitimate defences and explanations. They must, too, seek ways of avoiding damaging, even if ill-founded, rumours as well as of living up to the reasonable requirements of those who wish to take a positive view about their stewardship.

As they gather confidence in using any scheme of self-evaluation, managers must be prepared to go beyond the checklists of such approaches as those of the Guidelines for Review and Institutional Development for Schools (GRIDS). They will encounter tensions between self-appraisal and self-justification and will meet doubts which were summarized by Nuttall (1981) when he described the differences of attitudes which can exist between complacency and maintaining things as they are and the searching out of areas where change is genuinely needed.

The last decade of this century will have seen a considerable move away from the fears and uncertainties which Nuttall and others ascribed to teachers long before the legislative reforms of 1986, 1987, 1988 and 1992. Teachers have quickly amassed experience in explaining what they do, in observing firmer guidelines for their teaching than existed before teacher autonomy was questioned and in contributing their own views and questions to a school management plan.

Heads have moved still further. Their relationship with governors is managerial, and the delegated powers which they exercise give them control of the process of both clarifying and implementing the school's purposes. Even their salary position can be marginally raised or lowered on the basis of separate decisions made by governors.

If a parallel of self-examination led by management and shared with the members of a school's staff is sought in a non-educational field, one which was brought to light was described in a study by the University of Manchester Institute of Science and Technology. It examined the success of quality circles. These, in Japan since 1962, have as their purpose the improvement of the quality of industrial products. Even in the 1960s the Japanese quality revolution was already more than ten years old. The Manchester study turned to four companies with a reputation for excellence of product and strong management. The reasons for establishing quality circles were typified as the encouragement of an open management style, greater employee involvement, product price reduction and quality improvements. Early difficulties lay in the lack of middle management's commitment and support, delay in management response to suggestions from quality circles, difficulties in finding time to meet and selecting problems which were too complex (Dale and Lees 1986).

The implications from an industrial model of self-examination for the management of a school should not be pressed too far. Nevertheless there is a familiar sound to some of the suggestions which emerged from the Manchester study (Dale and Lees 1986:51):

circles work best when they are considered as being an intrinsic part of a quality management system which is supported and driven from within the upper echelons of the organization by the Chief Executive and where management are committed to listening to what their employees have to say and wish to involve them more in the business. Whilst the main ingredients of involvement, participation and quality are of equal importance to the success of a programme it is easier to identify with the quality commitment because it is the most visible and tangible . . . quality circles will work in organizations where the main objectives are to contribute to quality improvement even if the organization has an autocratic management style.

Quality in education is not always the most visible and tangible part of a managed system but one of the lessons emphasized by Nuttall (1981:42) is that possibly the 'most important issue is that strategies for implementing the consequences of evaluation must be prepared. Frustration and bitterness will ensue if the school is unsuccessful in remedying the failures which have been so publicly revealed.' In other words, school managers must not run the risk that views and recommendations of those who are involved are in some way ignored. And they must be prepared, whatever the source of criticism, to identify that part of the school's organization in which changes can or should be made, *before* it is known whether criticisms will in fact emerge.

Putting things right, in this context, means that the head has to accept responsibility for any failure of teaching. He or she has, in a programme which is agreed with colleagues, to devise an acceptable way of monitoring the work of all the professionals, including his or her own. And while the individual teacher can be guided, supported and counselled, it has to be decided in the end how far improvements can go. If they do not go far enough, governors must expect the head to take action – even if that has at times to be drastic. Governors must try not to make judgements on their own and even when it is the head who has to be improved or to depart they have to listen to professional advice.

Failure in the efficient use of resources – whether of people, money, accommodation or services – must be answered by the head and governors jointly. If too little teaching time is devoted to a subject or theme, if there are too few books and materials, if the allocation of assistance and other support is thin and if, above all, these deficiencies are noticeable enough to appear even likely to contribute to less effective teaching, the head must place a change in resource support high among factors to be altered in the next school development programme.

Responsibility for the strengths and weaknesses of the school's total performance should be divided between the head and the governors. The former has to be ready to put forward acceptable explanations and workable proposals for changes. Not all the initiative rests, however, with the head. Governors must also think ahead and offer their own expertness in the analysis of problems in the financial field as well as in matters which involve personnel, capital works and public relations. To this end both heads (and their senior colleagues) and governors must make time for learning, thinking, exchanging views, proposing possible solutions, trying ideas out and deciding what to pursue and what to drop. In his analysis of the organization and use of time in schools, Brian Knight has emphasized the importance of personal time management as much as the importance of reviewing and allocating time for the curriculum, for parents, for the community and for the range of ordinary activities which make up the school day (Knight 1989:171–81). No forward planning can be organized unless time is devoted to putting things right. In the words of Briault and West (1990:74):

every teacher has a management role and needs to reconsider the ways in which the precious resource of teacher-time is used and to evaluate the relative effectiveness of different sorts of use. There is a critical relationship between style of teaching, use of teacher time, the introduction of new material resources and the use of pupil time.

Each termly review of progress in the implementation of a school development plan (in the thinking of the School Development Plans Project (SDPP)) should be set 'against the success criteria associated with the target. The team will need some clear *evidence* of the extent of progress: if such evidence is recorded, the workload at a later stage will be reduced,' (DES 1989e:15–16). In the same project, the team suggested that regular progress checks involved somebody being given responsibility for checks to be made and making sure that progress was reviewed at team meetings, especially when taking the next step forward or making decisions about future directions. Regular checks also required agreement about 'what will count as evidence of progress in relation to the success criteria'. The checking process itself required the finding of quick methods of collecting evidence from different sources and of recording that evidence.

Advice about the most important and difficult aspects of each stage of formulating a development plan was given in a second SDPP report

(DES 1991a:). Even so not all the steps in a review will appear equally attractive or practical to a head, deputy, senior colleagues or governors. Nominating one person to be responsible for the check system may appear straightforward but it is a task which needs delicacy as well as time. The necessity for deciding matters on the basis of evidence of success or otherwise at meetings of a management team appears obvious provided that the school is large enough to have a working team and provided that the head can assume that reviews of past performance can be fed smoothly into planning for the coming year. But the most difficult aspect of the recommendations of the Development Plans Project's team is that which requires agreement about what will count as evidence and from what sources that evidence should be taken. Perfect though the whole programme of suggested checks would be, a management team must recognize its own imperfections. It is important that it knows what it is leaving out and whether that is unavoidable. If not, the team must make alterations in the plan for a school's future work.

Whether it aims at perfection or not, however, the Plans Project team has a clear sense of reality when, in suggesting eight possible strategies to overcome setbacks, it includes the temporary freezing of part of an action plan, the modification of its time-scale, the scaling-down of planned action to what it describes as more manageable proportions and postponing or substituting a target (DES 1989e:16). This is a reminder that too much should not be expected from self-evaluation.

Sizes of school

The process of altering a development plan – whether as the result of self-evaluation or of failures which have become obvious from other sources – differs according to the size of a school. That difference affects the structure of management most obviously in curriculum planning. If a school wishes to alter the way in which it provides, for instance, curriculum breadth it still has to manage effective continuity regardless of other adjustments. Progress between the key stage assessments has to be guaranteed.

The allocation of teaching time and the setting of priorities both play an important part in this planning. Increasingly there is pressure on secondary schools to provide a new combination of subjects. In part this is in response to the development of modular schemes of curriculum and partly – particularly after the age of 16 – in response to the gradual enlargement in the choice of examination and qualification routes. The fact that A levels, AS levels and BTEC National are available in sixth forms and that they make different curriculum requirements confronts management with a challenge.

As far as modular systems are concerned, managers have to plan what has been described as an integral coherence for each unit of learning in such a way that it can relate to or be exchanged with other modules. That relationship between modules may make difficult demands on teachers who specialize in a traditional way in specified subjects. Those demands can be met if the advantages of drawing together the processes of pastoral and academic counselling can be highlighted (Watkins 1987). But whether staff welcome or distrust modularization depends largely on whether the reasons for adopting it have been communicated and debated.

If teachers agree to a module approach, do parents, as well as students, understand it? Do employers sympathize with it? And can the school pass the test of finding out whether 'adjacent schools with overlapping catchment areas notice any difference in recruitment when one is known for its modular approach whilst the other offers a traditional curriculum?' (Watkins 1987:51).

For the manager the complexity of modular divisions means that a school's overall plan may need to take account of up to thirty subcategories of subject organization and continuity. To this can be added those national stages of assessment which lead up to Key Stage 4 and the relationship of that stage to GCSE. On top, too, of examinations and qualifications under the aegis of BTEC, A and AS levels, schools must increasingly take account of elements of the NCVQ network.

In this combination of qualifications the breadth of approach required from managers is daunting. In, for instance, the AS context alone, four different approaches and types of aim reveal themselves in the regulations and syllabuses of different examining boards. For example, the Oxford Delegacy of Local Examinations (1989:227) offered AS English literature for 1991 as a 'syllabus . . . designed to appeal to students who can profit from a course in English literature that is as demanding in its standards as an Advanced Level syllabus but has a much reduced content'. The syllabus here was intended to give a contrasting area of study to those who did not wish to specialize in English (the example given was that of those concentrating on science or mathematics) and to complement other subjects in the humanities field. The aims were to extend the student's experience of literature, to encourage attentive and sensitive reading, to develop a capacity to respond imaginatively to what was read and to encourage independence of judgement.

In the Southern Universities Joint Board's statement (1988:133), AS in biology, as set out in the syllabus for 1990, was intended to broaden the curriculum of A level students. 'This has provided the opportunity to develop a new type of syllabus . . . concentrating on modern developments and their impact on the needs of contemporary society.' The aims have a breadth comparable to Oxford's AS in English literature.

In contrast, the University of London's Art syllabus for AS did not dictate which areas of knowledge were to be studied but defined

relevant areas of experience. Seven aims were laid down, comprehensive even when compared with Oxford's English and Southern Universities Joint Board's requirement for biology. The Associated
Examining Board (1989:338), in contrast, stated the aim of its AS
level syllabus for 1991 in accounting in one sentence: 'To show the relevance and limitations of accounting as an information system for the
review of stewardship, measurement of economic activity and as an
aid to decision-making.'

Drawn from this mix of syllabuses and interconnected aims the
range of curriculum and subject offerings which is open to a school is
attractive, but in managing that mixture staff have to accustom themselves to many levels of planning. Examination preparation differs
from stage to stage within each school year and the work of teachers
becomes heavier at times when changes of syllabus or of schemes of
marking are introduced. Particularly time-consuming demands are
made when additional modular courses have to be organized or when
another subject is introduced into the range of school choices. Meetings to review the progress of class-groups, year-groups and individual
students have to go on at the same time as the task of re-gearing the
school's teaching. As the review of the progress of individual pupils
becomes more intense more depends, too, on counselling.

The quality of input from those who deal with syllabuses, timetable,
allocations of money for materials for the school library and for subject collections, with the organization of assessment or examination
preparations and with career counselling, each markedly affects the
quality of the school plan. Total success may be diminished if there
are inadequacies which cannot be put right from year to year and by
the use of revenue funds alone. And a plan can founder on poor buildings or inadequate allowances for the improvement of equipment.

Methods of planning, fixing priorities and allocating funds in secondary schools have not changed with the introduction of local financial management. What has altered is the point at which
decision-making takes place. While heads and governors, before the
effects of the 1988 Act were felt, were more or less committed to
priorities which had passed on from year to year and whose alteration
lay more in the hands of heads of department than of the school as a
whole, reforms now make the head more answerable for changes of
priority. But a school will only run well if everyone who is affected by
a change understands its causes and effects. In large schools the review and any subsequent shift of a development plan make demands
on the head, the deputies and senior staff. Few of the traditional gate-
keepers – into the upper school, into the sixth form, into special interest activities related to year organization or to a school's total social
organization – are now able to retain their long-established singleness
of view and of influence. Each contributor to the annual plan now
earns his or her place through a capacity to provide expert service in
the organization of teaching, in the passing-on of pupils and students

who are ready to benefit from the next stage and in assessing how his or her own part of the organization is contributing to the whole. This means, if we think of mission statements and indicators of delivery, that the contributors to a plan have also to be able to evaluate the contribution to the improvement or modification for which he or she is responsible.

How heads manage their senior colleagues and how these manage their co-professionals means little if the language of management borrows heavily from the giving of instructions. There has to be some level of ordering and obeying but it represents a minor part of management. If quality circles mean anything in the management of education, they underline the importance of a reflective, self-evaluative, shared and trusting style of collegial direction. All that the manager can do is to help others to manage themselves.

Smaller schools

There are schools which are small because they are isolated or because the organization laid down by their local authority does not allow mergers. As an example, some small country-town schools, even from 11 to 18 years, may never have more than twenty-five teachers. The complexity of management is less than in the large school but simplicity is bought at a price. Subject leadership, assessment and examination advice, the extent to which certain combinations of subjects or modules are practicable, the capacity to make significant changes in the time or money allocated to individual activities – these are likely to represent dual responsibilities among deputy heads and other senior staff. Heavy loads mean that these teachers often combine their efforts in making decisions about priorities but the fewer of them there are, the easier it may be to allow traditional interests to remain unchanged.

In a small school it is particularly dangerous for its stability and success if a head or a body of governors wish to move policies and practices quickly in new directions without enough reflection. If there is an uneven responsiveness to change among staff little good can come, for example, from an attempt to improve formative assessment and counselling without there being any changes in teaching to capitalize on that counselling. And there is little chance of success for those cross-curricular aspects of national curriculum which stress the importance of, for instance, economic awareness if the plans, wishes or hopes of governors, head, parents and employers are thwarted by staff incapacity or unwillingness to take action.

The smallest secondary schools of all, particularly those whose pupil rolls fell sharply in the 1980s or for which no reorganization into large units has either been attempted or approved, face the worst management problems. Small numbers of staff, linked possibly with the frustration of teachers being locked into a school or an organization from which there is no way out, mean that many tasks fall on few shoulders. The weight of the burden alone will not be new; small schools are accustomed to that. It will matter more that the shape of the burdens has rapidly changed. Complicated demands, however well intentioned they are in terms of national policies for improvement, at local level need discussion and mulling over. If a staff is large enough, colleagues act more or less unconsciously as mentors to each other. In smaller schools, the head has to find a substitute. The only direction from which it might have come in the past was outside the school, from advisers or local authority officers. But their role, too, has changed as has their capacity to respond to the new demands from schools.

In country towns, in run-down city suburbs, in first-, middle- and high-school systems where pupil numbers refuse to shift upwards – in each of these the small school faces particularly acute management problems. That they succeed in coping is a tribute to the devotion of heads and staff, to the understanding of governors and to the loyalty of parents and employers.

Primary schools

Primary schools are large if they have twelve teachers, very large if they have fifteen or more. Middle schools are unable to look for expansion at the top of their age range beyond the age of 12 and 13. They tend always to have lacked certain categories of specialized teachers and their management is often made more difficult by their having not only too few teachers to create a collegial unit but also too few who have senior responsibility in subjects or in overall school organization. Some of the demands are lighter: there is a less acute urgency about certain secondary school matters such as the preparation for examinations. There is a less pressing need for career counselling alongside public examinations. There are no connections between key stages and external examination syllabuses. The subject range is smaller. Modularity as such is not part of the teaching organization although primary schools in other ways have organized module-based learning (without calling it that) for many years. Nevertheless in primary schools of every size the priority which is set between academic and social concerns and the distribution of resources to match that balance poses sharp problems. Some of these were described after the Education Act 1964 made middle schools legal. For example, Jennifer Nias (in Hargreaves and Tickle 1980:77) pointed out that:

the ideal middle school, being collegial, adaptive and innovatory, is almost bound to be pluralistic as well. Like comprehensive schools, although for somewhat different reasons, middle schools allow for and sometimes even seek the cultivation of differences. For a start, there is no unified concept in the literature of what a middle school should be. Although lip-service is continually paid to certain key propositions (e.g. the unifying nature of the developmental characteristics of the middle years), these are differently interpreted and applied in different LEAs. Within authorities too, individual schools are free to develop autonomous cultures, deriving from their distinctive past and present circumstances, and based upon differing philosophies, sizes and forms of organization.

Organizing different interpretations of what was required made middle school management in terms of tutoring, co-ordinating, organizing the curriculum and communicating both with external agencies and with parents a demanding task (Gannon and Whalley 1975:45–65). And there were, all the time, the six questions which had been asked by the DES (1970) about the number and capacity of staff, the involvement of children in a broad and interrelated curriculum, about children's exploration in depth of their particular interests and about their opportunities to cross subject boundaries, to work individually on some occasions and at others to work either with a cross-section of the ability range or with their intellectual peers.

These questions have not altered. The NCC's guidance on the framework for the primary curriculum (NCC 1989) drew attention to the complex nature of primary education (and that should include middle schools) and to changes in teaching approaches which were 'designed to improve the match between teaching and learning and to offer an increasing range of opportunities to pupils' (NCC 1989:2). A curriculum audit would reveal the strengths, weaknesses and gaps of a school's curriculum when that was compared with the requirements of the National Curriculum Attainment Targets and Programmes of Study in foundation subjects. After that comparison a school's curriculum plan would have to cater for continuity at a variety of levels.

The key issues of planning were defined as the grouping of pupils, the development of staff, the management of resources, assessment, record-keeping and the monitoring of the curriculum (NCC 1989:10). But the smaller the school the fewer the minds which can be brought to bear on planning and implementation. The smaller the school, too, the greater the certainty that different subjects will fall into one teacher's hands. The NCC addresses the problem of overlap and consolidation solely in relation to the implementation of cross curricular dimensions, skills and themes. Its statements are placed in a predominantly secondary-school context and the NCC's view of flexibility in providing subject continuation is regarded as a matter of

using modular courses, reserving blocks of time for activities such as work experience, adopting a 6-day timetable or introducing an alternative structure for the school day. The primary curriculum is less frequently organised by subjects but teachers in Key Stages 1 and 2 must review the way the curriculum is organised. They must consider how far the National Curriculum programmes of study can be implemented in ways which are most appropriate to children at different stages and undertaking different activities (NCC 1990a:12).

Primary schools, small and large, are likely to do this even without advice from the centre. In small primary schools, in particular, there is genuinely no alternative to considering the needs, and the most appropriate way of providing for the needs, of individual children. And it would appear to teachers in those schools – whether they are considering mainstream curriculum or cross-curricular approaches – to be a luxury to be able to follow the advice that they 'must decide whether overlap between subjects reinforces and consolidates learning; whether it requires a more co-ordinated approach to provide consistency or whether it is no more than unnecessary duplication' (NCC 1990a:12).

Management of new educational demands in very small schools is not likely to founder at the first step of carrying out the curriculum audit. Because resources are limited, because pupil numbers are low and because staffing is small scale, questions about assessment and record-keeping may be so slight as to need little management. Even at the audit stage, however, the smallest school has to have unity between the teacher, governors and parents in the consideration which is given to two of the NCC's priorities, namely critical success factors and performance indicators. Teachers are still regarded by many parents as being those who are best able to judge a school's success. In 1984 Barrow pointed out (p. 262) that a great deal of scope should be allowed to the initiative and judgement of individual teachers. That was based on the view that

we know very little indeed about the best way to proceed in detailed terms, whether we are talking about teaching techniques or the organization of material, time and content. We do know something about the questions that need to be asked but we do not have any universally applicable answers of value. We certainly do not have any reason to suppose that there is a 'proper' way to design, develop or implement a curriculum, nor that there are any 'correct' ways to assess children's progress or the success of our curriculum. How a teacher should proceed stems essentially from a view of what the educational enterprise is all about, what the particular subject matter one is dealing with may contribute to that enterprise, and how dealing with it in one way or another may facilitate that contribution.

At the second step of the NCC outline of the planning process, that of producing a whole curriculum development plan, one item will need time before it is clarified, namely the distribution of resources. What is unlikely is that a small school will have the scope to redistribute resources. And if a small school attempts anything radical in setting long-, medium- and short-term priorities for curriculum change it is likely not only to find that what it is doing is difficult for parents to understand but also to expose itself to charges of unnecessary delay. Because of the very small scale of the strategic exercise behind a tiny primary school's curriculum planning, the third stage – of implementation – will also offer little choice about teamwork, co-ordination or overlap (NCC1990a:17).

In a three-teacher or even a seven-teacher school the personal variables of teachers are likely to provide 'a valuable corrective to views of management which rely exclusively on the abstractions of organizational charts and bureaucratic structures' (Hughes *et al*. 1985:31). Because of this it is wise of the NCC to steer clear of describing particular structures of management which have to lie behind curriculum planning. The Council seeks views and responses from a broad range of practitioners. These could include headteachers who place little reliance on concepts, techniques, theories and perspectives and who instead 'stress operational problems and their practical solution strictly in terms of the educational context. Moreover they prefer to rely upon personal qualities and wide experience rather than the findings of observation and research to inform the decision-making process' (Hughes *et al*. 1985:31).

Personal positions and training

In small schools heads are almost bound to be immersed in the total team. Some, however, believe in maintaining a position at a distance from other staff. This

can make the achievement of a genuine colleague relationship difficult . . . [because the superior is] an instrument of and arm of reality, a man with power over the subordinate but who is also potentially an agent of growth, a helper, trainer, consultant and co-ordinator. The two aspects . . . are liable to be in conflict and 'a commitment of maturity' is required on both sides to activate the two roles simultaneously (Hughes *et al*. 1985: 282).

Very small 5- to 11-year-old primary schools, along with the country's few surviving separate small infant schools and separate first schools have simplicity thrust upon them in the sense that the head has to take a lead and has to manage ways round obstructiveness and resistance. Not all schools can enjoy a 'commitment to maturity' because long-established teachers in small schools are as likely to take early retirement as their peers in larger schools. Instead small schools may be in the hands of young men and women who sympathize with the purposes and approaches of educational reform and who regard it as natural that they should secure the understanding and co-operation of governors and parents. These are not heads who seek an easy life. Their ambition is often to move as quickly as is reasonable to larger, more complex and, possibly, culturally richer schools. These are the heads, the curriculum leaders and the co-ordinators whose training for management is particularly important. They need to be given the chance to train inside some form of constructive tutelage within their small schools. In particular they need to learn how to cope with the movement of new ideas about educational organization before it rises to a flood.

Traditionally those who provide that tutelage have been heads who come from other schools. But tutoring in management has also come from inspectors, advisers and teachers-cum-administrators. Each group has the disadvantage of not being fully credible either because of the lack of recent and relevant experience – one of the tests applied to educators of teachers – or because the teaching profession is not so close-knit as to allow one category of practitioner to be confident that someone from another group knows the job thoroughly.

That practitioners should train others has the disadvantage attached to the pre-New Movement days of educational administration and the belief in the significance of practice and of training by anecdote. Training provided by practitioners also suffers from the fact that the education service is increasingly fragmented.

Because of the fragmentation of phases and types of education there has been compensatory emphasis on continuity and progression. That message used to come from LEAs, striving to create parity of treatment between schools and parity of opportunity for pupils across a range of different social environments. It was LEAs who until 1988 carried the responsibility for policies about curriculum funding, about staff ratios and about many different financial allowances. This single-ness of treatment led to bureaucracy but it also led to equitable and fair treatment of schools in differing circumstances. It provided an antidote to parochialism. The movement away from the LEAs started early: governors in FE had begun to exercise some autonomy after 1970 (DES Circular 7/70). Experiments with local financial management in schools in Hertfordshire and Cambridgeshire started a decade later. Staffing quotas had disappeared in the 1960s. As control loosened on one side, LEAs developed a capacity to give more help direct to schools: they were allowed, early in the 1980s for instance, to retain a small percentage of their capital receipts in order to subsidize restricted building programmes.

The pattern of control was slowly liberalized as local authorities gained a little freedom from Whitehall (not least in the funding of in-service teacher education). Authorities in turn remitted the power of decision on an increasing scale to schools. The main effect on LEAs in 1988 was to remove them from the field of non-university higher education, to limit their power over non-advanced FE, to force them to release their control over school decisions about local priorities in the use of funds and virtually to end their curriculum responsibility.

These changes were handled by practitioners who had experienced (or prepared for) little large-scale change. Thus, while the scope and purpose of school management had altered, the heads, governors and their allies (teachers and parents) had not been trained to take on tasks on the scale which legislation required.

Systems of training and familiarization had to be quickly launched by LEAs, institutions of higher education, organizations such as the Advisory Centre for Education and by one or two of the teacher associations. Apart from long-standing co-operation between LEAs and higher education those who separately provided training had little experience of managing education in concert with each other.

That separateness had to be diminished despite the fact that heads might not find it palatable to learn from other heads, nor governors from other governors. A concordat was necessary between vital groups of managers. For the benefit of both, LEAs, although their involvement in training in its traditional form might be only brief, needed to share experience. Their agents were local authority advisers and inspectors. Alongside them, HMI nationally continued their tradition of training based on detailed observation and a long perspective. Local advisers and inspectors and HMI had a record of collaboration but with the possible disadvantage of being respectively too close to the action and too remote from it. Nevertheless, their in-service provision spoke for itself. It was better still when higher education and the voluntary agencies joined forces with the two tiers of central and local government management training but it was revived once the swift 1991 review of school inspection services had been completed and new arrangements had been included in the Education (Schools) Act 1992.

Among the voluntary contributors the Campaign for the Advancement of State Education (CASE) has consistently trained – through day-meetings, materials, campaign packs and regular newsletters – both parents and governors for their part in management. Because CASE does not recognize divisions between partners, it regularly addressed governors and parents with the same message. In, for instance, its recommendations about the improvement of communications, it described nine possible methods of bringing parents and governors closer together (Parents and Schools 1988). Of these, three – the proposal that governors from different schools would find it helpful to meet one another, the stimulus to LEAs to clarify and publicize the law about time off work for public service such as that of being a school governor and the proposal that regular surgeries could be arranged for governors to meet parents or for governors to meet LEA officers – these and other ideas have become accepted. They are practical and they fill a need.

Nearer to the governors themselves, one journal, the *School Governor*, has regularly applied itself to improving their efficiency (Taylor 1989:2):

Just as the best education builds on what children already know and understand and encourages them to develop their own talents, so the best work with governors is based on drawing out the skills, knowledge and experience that already exist in every governing body. Once the governors have learned to work together as a group, respecting each others' different opinions and different abilities they can draw on that reservoir of talent to serve the school.

'To serve the school' is one way of explaining governors' responsibilities in management. It makes it clear that teachers do not have to submit to the jurisdiction of amateurs but it also makes the position plain of those who represent, in Joan Sallis's (1991:14) phrase, 'the captive participants'. They have a right to be heard:

If agreement on objectives, consent to methods, and assessment of outcome have been lost from the relationship between teachers and taught, it is serious, since the public are compulsory participants in a special sense: they are not legally obliged to use architects, plumbers or even doctors in the normal way. The school governing body has a special duty to represent these captive participants; to help determine the objectives and allocate resources on their behalf; to be satisfied as to the methods to be used; and to appraise the result. Yet significantly the school model is one of internal shared oversight, not just a consumer council. The head and staff, and the education authority have a right to participate also.

How the participation of the professional officers and advisers of a local authority will in future be treated by a governing body still has to emerge. In the past advisers sometimes had to give guidance before there was a new head. Ordinarily, when governors make an appointment they have to rely on references and on a professional view. That view may not always, now or in the future, be fully revealed. Advisers are sometimes suspected of harbouring secrets. But even if governors are suspicious it is still true that although inspectors may have a favoured candidate they are not necessarily wrong. 'Governors need to remember that officers are there to provide professional advice, which they should assess in the same way as any other advice or information they are given' (Taylor 1989:32).

Seeing the professional's mind at work can be helpful in another type of management training for lay governors, namely through 'shadowing'. A description by one governor, Angela Thody (1989:11), met with this response from the head whom she shadowed:

Our Curriculum Review has involved 1,700 students, 115 staff, 20 governors plus many parents and local employers, in developing a Statement of Intent, a collective vision of our destination. My job is to manage the journey towards this at a realistic pace. Judging this pace is difficult for, if change is to be effective, it has both to be thoroughly considered and understood by everybody. Angela Thody's visits have put her in the position of viewing the same journey from different perspectives. They will enable her, at governors' meetings to offer more knowledgeable and impartial advice. I can't get that in any other way and I value it enormously.

Heads who feel that governors should be involved only on the professional's own conditions need to be brought to see that that in time will breed apathy or resentment or, at the least, a damaging division between partners. Governors for their part need training because 'good will is not enough. Governors may be volunteers. They may be 'lay'. But they must not be unskilled' (Holt 1989:11). That is the message behind Action for Governors Information and Training (AGIT). The questions which AGIT posed when the first effects of the combination of the 1986 and 1988 Education Acts were beginning to be felt, were addressed to LEAs: was governor training provided? By whom and for whom? Could all governors receive some help eventually? Did the programme reveal careful planning? Had governors been asked to identify their needs and to evaluate what was being provided in order to inform future practice? Was there a consultative group? Did an LEA have a policy of governor support which included training, clear information and access to advice? Was there a plan to make governor support an integral and permanent part of LEA services?

These eight questions provide an idea of the depth and thoroughness with which governors have a right to be trained and supported. They are taken from an AGIT compilation (Holt 1989) where the total range of questioning also covers issues of participation and funding.

While governors are being trained to participate in management, teachers receive their stimulus to participate from heads, through peer discussions and activities, from their specialist advisers and in some cases from their own professional associations. Approaches differ but a common thread is easily picked out. The National Union of Teachers, for example, asked its members to monitor the effects of the local management of schools (LMS). The purpose was to enable the union to put to central government a well-informed case for modifications in or better funding for the scheme (NUT 1990:10):

The union believes that decisions over local management of schools should be a whole school issue. The union is firmly committed to the belief that the skills, experience and expertise of every member of staff should be a valued part of the monitoring process and that a 'top down' approach to LMS will not meet with success. Monitoring of LMS schemes is not about making a bad system of funding work. Rather, it is to ensure that the needs and circumstances of all schools are reflected within each scheme, and to assist the union in persuading the government to modify its legislation affecting LMS.

Seven items went into the pack which the NUT provided for its school representatives. These formed a basis for training, together with advice about seeking information within a school which previously had not been approached. Basic information, for instance, had to be accurate and easy to use and financial jargon or technical accounting terms had to be clearly explained.

There might be an understandable suspicion about a trade union's approach to questions such as advice in monitoring the effects of LMS. But whether or not they appear unduly suspicious, the questions which teachers are encouraged to ask do impinge on the effectiveness of the school. Four or five of the questions which, for instance, are suggested as being suitable for teacher representatives to put to school governors, have an obvious bearing on children's chances to learn (*The Teacher* December 1990:11):

Has the fabric and repair of the school buildings deteriorated or the standard of school cleaning dropped?

Are the staff not being replaced or are there attempts to replace permanent staff with teachers on temporary or fixed term appointments?

Has there been a change in staffing policies?

Has there been a change of policy on examination entries?

Has there been a reduction in the range or number of incentive allowances provided within the school?

Has there been a reduction in the number of non-teaching staff employed in the school?

These and other questions which include matters such as supply teacher cover and book purchasing relate to total management inasmuch as a trade union's defence of its members' interests is bound to be as much concerned with specific issues as with the wish to see the whole process of education being properly managed.

Gathering information in order to support collaborative action which would affect part rather than the whole of school management – again in the attempt to persuade central government either to review a gap in its rules or to make a new rule for the first time – lay behind the activity of another pressure group. In 1989 some parents disapproved of having their children, at the reception class level, taught in classes of forty. A movement, Ratepayers for Improvement in Primary Education (RIPE), came into being. It gathered information about a wide range of primary class sizes in Redbridge, looked at the averages and norms of some other London boroughs, noted the rules about class sizes in, as an example, West Germany and noted, too, that the five teachers' associations had their own suggestion for maximum class sizes (from 20 to 25 in reception classes, 25 to 30 in primary classes of children of a single age, between 20 and 24 for classes where children were of mixed ages).

The group also made use of recommendations from other sources – the 1984 report of the House of Commons Education, Science and Arts Committee, *Achievement in Primary Schools*, the Inner London Education Authority's Junior Class Project of 1984 and the 1990 HMI report on the implementation of the national curriculum in a sample of 100 primary schools. The conclusion which was important for managers and which was repeatedly underlined was that the 'satisfactory implementation of the National Curriculum will require even smaller classes, since pupils may be working at widely differing levels, and much teaching will have to be done with small groups, or individual pupils' (Matharu 1990:8–9).

In a manner comparable to that of the NUT monitoring scheme, this campaign was directed at school management. CASE asked its supporters to send to it details of individual LEAs' policies, together with examples of class size and age in individual localities. Supporters were asked to write to their MPs, to interest other parents in the campaign, to form a local group, to write to newspapers and generally to publicize their concerns. It was suggested that parent groups should speak to the local branches of the teacher unions.

To raise awareness about the significance of class size is an important but isolated contribution to the store of knowledge which parents need when they themselves join in the task of management. It is not a matter of repeating a rallying cry but of understanding about individual learning, about teachers' use of time and about the size of group in which young children best orientate themselves.

Building up knowledge on which to base their contribution to school management can be stimulated for parents by the efforts of schools themselves. They can remind them of the importance of good home–school relationships, as did the CASE and the National Confederation of Parent Teacher Associations when they produced joint advice. Of two recent key arguments one is related to a statement by the Senior Chief HMI that the disadvantages of under-achievement, inadequate school resources and poor teaching are more likely to occur when parents feel less able to influence the system. The other is that there are signs that 'the Education Reform Act has given fresh impetus to the development of good home–school relations – based on more than just the legal requirements of the publication of test results, complaints procedures and the requirements to have schemes of work available to parents' (Tulloch 1990:11). The reinforcement of this relationship can be regarded as part of the individual school's management task. While they still have influence, the same reinforcement is one of the responsibilities of LEAs. For their benefit CASE did draw up an eight-point code, including their need to have coherent policies about home–school relationships, machinery to encourage local links and in-service education for teachers about home/school liaison.

That link will be closer if it is well informed and if it is based on mutual trust. Isolation, particularly the isolation of a head, can reduce that trust but it is not necessarily the head who is at fault. Isolation can start elsewhere (Platt 1990:12):

For a career teacher one of life's ironies is that reaching the top of the profession is likely to mean you hardly teach at all. While secondary heads have been in this position for years, primary heads are also finding it more difficult to make time for teaching, barricaded in their offices as they are by the piles of paperwork and DES guidelines. The increase in administrative work and greater emphasis on financial control threaten the open, co-operative approach to school management.

The other element of success in school–home links – that participants should be well informed – extends to governors. How are parent governors regarded by other parents? Will there always be some governors who have been at the job long enough only to need occasional updating while other, newer members need support over a much longer period while they develop the confidence necessary to be effective?

To these and other questions one answer lies in long-term programmes of governor training, linked to university certificates, to certification by the College of Preceptors or to accreditation within the Open College system (Hunt 1990). But the more usual route for the knowledgeable governor is through short courses, day-meetings, videos, governors' handbooks, newsletters and occasional broadcasts.

And, particularly in smaller local authorities, where there are almost as many governors as teachers, governors can take part with staff in school in-service training (Dunt 1989).

If they work closely with the head and staff, governors quickly learn the essentials of planning. They learn, too, how to establish priorities because questions which need clear answers continually present themselves, particularly while new legislative demands are settling down. If, for example, a school can develop on top of its everyday work only three or four new activities, how is a balance to be maintained between particular subjects or parts of the curriculum, issues relating to social organization and personal education and matters of policy which require action in terms of both curriculum and ethos? Some governors may wish virtually all the planning to be carried out by head and staff. Nevertheless they still have to approve that planning and to know what are its effects. And in every case 'governors will find it easier to take part in the process where, as a body, they understand the stages of development planning and the potential for their involvement, where they have good working relationships and where they adopt appropriate methods of working' (Leask 1990:14).

Repeatedly the point is made by those who have experience of helping governors, heads and parents jointly to contribute to school management that all parties should know each other well. Governors may themselves be involved in action plans which form some subsidiary part of an overall school development plan. In these they work with teachers. In this relationship as in all their other connections with a school, governors have to gauge how much contact is desirable – with staff and also with pupils. They particularly have to gauge the weight which should be given to their visibility in the school, to defining their purposes during their visits and reporting on them to other governors.

Trust is central. There is no room for suspicion about secret reporting or about undue interference in matters which have not been jointly agreed – by head, staff and governors – as matters which form part of the legitimate concern of the governing body. Trust is important, too, in the agreements which are made with LEAs. Teachers and parents have not in the past had the same experience of local authorities as new heads and governors. Thus when the Audit Commission (1989) put forward its view about the future of LEAs it identified among six elements in their role that of visionary and leader. One comment (Kennedy 1990:25) about that identification came from a member of the commission who admitted that the terms 'visionary' and 'leader'

may sound far-fetched following the 1988 Act, because of the reductions in the LEA power which the Act entails. But even at a minimum, LEAs need some kind of strategic thinking to underpin decisions where they have discretion, such as provision for children below statutory school age, adult education and further education. In a number of less tangible ways, LEAs can set the tone for the education service in their areas, for example, by promoting co-operation amongst schools and colleges and by urging particular responses to the needs of pupils from ethnic minorities. For an LEA's vision to be more than rhetoric its aims need to be articulated into a clear statement of what it is trying to achieve and, crucially, this statement must be capable of translation into specific targets and actions.

Old influences will take some time before they completely lose their effect. Other forces will become more central to the way in which managers do their work while new national schemes of education take root.

In gauging how managers should be trained, trainers – and ideally these would for some time still come from LEAs – must present good examples of priority-setting and resource-matching which recognize the background of the local culture which has shaped public education since at least 1870. If trainers simply reflect short-lived municipal preferences, their contribution will not be relevant to the future. There were some traditions which were born with the establishment of LEAs in 1902, others developed in 1944 and yet others which were quickly generated after 1974.

Separately or in combination, strength is derived from past histories such as these. Local authorities particularly in metropolitan areas who set out to train the managers of new education can combine a clear sense of the past with enlightened programmes which cater for new populations and for comparatively recent shifts in culture. The realism of local government's flexibility from period to period carries important lessons for governors and heads.

In response to the Swann Report (1985) most areas of Britain were compelled to review education systems which had become increasingly involved in cultural pluralism since the late 1940s. The issues under review have always needed conscious, well-informed consideration and the planning and implementing of multicultural education call for managers to be ready continually to modify their systems. This has coincided with other major changes in the texture of society (Hulmes 1989: 24):

Society is becoming increasingly complex, but not only in consequence of technological change. This complexity needs to be acknowledged in education, neither merely described nor indirectly noted. Helping individuals to cope with the opportunities (as well as the tensions) which arise out of religious, ethical, political and technological diversity may be a task to which all teachers are finally obliged to make a conscious and planned contribution. This task can scarcely be undertaken without a lively interest in the practical implications of pluralism.

Connections between belief and action make a difference to both the content and method of education. Hulmes (1989:162–7) lists forty-four organizations and agencies which are sources of information about the religious and cultural diversity of British society of the present day. No individual school can hold a very broad brief on its own. If the services of LEA advisers change their nature, how many schools.

would buy expertness of advice from other sources? If the answer is that few schools would do very much other than rely upon their own judgement, the slide into parochialism and closed minds seems certain.

If a school chooses to review how it can improve its management of matters which are influenced by, for instance, multiculturalism, equal opportunity or gender difference it may arrange to buy the services of one consultant or more but the effect of that consultation itself has to be managed.

Consultancy and performance indicators

The management of large-scale issues which are new to a curriculum or so recent as to need to be kept up to date call for in-service education and staff development. In common with all other types of staff development, an outside consultant who helps a school with, for instance, the revision of its multicultural curriculum and the appropriate aspects of its social organization has to assume that the unit of change is the whole school rather than individual teachers. The consultant also has to assume that all staff are involved in determining the process and the content of their professional development because in essence that development 'should be conducted on the basis of a genuine exchange of views, should produce negotiated and agreed actions, should be directly related to the roles played by teachers in their schools and should be implemented through a structure that is understood by and open to all staff' (Aubrey 1990: 45).

Handled with assistance from a local authority, supported by the experience of an adviser or consultant, a head still has to ensure that staff attitudes and practices move in the direction of the policy which is being reformulated. The head who is committed to staff development on an entirely open basis of staff choice cannot make top-down judgements about the speed or thoroughness of change. And whether staff development is open or directed, there has to be an evaluation based on some form of performance indicator.

Because it is thought that such indicators cannot measure many aspects of an institution which is as complex as a school, they are distrusted. Appeals to common-sense judgements (examination results, pupil assessments, pupils' out-of-school behaviour, the opinion of the local community or the parents) fail because common sense is not universal. And if performance indicators have to be used they need to be broken down into as specific measures as is possible and with as much reference as possible to the changes which are looked for in those pupils whose education is being evaluated. Performance indicators can work if data from the process of evaluation are fed back into the school's own development process. To that end the data must be accessible, intelligible and credible.

In this process Hopkins and Leask (1989) have drawn attention to three approaches which the formative use of evaluation can adopt after the feedback into the school's development process. First, the making of almost immediate changes in the matters which have been evaluated. Second, a more formal stage of making changes to the school development plan at the time of its annual revision. Third, action in which

the school/college management team discuss the evaluation with the local inspectorate or external evaluation consultant. The inspectorate will be concerned to monitor the school's development and to make certain it is in line with national and local priorities. The evaluation consultant's questions are normally of a different order to practitioners' questions, which tend to be related to the day-to-day activities of the project. These questions, or 'sensitising concepts', are usually to do with trends or ideas which transcend individual classroom concerns and relate to the wider implications of the scheme (Hopkins and Leask 1989:18).

In its own contribution to performance indicators central government in 1989 built up an item bank drawn from eight local authorities and forty primary and secondary schools. In publicizing these, a Minister of State at the DES emphasized that the indicators originated in schools themselves. The DES, it was said, had wanted to move on from quantitative indicators and had consolidated a checklist of qualitative items. The Minister pointed out that

each school need not re-invent the wheel entirely. There is a vast resource of knowledge and experience which schools should be able to tap – in particular within the LEA inspectorate and Her Majesty's Inspectorate. These groups of professionals are excellently placed to advise on what makes a good school, on what are the criteria for evaluating success – and on what range of indicators might help schools to judge whether they are achieving their goals (DES 1989c).

Local education authorities had, in preparation for the introduction of LMS, been encouraged to advise and support their schools in developing their own school-based indicators. They had also been asked to develop indicators for financial and other management functions.

The DES checklist consists of 50 items, covering a school's basic data (13 items), its social, cultural and economic context (11 items), its pupils' achievements (4 items), its objectives for parental involvement (4 items), the processes used to identify and discuss pupil attitudes (8 items) and its management arrangements (10 items) (DES 1989d).

The reference to inspectors as guides and assistants may indicate central government's wish that significant influence should still be wielded from the centre of the system. This is a long way away from an earlier expression of certainty by the National Association of Inspectors and Educational Advisers: 'The inspection of educational establishments, a fundamental duty of a local authority, underlines the fact that the work of those who administer policy decisions and allocate resources, and of those who evaluate the impact of those policies on establishment make an indivisible whole' (Winkley 1985: 201). It is a long way, too, from the narrowed definition of HMI responsibilities which is all that is left after the enactment of the Education (Schools) Act 1992.

The dissolution of LEA responsibilities will contradict what the Audit Commission said in 1989, that advisers and inspectors were there in order to monitor schools, to guarantee for the LEA and the electors that an appropriate service was being provided and to assess needs. There will still need to be a system of advice, support and monitoring. Not all of it can be left to be bought by schools unless central government wishes – and it may well do this – to give up its responsibilities for a national system of safeguarding educational quality.

While the tiers of government and the levels of responsibility for education are revised it has to be noted that the connections between the head as local manager, those who carry out the day-to-day teaching of a school, the external adviser as consultant and HMI have already been damaged almost to the point of severance. There was benefit when teachers, advisers and HMI could work in concert in re-appraising the curriculum (DES 1983b:6). But now one can either take the view that the benefits were lost without any real effort having been made to save them or assume that what was once regarded as an important process of evaluating the work of schools has made way for school-by-school judgements based on self-evaluation, on parent choice and indicators of performance. But the fifty items on the DES checklist in 1989 were less about quality than about those parts of a school's organization which are regarded as likely to *lead* to an improved quality of education. If management pays heed to very thorough indicators the question still remains of how a certain level of quality in management can be guaranteed. The user of education (namely the student), and the beneficiary of a service of education and training (namely the employer and the community) can only accept assurances about quality if its control and management can also be guaranteed.

Conclusion

To apply stimuli or correctives is part of every scheme of management. When there is much that is new to manage, the question has to be answered of how often a review of progress should be made. If some years have to pass before new examinations in secondary schools, new schemes of assessment in primary schools, new approaches to subjects, modules and cross-curriculum themes are capable of being evaluated, the managers have to maintain their confidence in existing systems of working. They do not always operate as equals and it is important that they should share what they know with each other in order to build up mutual trust. This is likely to emerge if honest and thorough attempts have, at the start, been made to foresee difficulties and to plan a way of solving then. It requires every party to know about any plan at each stage of its development. If some members of the partnership need to be led more quickly or to be taught in more detail than others, the right trainers working at the right pace have to be sought.

Within a system where there has to be less and less dependence on local authority services and particularly on LEA advisers, managers must decide how broad a view they have to take of their duties if they are to avoid the inward-looking parochialism of separated schools. If they go outside their own personnel they have to afford to bring others in. If they pay for outside advice they will probably decide to pay for the services of those who will validate the outcome of their self-evaluation. When they have confidence in an external moderator this has to be felt by parents and governors as well as by teachers.

CHAPTER 12

New responses from management

Management has to master a changing variety of legislative and social requirements. These have not always been acknowledged, nor has there always been a concern to ensure that managers have the resources to manage new demands.

Legal requirements about the organization of teachers' time were the first aspect of reform which assisted new approaches to management. There was alarm when the Teachers' Pay and Conditions Act 1987 defined the teaching year and when distinctions were drawn between directed and non-directed time. Fears sprang from the impending loss of the element of goodwill in the relationship between teachers and employers. At its best that had meant that teachers could be expected to carry responsibilities which took time outside the processes of preparing and teaching and, where it applied, of marking pupils' work. In the name of goodwill teachers looked after clubs and non-curricular activities during lunch hours and after school. School sport was largely a matter of out-of-hours (and therefore voluntary) involvement on the part of teachers. School visits, the use of residential centres, school holidays abroad, each added to the burden of time which teachers (most of them willingly) gave to their schools and to their pupils.

Bad feeling over salary settlements, protracted disagreements about whether teachers could be compelled to supervise school meals, disagreements about teachers' responsibility on school premises after pupils had started to arrive in the morning but before the school day had formally begun – these created enough bitterness to drain goodwill of much of its meaning.

This was the background of the 1987 legislation which gave employers an assured position about the amount of time they could ask a teacher to dedicate to professional duties. It gave heads certainty in organizing school years and terms in such a way that they could require teachers to be present at meetings concerned with planning and review. It offered teachers the certainty that if they gave 1,265 hours a year to their work, if they attended meetings and conducted other required activities in the fixed period of directed time, they would then be free to use their time as they wished.

Many teachers choose to spend their free time on professional work. Although this, by and large, is a genuinely free choice, there can still be some exploitation of good nature. The rules about available teacher time are on the whole respected by heads; they can be turned to advantage if a head wishes not to consult his or her colleagues very widely or in much depth about a change in school organization. The less time there is available, once the limits are being reached, it might be claimed that it is excusable for the head to make a decision without consultation.

But heads also now make use of the time that is available more economically and purposefully than in days when staff meetings after children had left the premises had sometimes been protracted, poorly planned and excessively fatiguing. Some schools now, if they can, hold two staff meetings a week simply to keep up with the matters emerging from the national curriculum and from assessment requirements, one for updating and one for more general matters. Exceptional though such frequency may be these meetings take place during lunch hours, when available time is limited and has to be used in a business-like way.

The fear that heads would be preoccupied with totting up each teacher's hours and then be held to account by their local authorities never materialized. If there were irregularities, the system managed to cope. The overall impression has been, from soon after the implementing of the 1987 Act, that teacher–employer and teacher–head relationships are relaxed and trustful. In particular the change of law freed heads and deputies in large schools from a position which had become stressful: heads and, by a definition which was seldom challenged, their deputies were unable to leave a school while there were still pupils to be overseen. Assistant teachers leave but heads had to attempt the near-impossible task of covering each and every corner of the premises during lunch hours and immediately after school.

Without the 1987 Act it would have been difficult to plan the reforms of 1988. The involvement of teachers in the process of professional change had to be guaranteed. The most important part of that involvement was their preparation and planning for changes and developments in curriculum and assessment. It was important, too, that they should attend as much in-service training as was available. This was markedly in contrast with two earlier periods of reform in the second half of this century: the early 1960s saw the improvement of mathematics, science and language teaching in primary schools through the combined efforts of HMI and of Nuffield Foundation-funded schemes of innovation in materials and teaching methods. These changes coincided with, and then became part of, some of the curriculum development programmes of the Schools Council for Curriculum and Examinations. New methods and materials were devised, tested, changed, tried more widely and again revised. The whole curriculum in primary and secondary schools, from 5 to 18 years, was under scrutiny. But the additional time which was devoted to this work was voluntary and, in contractual terms, unrecognized. Little credit was given by central government to a great range of activity, commitment, ideal-ism and vision. Goodwill seeped away and what was left was the im-pression that teachers wished not to be accountable to their paymasters or to central government. Against this background the reforms of the late 1980s had, in the minds of central government, to avoid the repeti-tion of mistakes about teacher power. It was the impediment of recal-citrance and organized apathy on the part of teachers which first had to be set to one side. The 1987 Act secured that. Unfortunately the Teachers Pay & Conditions Act 1991 drew further distrust from the teachers and, in particular, dissent from governors (TES 1991F).

As far as local managers were concerned the most important needs which underlay reform and which had become clear over the two de-cades before 1988 were those which made it necessary to make in-ser-vice education frequent and accessible, and which made teachers (particularly through the organization of local teachers' centres) more responsible for deciding what training they wanted. Teachers were in particular helped towards clarification about curriculum leadership and co-ordination. In infant, first, primary and middle schools this had been continuously encouraged in successive HMI reports over fifteen years.

Management of the curriculum alone was, however, some way from the top of the list of management priorities. First, there were increases in school population followed by a tapering decline between 1979 and 1991. This decline was to reach post-16 education in 1993 and in one way made it easier for the shift of control over FE from local to cen-tral government to be made in that year. But the effect of demographic change was to lead to crises about the supply of specialist teachers and about costly over-provision of classroom and specialist accommoda-tion. At a time when pupil numbers were going down there was con-siderable pressure to sell off unused buildings. But there was also pressure for schools and authorities to allow spare space in primary schools to be used by admitting children to school at an earlier age. The managers of primary schools had to handle liaison with and conti-nuity from nursery units and, perhaps more testingly, the maintenance of constructive relationships with pre-school playgroups.

A comparable task in managing relationships between schools, par-ents, interest groups and pressure lobbies had been tackled at the time of the 1981 Education Act. The integration of pupils with special needs into mainstream schooling required yet another range of man-agement skills, as much concerned with allaying the anxieties (and meeting the aspirations) of parents as with altering a school's curricu-lum organization. In this connection and as a result of steadily more confident links with parents, primary schools had to manage the con-solidation – alongside professionally trained teachers – of non-teaching helpers and classroom assistants.

Secondary school managers had had two major problems before the late 1980s: fluctuating pupil numbers, added to the question of whether there were enough specialist teachers available, intensified the importance of who should and who should not be entered for public examinations at 16. With this issue arose the question of how best those 16-year-olds could be prepared for what came after they had passed compulsory school age. This was at a time when the country's employment pattern favoured the adult worker. For the young adult, unemployment after leaving school or the alternative of poorly paid, low status and unskilled employment led to a disaffection which was sharply felt even before school was left behind. Methods of continuing from schooling to training were undeveloped and although progress was being made before 1991 into BTEC Firsts being available below the age of 16 in schools and BTEC Nationals after that age, the sudden announcement of the separation of school and FE funding to take effect in 1993 risked driving education and training apart after three decades of work to bring them closer together.

Another large management issue for secondary schools was the development of the entitlement curriculum in the 1970s and 1980s. This held promising implications for the post-1988 era and a curriculum on the basis of which schools attempted to create contracts with pupils and their families led to a growing pressure for the universal development and use of records of achievement. Each addition to the list of matters which managers had to handle was regarded as stimulating by those who saw that local school management would before long be virtually the only level of management which mattered.

Up to 1988 managers of schools were involved mainly in matters which were regarded as being directly linked to teaching and learning. There was little concern for premises, meals, transport, the upkeep of grounds, anti-vandalism policies or policies about health and safety. Those were left to LEAs. Schools dealt with practicalities and implementations. The success of heads was measured mainly in terms of the range, quality, interconnectedness and results which they could show in the spheres of curriculum and pedagogic planning. In secondary schools the GCSE was launched with confidence and success. Earlier, TVEI had settled in and expanded at the same time as pre-YTS schemes had been attempted, together with a range of other minor prevocational qualifications. In primary schools between Plowden and the 1988 Act the manager had been busy with curriculum development and with cross-curricular themes. Primary schools had, too, been increasingly involved in that part of education which was connected with personal, social and moral growth. Primary pupils in the early 1990s drew benefit from an education which was better than that of 1944 and better than it had been in 1967, at the time of Plowden (Thomas 1990).

In the two decades before 1988 the main impediment which local managers inherited was the continuing position of a head who was still regarded mainly as a teacher and only secondly as a manager. Heads, at both primary and secondary schools, had certainly had to shoulder responsibilities related to institutional management but their local authorities, HMI, employers, parents and the local community gave the impression that it was a committedly educational wisdom in the running of a school which was appreciated in preference to a neutrally functional management skill.

It is surprising that the picture had not changed long before the 1988 Act. From the standpoint of central government it was HMI, historically independent of the Secretary of State for Education and Science, who had supported the development of managerial skills among heads. In the 1970s a small group of HMI organized courses which became known by the initials of their originating body, the Committee on the Staffing, Management and Organization of Schools. The typical COSMOS course was concerned with heightening the awareness of, and the skill exercised by, heads and deputy heads in respect of staff, time and buildings. They were among the earliest courses which were intended to train people in new ways of making decisions about the disposition of resources. They encouraged timetable analysis and curriculum analysis in such a way that a school's purpose could be more realistically linked with the way it organized its staff and material support (Owen 1973).

Local authorities appreciated and encouraged this approach and themselves built some local management in-service training upon it. Later, as a result of Circular 3/83 (*The In-Service Teacher Training Grant Scheme*), a four-year programme which reached 6,000 heads and senior staff from primary, middle, secondary and special schools was mounted at 45 training institutions. One-Term Training Opportunity (OTTO) courses were the first fruits of a policy of earmarked funding by the DES of particular areas of in-service teacher education.

The OTTO courses signalled that management training had arrived. Both the success of and the future risk to policies of in-service work in management training have been well described by Poster and Day (1988). But new legislation meant that the partnership of DES, local authorities and, for example, the National Development Centre for School Management Training (NDC) had to change. The latter, at the University of Bristol, had changed its character by 1988 because it was required to be self-financing. The trainers of managers had to face the same challenge of financial organization as school managers themselves.

The tendency to concentrate on individual institutions – which is a notable feature of LMS and of the feeling of school governance, meant that although LEA and HMI training, helped by the NDC and higher education institutions, had started to widen the role of the head, their efforts had reached only a minority of teachers. Some heads approached the reforms of 1988 with little more than one or two locally provided days of induction training – often when they themselves had been newly appointed. And, as though to contradict constructive approaches to longer training, a national project which examined how to improve the selection of secondary school headteachers found that there was almost a positive antipathy towards the idea of the head as manager even as recently as the mid-1980s (Morgan *et al.* 1983:35).

Headteacher selection has to combine democratic control with technical efficiency. Further, this democratic control is unusual in that it is exercised by two groups of selectors: members and governors. The balance between these two and officers is unspecified and varies between authorities and selection stages in the same authority. The organization of local education authorities' headteacher selection practice is, partly because of its perceived episodic nature, far from adequate. More importantly, though, the culture of the education service is antithetical to systematic selection: it stresses individuality and personality, and tends to reject management notions.

The Project on the Selection of Secondary Headteachers (POST) ran with research funding from the DES between 1980 and 1983. It revealed that the selection process did not take account of the variety of specialized and technical skills – in addition to personal traits, gifts and experience – for which a head was appointed. After the early 1980s more LEAs intensified and prolonged the process of seeking information. Brief one-off interviews for appointment became rare even in very small primary schools. This improvement should have meant – but there is no proof – that subsequent management training could build on known strengths and could remedy possible weaknesses in any head's earlier management experience.

The significance of earlier experience in management can be obscured by heads who describe their earlier careers in terms of functions. Confronted by the need to judge any large issue in education they fail because they launch on hypotheses of which they have no experience. Heads only succeed if they have the capacity to build a case for improvement or change on the basis of activities which have already forced them to think – and to work their way – through the handling of specific issues.

The inevitability of making appointments on the strength of verifiable experience was one of the factors which led the POST study to recommend an extended investigation of a head's past professional career. It is not enough to confine such an enquiry to the institutional setting through which the head has progressed unless management is seen solely in local terms. There are disadvantages in this; there is a narrowness in a head's experience if his or her previous institutions have been of one kind or have been confined to one phase or age-group. But if experience has allowed an insight into the connections and discontinuities of education the manager is better placed. He or she was, until the split-off of FE from 5 to 16 schooling, placed even more strongly if there was also a capacity to think and to plan across the division between education and training. This was because, regardless of the artificiality of separating schools and FE through establishing separate funding mechanisms, it should no longer have been regarded as right to define vocational or professional training as something which does not include an earlier and broader connection with general education.

In addition to seeing the connection and gaps of education through their past experience, managers need to combine different types of institutional activity in their record. To organise a curriculum is an incomplete piece of work unless the organizer can find, substitute, exchange or persuade the right resources to be forthcoming. And no manager of education can properly claim that title unless he or she can handle the availability of people, time and accommodation.

If a manager is incomplete in the range of experience, can the lack be made good through book-knowledge? That seems unlikely in a society in which empiricism is still a notable basis for choice, decision and action. Clothing ideas in the language of practicality is difficult unless the details of practical knowledge can themselves be verified. In Britain, in other words, it must be rare for a head or any other senior manager in education to be appointed because of theoretical skill alone.

Short, hands-on secondments can be of assistance in giving the manager enough breadth to manage education rather than simply to look after the details of day-to-day organization. This has proved effective in schemes of linkage between education and industry. It works, too, when a manager who is moving from one sector or function to another (secondary to primary or headteacher to inspector) can rapidly learn lessons – and observe – at first hand. This method represents, however, the oldest weakness in management training: it takes us back to anecdote and anecdotal theorizing and to the need to avoid the inadequacies of outdated approaches.

Inadequate experience

It is because book-knowledge and learning-from-your-neighbour are inadequate bases for senior management that, despite the reservation of the POST project, employers sometimes make judgements about the unverified capacity of their appointees. Analogy takes over: if you were good at managing one type or size of department, school, system or organization then, by analogy, we judge that you will be good at this new appointment which we are trying to fill. Analogy is helped by faith, too, in the capacity of people to learn on the job. Mistakes and the position of those who suffer from their mistakes are not often publicized. Further, we show sympathy for the belief that an ill-managed education is not the worst difficulty which can befall the learner. The recognition that we cannot compare senior managers in everyday roles in the undramatic parts of civilian life with surgeons, airline pilots or captains of mega-tankers nevertheless ignores the fact that insidious damage *can* be wrought by poor management in any field. But in the final analysis we cannot trace damaged lives or frustrated opportunities back to the bad management of education.

Lazy or neglectful management may lead to measurable deficiencies in output. In secondary schools poorly organized courses, inadequate counselling or a failure to cope with the mechanics of organizing examination entries can be a reason for poor examination results. In primary schools oversights and poor estimating can leave too little money for readers and support material. As a result, children may fail to read as quickly as they might. In the field of physical education, too, apathy or neglectful surveys of the state of buildings and grounds can lead to dangers not being removed and to spaces for games, practical activities or dance being rendered unusable. As a result, children's experiences and development in activities which lie outside formal assessment may fall behind what teachers expect.

Do these defects about the management of routine details matter as much as the incapacity of a head as manager to develop a long-range view and a vision? Do they matter as much as his or her incapacity to consider where pupils will stand when they look at themselves ten years from now? In the past few would have regarded this type of short-sightedness as a serious managerial fault yet nationally, if the majority of managers were unconcerned about a long-range future, it could be claimed that it was this, at the start, which damaged the quality of the adult workforce in terms of training and skill.

Looked at separately, the primary-school head in a small locality is unlikely to be stigmatized for lack of vision in the guaranteeing of quality. Short-sightedness is not regarded as an insuperable flaw in management and this lack of concern for a manager's range and breadth of vision leads to the idea that we do not need skilled managers of education if by skilled we mean anything other than efficiency in the manipulation of resources. If good management is defined in that limited way we do not need a view about connections between different parts of education and between education and adult life in education or in society. Properly to manage a particular school in an individual locality calls, in this way of thinking, for more limited skills.

The comfort of taking a constricted view of management is that heads as managers who do not wish to move out of a short-range role can remain quite secure, provided that their governors are of the same mind. If governors take a broad view while the head's vision is limited, that in itself might be a reason for stress and division. Governors may only then be ready to stir over-complacent heads. Heads, on the other hand, have to conceal their own frustration as managers who possess skill and vision if their governors are blinkered. They may even claim that they did not expect anything different, that governors are unchangeable and that regardless of other claims it is still the head who has to shape as well as to run the school.

If cynicism is not to breed tension and mistrust heads and governors have to negotiate a way of acting together. Each side needs to stimulate the other and yet draw attention to the limits of practicality and public acceptability of certain proposals, whichever side they come from. They should be able to curb any tendency towards over-optimism. If they do not, the scepticism of parents or the caution of teachers should continually bring matters back to the level of real life. If a head and governors are inactive and unconcerned, parents can ginger them up. For teachers to try this is more difficult. It is not safe for them publicly to draw attention to neglect inside a school. Responsibility can easily be turned back on someone else and remonstrations by either parents or teachers can lead to divisions in the partnership of those who should concertedly support a school.

In the past LEAs were able to restrain or stimulate heads and governors to a limited degree. For this the main point of access was the curriculum plan and the implementing of that plan. Authorities had to make and keep up to date a written statement of their curriculum policy, but except for one national exercise between 1983 and 1985 they were not in a position directly to comment on curriculum policies put forward by governors nor were they asked to do so. This was despite the fact that governors themselves had to create a curriculum policy statement which showed how they intended to meet the requirements of the national curriculum in the light of their LEA's curriculum policy. The dwindling importance of LEAs removed them from the position of stimulator and corrector despite statements made by government at the time of the 1991 poll tax changes to the effect that local authorities were necessary if only to distribute money and to do some monitoring (Secretary of State for Education and Science, *The Independent* p. 1, 22 March 1991).

The promises of the immediate post-legislation period of 1988/89 are now almost forgotten. The hopes held out by Maclure (1989:25) that it would be mainly through monitoring school performance and through in-service training and local authority support services that the local authority would be able to give expression to its own curriculum policy may not be realistic. In due course it will no longer be possible for an LEA to use flexibility in the organization of its training grant schemes or education support grants. The changes planned in 1990 and made through the introduction of GEST (Grants for Education Support and Training) from April 1991 effectively put an end to LEA co-operation with, and delegation to, schools in the use of common training funds (Plummer 1991).

The shared planning of in-service work, the duty of monitoring and a partial responsibility for distributing central government money provided LEAs at best with a very indirect route for intervention. After the changes of 1988 and 1990 authorities were able to do little more than formally make a representation to governors when their management was proceeding in a way which might seem likely to damage children's education.

The picture which is left is that of heads and governors not so much negotiating how to act in partnership as accommodating each other.

The process of fitting their preferences and prejudices together is neither publicized nor deliberately secret. An account after all has in the end to be given to parents and only a very unskilful head or body of governors will fail to stay within the rules and yet maintain their own preferences. But they must pay heed to the school first and foremost and no activity, curricular or otherwise, will flourish unless they jointly agree that it sits properly alongside government requirements. Given this no one can be very clear whether decisions are taken in concert or separately by the head, governors or staff. Parents in particular have an undefined role, other than that which they don for themselves, fashioned by interest groups, by outside organizations and by campaigns. Their capacity to see into the inside of the system is limited. Penetrating the camouflage of management might lead to the uncovering of managers who are best left to do what they are already doing. And not all teachers relish the prospect of being forced into collegial structures if they feel that parts of their normal professional work can remain untouched by new systems and new demands. No amount of parent activity or government questioning is likely to change this.

The advantages of new requirements

The suspicion soon after the 1988 Act that schools would be dragooned into following policies which they neither enjoyed nor trusted gave way to some sense of relief that teaching methods were still regarded as a matter for the teaching profession. It was comforting too that the planning of the curriculum required nothing more than a corporate plan which embraced all aspects of the whole curriculum as outlined by the National Curriculum Council and as augmented by each school in the light of its individual circumstances (NCC 1990a:7). This may seem to understate the task which confronted schools but for heads and for senior teachers the whole curriculum, in the terms of the NCC, had shape and purpose. Those terms allowed planning to be orderly. They also quietened some of the more repetitive aspects of staffroom debate. The orderliness of curriculum planning, however, did not conceal the more pressing and onerous demands of legislation in pupil assessment and in the recording of achievement.

Good management in the meeting of those demands has made it clear that teachers can regard themselves as either the managers or the managed. They can see for themselves that at times they need to get deeply involved in planning and self-monitoring. In the process of performance management they become part of a positive working ethos (Trethowan 1991:243). At other times they can simply observe the work of those who make decisions on their behalf but even then they cannot opt out of the school's corporate effort. When they are involved in matters which are relevant to their own particular tasks they are managers. When they observe others they are being managed. The comforting thought is that it is right that not everyone should try to do everything, that confusion and ambiguity can be avoided and setbacks can be kept to a minimum.

But what are teachers, as contributors to corporate planning, to do when there *are* setbacks? They can, among the eight suggestions from the School Development Plans Project (SDPP), temporarily freeze part of an action plan, scale down the action which they have planned or postpone the attempt to reach certain targets (DES 1989e:16). If they are acting corporately, the particular alteration or postponement which they choose has to be agreed between each interest. The process of reaching that agreement has the advantage that misunderstandings and suspicions are removed. Individual teachers cannot privately postpone or cancel one aspect of teaching or one aspect of assessment when the school's plan needs these to be carried out in order to maintain progress and balance.

The second advantage of the 1988 legislation for heads and other teachers as well as governors and parents is that it is now essential that every school does take a view about education as a continuous activity between specified ages. They are not asked to confine themselves to planning or working through one year group or one class.

Taking this larger view of their work is not a burden for teachers. At the stage when they themselves were still students during their own professional education and training they were asked to prepare themselves for entry into a whole educational system, not into an individual school. Some breadth of concern should continue to be felt during the whole of teachers' careers. The national curriculum constantly reminds them that each part of it and each stage of learning is important within a child's and a young person's total education and whole-school planning reinforces the importance of that view.

For governors and for parents one result of now being publicly involved in supporting complete education is their inclusion in the responsibility for total quality. They are still not the arbiters of how much money each school can handle but they are critics and approvers of what a school does with its money. More important, the national curriculum allows them to see what comes next.

Another advantage is that heads, other teachers and governors can now explain to parents what is happening to their children by referring to shared, clearly expressed and accessible statements of aim. This diminishes some of the difficulty of finding a bridge between the languages of professionals and lay people. It diminishes the criticism that it is educationists alone who are dominant in deciding what children should learn. It is an elected government which now underwrites the aims, purposes and control of much of a child's schooling.

The changes of 1986 and 1988 take away the puzzlement of parents who not only want to understand the present state of education but also want to know whether their children's education fits in with that which everyone else receives. This reduces the risk that parents who are governors or members of the school associations may, because they are interested solely in the success of their own children, be unwilling to share their specially acquired knowledge and insights. Parent governors are an important part of a school's management and they must communicate freely with other parents.

A connected advantage is that a common bridging language allows the mystery to be taken away from the meaning of cross-curriculum work, of the stages of assessment and of the NCC trinity of dimensions, skills and themes. All five of these now have to take their place as part of the total curriculum. A school has to be clear why all and each forms part of the school plans and needs the understanding of parents.

Another benefit of the Education Reform Act will in time emerge but will need two or more complete cycles of curriculum planning. The organization of education at school enables the family and the child to know where they are going next. At present the NCC and SEAC are thin in their statement about post-school education and training. Each school plan, although it takes a local view should, as has been said already, take account of the activity of the National Council for Vocational Qualifications (NCVQ) and of the changes in non-advanced FE which emerge from the strategies of Training and Enterprise Councils (TECs).

There is a risk that this continuity into the post-16 world of education and training is regarded as more difficult because the funding of FE is now separated from school finances. But shifts in the mechanism of finance should not be regarded as dictating a shift of schools and colleges into separate spheres. They still have to meet common objectives. Managers at school level need to seek out information about national and local plans for education and training which complement the later stages of secondary education. They need, too, to take particular note of the pointers in NCC guidance papers about the relevance of Key Stage 4 to post-school experience.

A final advantage for managers is that they can choose (but also pay for) their sources of expertness. They can define what kind of advice they want and when they want it. They are, as has been noted already, less likely to seek advice about generalized improvements than about the improvement of education for pupils and students within particular limits.

All the advantages of legislation assist the manager in attracting the understanding, support and loyalty of parents. As for employers, their interest is neither as immediate nor as long-lasting, and the definition of community, as another partner, is not tight enough for it to be said that a school *must* attract loyalty from that direction. Nevertheless the benefits of school–community liaison are morally important and parents can claim to be the most significant part of that relationship. In maintaining the support of parents, managers realize that a family will certainly want its children to fit into what can only be described as society – as defined by the ways and traditions of the country as a whole. That society is full of variety. The process of fitting in may only seldom be perfect. But parents do not want education to turn their children into misfits or, if they do tend towards misfitting, many parents will still seek to have their children's individuality retained and their capacity to get along with other people improved.

Hence managing a whole school programme has to be concerned with supporting the personal and individual development of each pupil and student and with ensuring that both the school's curricular pattern and its social structure can enhance self-esteem and self-discipline.

The confidence and the achievements of children reflect the wish of their parents. They want their children to do well. They may think in terms of competition for local employment, in terms of training which will lead to employment elsewhere if local prospects are poor or in terms of a qualification which will give admission to employment which in either professional or vocational terms is available throughout Britain or internationally. The only key to these latter stages of which the parent may be aware is the importance of entry into further or higher education. The manager's responsibility is clear: for every ambition a school (whether primary or secondary) must organize each pupil's preparation and sharpen his or her capacity to choose the right next step.

About this little is said in government statements about the curriculum, about school development plans or about the development of school management. The career education and guidance approach of the NCC goes some of the way but beyond that managers have to plan an education which more broadly permeates the lives and aspirations of families and students. This is particularly important because the long history of the importance of personal, moral and social values in British education does not receive justice in the NCC guidance paper about the whole curriculum. The impression is given that cross-curricular elements and themes together with subjects both within and outside the national curriculum will make their contribution and that that will be enough. Little is said of the contribution from outside the school. And yet those who manage education have to satisfy their own and their staff's ideals and ensure that governors know and, at the least, do not disapprove of, those aims. They need to communicate their purposes and methods to outsiders in such a way that homes and schools can build on an established partnership.

Parents have always expected schools to regard moral training as an important function and they have expected schools to help their children to acquire confidence to be at ease as young adults and to be able to make the most of themselves (Schools Council 1968). If this together with other aspects of care forms part of the long-established pattern of education, does its management today need anything more than a virtually intuitive and traditional skill? Yes, because the defining lines between the national curriculum and every other part of learning and experience need attention. The divisions between subjects and themes as well as between disciplines and cross-curricular studies have to be observed in order partly to maintain the integrity of the national curriculum. The other part of the reason for observing the division of learning is to make sure that broad programmes of personal and intellectual development are handled with exactness. Managers have to make sure that the edges of what they provide are not blurred by loose thinking.

Conclusion

The task of managing new demands is rewarded with advantages. Large-scale reform could not be handled if there was still the voluntaryism which both helped and hindered attempts at large scale curriculum development in, for instance, the 1960s. The manager is assisted towards efficient planning and use of time by the 1987 Act. The legal definition of teachers' time and responsibilities makes it possible, too, to handle in-service training on a rational basis.

There are continuing difficulties for the manager if total resources and if both staff members and staff specializations are subject to severe variations. In part this can be controlled through the financial aspects of local management and through policies for the curriculum-led use of personnel. Both these require firm institutional handling. To concentrate on the institution can have the effect of preventing a head, other staff and governors from seeing larger aims which must not be lost to sight. The head has in the past not always been encouraged to concentrate on much other than the school. Methods of headteacher selection and limited programmes of training have placed school organization and its maintenance at the centre of the stage.

It is unlikely that management quality can be ensured without an awareness of practice and policies which lie outside the head's own school. Without knowing how things are managed differently elsewhere, a head may lack the stimulus to think anew. This limitation can communicate itself to governors. If not, they and the head become inward-looking and risk becoming complacent. That in turn communicates itself to other staff. They too need to see their work in a broad framework since the more confined is the view of the top managers, the more uninterested others can become in paying heed to other people's practices.

In striking a balance between complacency and excessive enthusiasm heads and governors now lack the mediating effect which could once have been exercised by the LEA. Local authorities used, too, to provide some of the colouring and flavour of the style of education which was expected in particular schools – and that in itself sometimes gave heads a framework against which to judge their own thinking. It would be valuable if a comparable framework could emerge from the ways in which heads and governors deal with each other in the post-1988 world.

Both governors and heads are helped by the certainties of the Education Reform Act: they know what has to be done, they are encouraged to take a longer view of education than used to be expected of them, they need to explain and to share, they need to plan for the breadth of curriculum and for individual pupils' development alongside a closely defined national curriculum.

The changing demands made on management can appear to be excessive when one part of the national machine emphasizes obvious connections between curriculum provision, pupil assessment and continuity at the same time as another part of the machine seems to separate the providers of general and vocational education. Even if that separation in post-16 policies limits itself to separate funding, it would surprise everyone if it did not also carry with it a range of different educational expectations. Only local managers can limit, by their joint strategies, the disadvantage of separation.

CHAPTER 13

Responsibility and self-justification

New demands on management have to be met explicitly. Managers cannot rely on unspoken assumptions. They need to get as near to the reality of each issue as not to leave others who are involved suspicious or confused. They need, too, allies who can support them in their interpretations and who can explain them to a yet wider circle of participants.

For example, the National Curriculum Council (NCC) in the definition of widely attempted cross-curricular elements distinguished between three elements or aspects, namely dimensions, skills and themes. Some dimensions of the curriculum are to do with knowledge, making connections, connecting ideas, explaining and questioning. Other dimensions are those through which knowledge, awareness and attitude rise to the surface without an exclusive link with any one particular subject. Dimensions such as these permeate parts of a school's organization over and above the curriculum. As an example, schools are committed to providing equal opportunities for their pupils regardless of gender, race or cultural background. As a second example, schools have to guarantee that they can provide for children who have special educational needs.

Schools have long pursued policies which equalize opportunities and the NCC (1990a:3) underlined a practice which might have needed no further emphasis when it said:

In order to make access to the whole curriculum a reality for all pupils, schools need to foster a climate in which equality of opportunity is supported by a policy to which the whole subscribes and in which positive attitudes to gender equality, cultural diversity and special needs of all kinds are actively promoted.

However obvious this statement may seem to a manager he or she has to treat it on the basis of its being an explicit demand. If the curriculum comes first, does it mean previously adopted teaching attitudes may have to be set aside? One answer has already been quoted where Shah (1990) pointed to the risk of diminishing the effect of 'spontaneous teaching'. In other words, although a whole school policy about equality of opportunity means that every teacher has to understand his or her contribution, this still has to allow for flexibility.

It would be an unreal school which drew up its plans in such a way as to restrict spontaneity and it would be an ill-thought-out management plan which tied itself solely to the national curriculum. It may be surprising that the documents of the NCC do not do more to acknowledge the care with which schools have developed their practices. For instance, in seeking a rationale for the preparation of teachers in the multicultural field Maurice Craft (1981) long ago drew attention to the lack of a formulated analysis of the curriculum needs of a multicultural society. That is still missing and controversies about mother tongue teaching, bilingualism and culture maintenance live on.

In contrast to the question of how teachers should be trained in this work, the importance of leadership in building up a guarantee about a cast-iron commitment to equalizing opportunities for ethnic minorities has become very clear. Here the NCC message is correct in locating that commitment within the process of planning a whole school's curriculum organization. The head must make the first move in that commitment and must use the armoury of skills and of home–school relationships. The head must pursue the same enquiry as that outlined by Shah and the school must be clear, subject by subject, about what it can contribute.

It is the responsibility of the head to ensure that each teacher does fully contribute to a dimension of learning such as that which is brought to life in the improvement of multicultural opportunity. But if we turn from multicultural education to the job of ensuring equality of opportunity between the sexes, management is not likely to be assisted to the same degree by the national curriculum. This may be because, in a profession in which proportionately more women hold senior posts than in other fields, equality will be looked at in terms not so much of day-to-day learning as of jobs and seniority.

That this is still an issue over which education is divided is borne out elsewhere in a study of higher education (Lees and Scott 1990:343):

For equality of opportunity initiatives to be in any sense meaningful, there must be a clear acknowledgement that change involves conflict and that conflict may arise not only between the demands of the unrepresented and powerful but also between the disadvantaged groups themselves. . . . With scarce resources, priorities will need to be set between the needs of teaching versus non-teaching staff, manual versus non-manual workers, black versus white, disabled versus abled and men versus women; this will raise dissension.

The openness of dissension in this suggestion is in contrast to the obscure and intangible influences which a school brings to bear on pupils. Those influences create and strengthen sex stereotypes. The hidden curriculum has deep layers and because 'it is not a planned, articulated, ostensible part of the school, it is difficult to work on. There are no accessible channels of influence and control' (Marland:1983:3). Marland makes the point, too, that although curriculum control may become more centralized, schools – particularly those which concentrate their efforts on being part of the community – deliberately make themselves open to local influence. Local influence can include local prejudice and 'the more sensitive the school is to society's views, the harder it is for the school to work against them' (Marland 1983:3).

Prejudice and scepticism in the local community – among parents, voiced in workplaces, shops and pubs – imposes on those who try to manage policies of enlightenment the obligation to avoid naïvety, not to retreat and yet not to work so much against the grain of local thought as to make the school's efforts counter-productive. If schools are, in Marland's words, sexist amplifiers, the messages of the NCC do not penetrate anew the problems of creating and maintaining policies of equal opportunity. The question is not what the national curriculum can do to help but what might LMS and the policies of competition do that is adverse. It is difficult to find room for altruistic considerations when school staff and governors are trying to decide a reasonable basis for policies which are, for instance, basically self-centred (Dennison 1990).

More concrete than their method of organizing a school in such a way as not to have its work distorted by prejudice, managers find their responsibility to meet special needs in ordinary schools less ambiguous. Since 1981 much has been done in setting out their aims in the organization of the curriculum and in their teaching programmes. This has led to their becoming accustomed to reviewing their curriculum year by year and to the steady improvements in the pastoral curriculum. This has been described as being successful because personal and social education contributes 'to a climate throughout the school which accepts and respects individual differences. . . . A task for the guidance programme is to develop in pupils a constructive awareness of disability and an attitude which recognizes disabled people's right of access to resources in the school and in the community' (Jones and Southgate 1989:73).

Skills

Of the two other aspects of planning which are taken by the NCC as a salient feature of school organization, one (the nature of cross-curriculum *themes* and their management) has already been noted.

A third aspect is that of skills 'which can be developed coherently throughout the curriculum provided that teachers adhere to the principle of sharing responsibility. All these skills (oracy, literacy, numeracy, problem solving and study skills) are transferable, chiefly independent of content and can be developed in different contexts across the whole curriculum' (NCC 1990a:3).

The management of the process of developing pupils' skills underlines the importance of the connection with homes and parents but that apart, the skills of education lie in the heart of much which can only be provided and managed by teachers themselves.

Five studies by HMI, in their *Aspects of Primary Education* series, traced the development of practices between the 1978 primary survey and the late 1980s. Two of these – on the teaching and learning of mathematics and the teaching and learning of language and literacy – related to the years of development up to the time of the requirements of the national curriculum.

As an example, the document on language (DES 1990c) draws attention to there being an increasing need in a rapidly changing and complex society for more than literacy. Good practice in individual classrooms needs to be more than intermittent and 'where good practice is consistently achieved throughout the school, the teachers share a common view of language development and of how the teaching and learning of English contribute to, and are extended by, work in other subjects' (DES 1990c:32). Much is asked of the class teacher, the only adult with whom the majority of children communicate during the school day. Much depends on 'the quality of the teacher's explanations, clarity and structure of speech, the skilled construction and use of questions, and the ability to engage children in intensive discussion of increasingly complex ideas. These are all crucial not only for the development of language but also for helping the children to understand and to think in all areas of the curriculum' (DES 1990c:32).

Language and thinking are part of each other. All parts of the curriculum call for the development of habits of clear thinking. On the repeated theme of work across the curriculum HMI noted that there was 'a welcome trend in some schools towards helping children to reach a further understanding of how language works. This emphasis is strongly supported by the Kingman Committee and the Statutory Orders for teaching English in the National Curriculum' (DES 1990c:33).

These are clear messages to managers. They amount to an encouragement of partnership between teachers and they connect with a further message about assessment. Commenting on that, HMI pointed out that too narrow an approach contributes 'little to the planning of children's work within the class and [fails] to influence the policy for the teaching and learning of language and literacy throughout the school'. There would be a demand for far greater attention in the future to be paid to assessing, recording and reporting children's progress and, in the by now familiar way, it was added that these assessments would be crucial for purposes of planning, monitoring and communicating progress to parents and others (DES 1990c:33).

This document on literacy, when read alongside NCC statements about cross-curricular skills, provides a virtually perfect commentary for the management of skills education. It is not surprising that schools should be urged to award more of their designated posts for English to curriculum leadership. What is, as an extension of this, a yet more powerful piece of advice is that the example of high quality work should be helped, in its permeation throughout a school, by language consultants. These 'can be highly effective in influencing practice in the classroom and in co-ordinating work across the school. To fulfil such a role they need scope to develop and practise management skills, as well as providing advice in relevant language matters, to act as exemplars of good teaching and to help other teachers to assess their work' (DES 1990c:34).

It is in connection with finding a more effective role for consultants that HMI draw attention to the need for them to work between infant and junior schools, between departments in a 5–11 primary school and between primary and secondary schools.

This model of the handling of something as far-reaching as a language policy takes us slightly away from that introspective view of management which might become the norm if the outsider's view and the consultant's evaluation and advice are not brought into play.

In contrast, inside the school the most important activity to manage is teachers' adherence to the principle of shared responsibility. If the head and other teachers take examples such as that of the NCC text about the dimensions of the whole curriculum together with the HMI report on literacy and language as dual guidelines of how to observe the national curriculum, how to get the most out of its interconnected parts and how to encourage, justify and organize the development of pupils' skills, they are likely to manage the curriculum well.

In protest against this, however, it will be said that schools have always known how to manage the curriculum. But a denial of that has repeatedly come from HMI reports and from their comments that while most schools, classes or teachers do things well, some do not. The purpose of the national curriculum is after all to draw together several strands of improvement – at national, local authority and school level – which had been noted in the period 1978–88 by successive Secretaries of State, the DES and HMI. And, while the local authority role in the curriculum may itself be diminishing it is still 'the national curriculum which provides the local authority, the governors and the head teacher with their marching orders. A school which is implementing the national curriculum is working within the law' (Maclure 1989:9). The managers, be they the head and senior staff or the head and governors and parents, need not only to work within the law but also to provide, by their own lights, a good education. They are, to return to an earlier point, certainly serving and managing their schools but they are also managing education. They do this in the real sense that the management of a national education system is an agglomeration of small schemes and practices of management. The Secretary of State does not manage the education service. Those in schools at present do so. To do it well they need to look beyond their own institutions but, before they lift their eyes, they must make sure that those institutions are well run. Are they safe in trusting their own judgements?

Monitoring the manager

As local authorities change their functions and their size, their capacity to monitor schools will alter. New systems will preserve two functions: the distribution of funds and the task of ensuring that education is provided in the terms of the basic 1988 statute. It will be the duty of Secretaries of State, LEAs, governors and heads to exercise their functions with a view to making sure that the curriculum of each school satisfies the requirements of the Act. Local authority schemes of review and reporting through their own advisers and inspectors will survive for as long as those advisory services themselves survive. The more grant-maintained schools that come into being, the broader the exercise of LMS power in maintained schools, the more will advice become a consultancy matter. In the task of inspection local authority advisers can take only a very small sample and this is true, too, of HMI. This in itself will not change when HMI become a separate agency, responsible to a Secretary of State and placed in a position where they can vet and monitor a virtually privatised inspection service which schools managers will contract to employ – under the Education (Schools) Act 1992. As the size and range of local advisory services diminish, local monitoring will change its character. The significance of that monitoring, too, will diminish as reorganized authorities alter their roles in criticizing or seeking to put right curricular inadequacies. The 1986 Act allowed governors to vary local authority policy, and although the 1988 Act required both governors and local authorities to adopt curriculum policies which would implement the national curriculum those requirements will, as far as local authorities are concerned, become a dead letter. Schools will be free and, as predicted 'they will not be forced to toe the authority's line so long as they remain firmly within the terms of the national curriculum' (Maclure 1989:142).

It is heads who formulate the school's policy for acceptance or amendment by governors. Governors and heads seldom fall out – and only very occasionally will parents exercise their right to make a formal complaint. The power of the head and staff over the curricular efficiency of the school is, thus, considerable, but even so it has to be remembered that heads and other teachers have not been accustomed to meeting public criticism. Their LEAs until 1988 handled complaints and criticisms, took responsibility and put things right when that became necessary. Behind that defensive barrier there was no need for professionals in schools to give reasons or to attempt exercises of self-exculpation.

To have to face and answer criticism without help from a local authority, without the guarantee of governors' support and with a continuing uncertainty about the degree of approval which parents feel, professional managers need, alongside the feeling of unfettered influence which they possess if they act within the law, to develop the habit of looking over their shoulders. They need to have, through the exercise of self-evaluation, a mind which is ready to explain and defend and, if a middle way has to be found in order to meet criticism, to conciliate.

It is largely heads who need to develop these skills of management in contrast to governors and parents. Parent/governors indeed may feel either disaffected or left out. Attention has been drawn to the plight of a sample of parent governors who do not see curricular matters being made either a part of the termly record of a school's activities or of a regular agenda item at governors' meetings. They do not know who makes the decisions. They are unlikely to support a head who does not take them into his or her confidence (Morgan 1990:86):

The final decisions (about curriculum) are probably with the education authority . . . I don't know . . . I just don't know.

I suppose the head decides . . . that is a bit beyond me who decides what schemes for what schools. I don't really know where that comes from.

I have no idea who decides at all . . . I couldn't say it's each individual education committee . . . I have no idea. Isn't that frightening. I don't assume it's discussed with the chairman of governors or any of the governors.

In essence it takes time for parents to feel that they need to know much about a school's responsibilities. Without that knowledge they cannot regard themselves as being involved in its management. The professionals – the head in particular – must fend for themselves when things go wrong. Morgan again (1990:89), in the analysis of a sample of parent governors:

Accordingly the public consciousness may yet remain to be informed. If so then there is an especial obligation on those parents holding office or on those who have recently held office to assist other parents in realising their opportunities for involvement in education and for the acquisition of curriculum information. The parent governors . . . have been elected to such a position and have such a responsibility. Yet . . . they have not been empowered to discharge it.

In contrast to parent governors, teachers can be claimed to have been fully empowered to know about and to take responsibility for the professional decisions of the school. The use of their directed time is one of the means by which to secure this empowerment. One survey showed that there were some advantages in this for both teachers and for the running of the school. These were, however, outweighed by disadvantages when heads misused time, called too many meetings the purposes of which were not clear or failed to run meetings efficiently.

Pointing out that the 'impact of [directed time] on the management of individual schools has far-reaching implications for styles of leadership in the future, for the organizational health of schools and for the role of individual members within the organization', Cowan and Wright (1989:381) underline the disappointment of those who had hoped that the efficient use of directed time would facilitate collegial or corporate types of management. What had been hoped for was that there would be opportunities 'for all members to experience an owner-ship of the organization's aims, new initiatives and systems of evalu-ation'. As a result 'goals will be achieved, staff will be committed and motivated and quality of output will be directly influenced' (Cowan and Wright 1989:381). The disappointment about the failure of di-rected time to produce these benefits is 'depressing for those schools seeking to develop such [collegial] philosophies within their organiza-tions, to find that increasing pressures to react immediately to external forces constrain such endeavours and encourage a return to more auto-cratic styles' (Cowan and Wright 1989:381).

A return to autocracy isolates the head. If things go wrong sceptical teachers will be unlikely to join in the defence either of the head or of decisions made in the name of the school. In answer to this the head's degree of strength in single-handedly speaking for and defending man-agement's policies and actions depends on self-awareness, honesty and the capacity to put matters into perspective. Johnson (1990) drew at-tention to the need for heads to assess and parcel out time and energy to different parts of the workload, to the importance of their making time for reading and reflecting on their organization and to the likely value of their having formally studied educational management and administration. In particular heads need to reduce their isolation since, while they will be in the habit of frequently commending other people, their own position is different. In terms of their self-esteem

underconfidence is normal, even among highly effective managers. Few ad-ministrators seem to be sure they are doing the job well: many are uncertain and would be grateful for the assurance they so rarely receive. Whilst teachers find peer support in the workplace, it is just as vital for headteachers and deputies to derive professional support and understanding. But they must look beyond the school for their peer support: headteachers need to establish struc-tures that involve regular contact with fellow headteachers and other managers (Johnson 1990:283).

Headteachers' associations and conferences can temporarily seal their members off from the harshness of the outside world. They can provide them with the professional camaraderie which either reduces self-pity or engenders the confidence of knowing that everyone is ex-periencing the same problems as oneself. Associations and conferences also allow other people to be identified as the ones who are at fault – employers, the DES, governors, other teachers, parents. But the con-fidence gained from comparing notes with members of the same club has to be translated into the skill of justification, explanation and defence back on the job. It is there that it is wise for the head and the senior professional team to make sure that parent governors do indeed know what is done in their name. Parent governors – and all other governors – need to be brought to the point that they genuinely share a sufficient degree of commitment and understanding to be able to speak for the school.

In the same way – it need scarcely be said – the head has to try to cope with sceptical staff. The likelihood is that this will not be so much a matter of winning teachers over, since attitudes of genuine mistrust are often long-lasting, as of a positive search for ways of limiting the effects of excessive scepticism.

Heads need to decide how much isolation they can stand and how much scepticism is tolerable. They cannot go the whole way and altogether dismiss the support and understanding of other people. Unless they really are bent on autocracy they must connect the management of several different issues but they must first find out how much consensus is needed in making a management plan.

Second, they must determine how to achieve that consensus and what to settle for if it is not complete. Third, they must translate that unity of ideas which makes up a consensus into a shared strategy. The strategy must include a constancy of aim and a variety of tactic. The aim should not be changed unless the whole plan is to be revised. Tactics can be altered again with as many partners as possible contributing to their revision – even as often as from half-term to half-term.

The fourth part of a connected scheme of management is the securing of each teacher's teaching plan as part of the whole. Along with this goes the gauging of how far the teaching plan is being followed. After that comes the fifth task, namely to work out how to gain agreement for the self-evaluation through which each contributor passes. An extension of this is the development of a scheme for evaluating the whole school plan, again with emphasis on securing voluntary views and contributions from each teacher.

The seventh and final task is that of reducing the plan, its implementation and its evaluation into the threefold form of, first, a mission statement which can act as the basis for the next cycle of review, second, a summing-up of the effect of the most recent statement of intent and, third, a report on the year's stewardship.

Not all heads will adopt these approaches. Their differences have been described in one study as amounting, in the one case, to the head being regarded as a teacher-educator, in another as a leading professional, in the third as a pastoral missioner and in the fourth, as a combination of pastoral missioner and leading professional (Morgan *et al.* 1983). This was a picture of leadership in secondary schools before the Education Reform Act when the authors had described and evaluated the POST project in the mid-1980s. They were not surprised that the method of appointing headteachers led to there being a considerable variety in the way they looked at and performed their jobs. Thus of the four quoted, the first (the teacher-educator) was highly visible but not easy in communications. Uneven in the handling of staff, this head relied on vested authority and practised a high degree of centralized activity. The second was again highly visible but inaccessible and not frequently available to other teachers. The approach to 'decision-making was more autocratic than participatory . . . attempts to involve staff were tempered by scepticism regarding their motivation..' (Morgan *et al.* 1983:209–210). The third taught a good deal, attached high importance to the school's instructional goals. Otherwise he delegated much work to others, yet 'encouraged participatory forms of decision-making, emphasising good interpersonal relations . . . though not always clarifying on a systematic 'whole school' basis the factors contributing to the achievement of school goals' (Morgan *et al.* 1983:210–11). The fourth head was characterized by a 'systematic involvement in the whole range of the school's activity in spite of extensive commitments to activities outside the school . . . by a strategic view of school matters, ensuring continuing attention to longer-term planning and by a proactive stance towards innovation and change' (Morgan *et al.* 1986:211).

Effective heads need a combination of these attitudes and skills. They also need to establish how much has changed in the position which they might take about leadership as something which should be defined in different terms before and after 1988.

More systematic power is now given to the head than was possible at the time of the Hall study. There are now materials and ideas on which to build the curriculum. Much, too, is available in terms of information about practice and experience in the whole organization of pupils' learning. This, even if it is prescribed by central government, must nevertheless be organized, school by school, with a view to the complementarity of subjects. They have to be locally managed in such a way that they lead to the continuity of experience.

The head is the principal manager not only in the professional field. How well the school is understood, how much sympathy and support it can attract depends as much on ethos as on those dimensions and themes of learning which need the collaboration of families and of the community. Among these partners none can be singled out as the target of questioning, criticism and occasional praise as easily as the head. Hence the head's grasp of management has to be, if not perfect, at least several steps ahead of those of governors, other staff and parents.

Conclusion

Because managers have to provide teaching and assessment beyond simply the subject content of the national curriculum and because they have to work in territory where there are dissensions and disagreements, they need reliable allies and accurate interpreters. There are layers of management which lie outside schools, when firm and well-argued views can be exchanged between those who have no direct input into the activities of staff or governors. Support for radical ideas from such sources is balanced by resistance and scepticism. The internal manager must weigh prejudice and scepticism against uncritical enthusiasm.

To venture into policies which some outsiders will regard as too concessive brings with it the criticism that where there is genuine freedom of choice for parents between schools, traditions are more attractive than innovations. The manager has to keep the edge of competition sharp without severing channels of support from the world outside the school.

In setting a school up as expert in each of its fields those who set out to make and manage policies which are acceptable have to manage the monitoring of those policies. The capacity of the traditional sources – particularly LEA advisers and HMI – to offer school-by-school monitoring is changing. Managers may, instead, have to afford consultants who can combine external monitoring with the initiation of any corrective work which is needed.

Managers are learning how to justify the expense of external evaluators and why not to rely wholly on self-evaluation. This comes at a time when central government's interest in reaching its own conclusion about success is not matched by the funds and the organization which national school-by-school assessment would require. This is one of the points where schools can first feel they are drifting away from a national system of policy-making and assessment.

The greater the isolation of individual schools, the more inevitable it becomes that heads and governors must make their own judgements. Yet at a time when the work of the NCC is giving useful and clear indicators about priorities of management, schools cannot afford to lose allies and interpreters. If local authorities in their old form are no longer able to act on behalf of aggrieved parents or are no longer able to meet teacher organizations promptly enough to defuse their professional dissatisfactions, there is little chance that new regional boards or councils of education can provide immediacy of reaction.

The combination of changes in the law of education and the law which controls the organization of local government tend to leave schools to fend for themselves. Heads, too, are left in a position where they have to take the first step in creating policies, in implementing them, in evaluating them as well as in modifying future practices. They are the first to be required to be constructive and they are the first to receive complaints. Unless they do create corporate structures of management, heads will fail to cope and schools will slip into a type of independence which in time will be akin to modest anarchy.

END NOTE

At some distance from schools, arguments are conducted about the weaknesses of British education. They catch the eye of the media and are presented in the language of hostility – between politicians and educators, between left- and right-wing politics and between tradition and experiment.

Although these confrontations occur at a national rather than a local level their echoes are still heard in provinces and distant corners of the Education service. Reported disagreements between government ministers and those who advise them on English degenerate into squabbles about nationalism. The responsibility of educating children in any physical activity converts itself into an argument about learning to swim and about who pays for the swimming pool. The arts in education are not roughly handled when their experts report on their future in the curriculum but instrumental music, because of other parts of the 1988 law, loses much of its institutional base.

Managers have to watch the trend in each of these arguments but cannot take them seriously into account until one side or the other has won its point. Continuing disagreements, notably about the curriculum but also about the local management of funds, do not badly damage education but they do weaken it by showing that trivial points taken seriously can unbalance the main part of a school's efforts.

It is fortunate in some ways that all the words which are used to expose the rifts which are seen by those who speak from important public platforms as politicians, economists or industrialists do not reach the schools. But while the criticisms mount, the activities and aims of schools are, if they are primary, predominated by the assessment of pupils. Managers are more concerned with avoiding ambiguities and injustice in their treatment of individual pupils than with competition with the school next door. In secondary schools assessment also predominates: how do the assessable needs of the national curriculum match the increasing range of public examinations and qualifications at the age of 16 and 17? How can subjects be broadened and yet avoid the complicated coils of excessive modularization? And when will a five subject approach be accepted as the junction between schools and higher education?

Management of new demands inside old boundaries asks for a good understanding between existing partners. In maintained schools the trinity of head, other teachers and outsiders (to assess, comment, advise or support) in the shape of people from the local authority or from HMI is weakened because the position of external partners is jeopardized. Just as the narrowing down in the number of LEAs in 1974 meant that 104 authorities could build strong advisory teams, so the sixfold increase in the number of authorities after the local government commission in 1993 will lead either to a great dilution of external services or, because the period of change coincides with the completion of local school management (including finance), to their disappearance.

With or without the external framework to which they were accustomed, schools will get on with the central activity of learning. With that goes a concern about the quality of teaching. They have to devote much time and thought to their connection with the processes of initial teacher education and staff development – more time than the Education Reform Act and its surrounding changes envisaged.

Management need attract little attention to itself in the manner in which it balances the response to differing pressures on a school. It has to be conducted in such a way as to make sure that the sources of pressure, of interest and support are fed with information and with opportunities for direct involvement. This in particular refers to parents but it has to encompass those contributors from the wide community who are still only slowly making their impact on schools.

Finally, the fact that management in its diversity is channelled through governors may be the most significant factor in avoiding the disadvantages of too much isolation in the process of self-management. Lay people, however satisfied they are with their own schools' reports, still want to know how others are doing. The professional educator can turn to professional resource centres, unless these, too, disappear with the changing organization of LEAs. Even when local frameworks wither away, the larger out-of-school picture will still be available to professionals through their associations and through their professional journals. But for one side of the partnership to be well informed about broad movements in the approaches to improvement and for the other, the lay people of parents, families, governors and employers, to be left to look inward will lead to narrow-minded education. It was this from which the schools escaped in 1944. Management's task is to create new partnerships for the sake of a renewed broadening of goals and for the sake of guaranteeing agreed levels of quality.

REFERENCES

Associated Examining Board 1989 *GCE Syllabuses 1991 A Level, AS Level.* AEB, Guildford

Aubrey C ed 1990 *Consultancy in the United Kingdom: its role and contribution to educational change.* Falmer Press

Audit Commission 1986 *Towards better management of secondary education.* HMSO

Audit Commission 1989 *Assuring quality in education.* HMSO

Audit Commission 1991 *Management within primary schools.* HMSO

Baginsky M *et al* 1991 *Towards effective partnerships in school governance.* NFER

Ball C 1985 *Fitness for purpose.* NFER/Nelson

Ball C 1991 *Learning pays: the role of post-compulsory education and training.* Royal Society of Arts

Ball S J 1990 *Politics and policy-making in education.* Routledge

Baron G, Taylor W 1969 *Educational administration and the social sciences.* Athlone Press

Barrow R 1984 *Giving teaching back to teachers.* Wheatsheaf Books, Brighton

Becher T, Eraut M, Knight J 1981 *Policies of educational accountability.* Heinemann

Beck C 1990 *Better schools: a values perspective.* Falmer Press

Bell L 1988 *Management skills in primary schools.* Routledge

Bennett S N 1985 Time and teach. In Entwistle N (ed) *New directions in educational psychology.* (p. 206) Falmer Press

Berg L 1968 *Risinghill: death of a comprehensive school.* Penguin

Billings D 1989 The curriculum framework associated with NCVQ. *Education in Science* **134**: 12–13

Bogdanor V 1979 Power and participation. *Oxford Review of Education* **5**(2)

Briault E, West E 1990 *Primary school management: learning from experience.* NFER/Nelson

British Standards Institution 1991 BS3750 *Guidance notes for application to education and training.* Milton Keynes BSI

Broadfoot P, Grant M, James M, Nuttall D, Stierer B 1991 *Records of achievement.* DES HMSO

Brooksbank K ed 1980 *Educational administration.* Councils and Education Press

Burstall C 1974 *Primary French in the balance.* NFER

Campbell R J 1985 *Developing the Primary School Curriculum.* Holt, Rinehart & Winston

Careers and Occupational Information Centre 1990 *Knowledge and competence.* HMSO

CASE (Campaign for the Advancement of State Education) 1988 Good practice. *Parents and schools* Winter

CBI 1990 *Towards a skills revolution.* Confederation of British Industry

Central Advisory Council (England) 1967 *Children and their primary schools.* HMSO

CERI (Centre for Educational Research and Innovation) 1973 *Case studies of educational innovation* vol. 4. Organization of Economic Co-operation and Development

Chelune G *et al* 1979 *Self-disclosure.* Jossey-Bass

Clarkson M (ed) 1988 *Emerging issues in primary education.* Falmer Press

Cohen G 1989 Managing change in education. *International Journal of Educational Management* **3**(3)

Cowan B J, Wright N 1989 Directed time, a year on: staff perspectives. *School Organisation* **6**(3)

Craft M 1981 *Teaching in a multicultural society: the tasks of teacher education.* Falmer Press

Coulson A 1990 Primary headships. In Saran R, Trafford V (eds) *Research in education management and policy.* (pp. 106–7) Falmer Press

Cullingford C 1985 *Parents, teachers and schools.* Robert Boyce

Dale B G, Lees J 1986 *The development of quality circle programmes.* Manchester UMIST

Dale R, Esland G, Ferguson R, Macdonald R (eds) 1981 *Education and the state.* vol II: *Politics, patriarchy and practice.* Falmer Press

Dalin P, Rust V 1983 *Can schools learn?* NFER/Nelson

Dean J 1991 *Professional development in school.* Open University Press

Dennison B 1990 The competitive edge – attracting more pupils. *School Organisation* **9**(2)

Department of Employment 1989 *Training and Enterprise Councils: a prospectus for the 1990s.* Department of Employment

DES (Department of Education and Science) 1970 *Towards the middle school.* HMSO

DES 1972 *Educational priority.* vol 1: *EPA problems.* HMSO

DES 1975 *A language for life: report of a Committee of Inquiry.* HMSO

DES 1977 *A new partnership for our schools.* HMSO

DES 1980 *The APU: an introduction.* DES, COI

DES 1981 *The school curriculum.* Circular 6/81, HMSO

DES 1983a *Teaching quality.* HMSO

DES 1983b *Curriculum 11 – 16: towards a statement of entitlement.* HMSO

DES 1989a *Discipline in schools.* HMSO

DES 1989b *The curriculum from 5–16.* 2nd edn. HMSO

DES 1989c *The development of performance indicators.* DES

DES 1989d *School indicators for internal management. Aide-mémoire.* DES

DES 1989e *Planning for school development.* School Development Plans Project, HMSO

DES 1990a *Developing school management: the way forward.* School Management Task Force

DES 1990b *Records of achievement.* Circular 8/90, DES

DES 1990c *Aspects of primary education: the teaching and learning of literacy.* HMSO

DES 1991a *Development planning: a practical guide.* School Development Plans Project, HMSO

DES 1991b *The parents' charter: you and your child's education.* DES

Devon County Council 1990 *Governors guide to local management of schools Part 1*. County Hall, Exeter

Docking J W 1980 *Control and discipline in schools*. Harper and Row

Docking J W 1990 *Primary schools and parents*. Hodder and Stoughton

Dunt P 1989 Not all cream and pasties. *School Governor* June

Earley P (ed) 1988 *Governors reports and annual parents meetings*. NFER

Earley P, Fletcher-Campbell F 1989 *The time to manage?* NFER/Nelson

Edwards J, Sutton A, Thody A 1990 TVEI cluster co-ordinators: inter-school management role. *School Organisation* **10**(1)

Employment Department Group 1990 *The management of quality: BS 5750 and beyond*. Department of Employment

Entwistle N 1985 (ed) *New Directions in educational psychology 1. Learning and teaching*. Falmer

Entwistle N 1987 *Understanding classroom learning*. Hodder and Stoughton

Eraut M (ed) 1991 *Education and the information society*. Cassell, Council of Europe

ESAC (Education Service Advisory Committee) 1990 *Managing occupational stress: a guide for managers and teachers in the school sector*. Health and Safety Commission, HMSO

Everard K B 1986 *Developing management in schools*. Blackwell

Farley M 1990 Let's make new friends. *Education* **175**(3)

Finegold D, Keep E, Miliband D, Raffe D, Spours K, Young M 1991 *A British 'Baccalaureat': ending the division between education and training*. Institute for Public Policy Research

Galton M, Simon B 1980 *Progress and performance in the primary classroom*. Routledge and Kegan Paul

Gannon T, Whalley A 1975 *Middle schools*. Heinemann

Gibson D, Wickham D 1987 Success criteria for the implementation of management systems. *Coombe Lodge Report* **19**(8) Blagdon

Gilbert G (ed) 1990 *Local management of schools*. Kogan Page

Gipps C, Goldstein H 1983 *Monitoring children: an evaluation of the Assessment of Performance Unit*. Heinemann

Glatter R *et al* (eds) 1988 *Understanding school management*. Open University Press

Haffenden I, Brown A 1989 A study of the new vocational qualifications. *Journal of Further and Higher Education* **13**(3)

Handy C, Aitken R 1986 *Understanding schools as organisations*. Penguin

Harding L, Beech J R (eds) 1991 *Educational assessment of the primary school child*. NFER

Hargreaves A, Tickle L (eds) 1980 *Middle schools*. Harper and Row

Hewton E 1988 School focussed staff development. Falmer Press

HMI 1980 *Matters for discussion: a view of the curriculum*. HMSO

HMI 1990 *The implementation of the national curriculum in primary schools*. DES

Hodgson V *et al Beyond distance teaching*. Open University Press

Holt A (ed) 1989 Governor training: what does it look like? *Parents and Schools* **56** Winter

Honey J 1990 *Does accent matter?* Faber and Faber

Hopkins D, Leask M 1989 Performance indicators and school development. *School Organisation* **9**(1)

Hughes M (ed) 1975 *Administering education: international challenge*. Athlone Press

Hughes M, Ribbins P, Thomas H (eds) 1985 *Managing education: the system and the institution.* Cassell Education

Hulmes E 1989 *Education and cultural diversity.* Longman

Hunt C 1990 Certified school governors. *School Governor* March

ILEA (Inner London Education Authority) 1984 *Improving secondary schools.* ILEA

ILEA 1986 *The junior school project: the main report.* ILEA Research and Statistics Branch

Jenkins H O 1991 *Getting it right: a handbook for successful school leadership.* Blackwell Education

Jewell D 1990 Advance on two levels. *Times Educational Supplement* no 3858, 6 June:A22

Johnson N 1990 Self management strategies for head teachers. *School Organisation* **10**(2) and (3)

Jones K 1989 *Right turn: the Conservative revolution in education.* Hutchinson Radius

Jones K, Clark S *et al* 1989 *Staff development in the primary school.* Blackwell

Jones N, Southgate T 1989 *The management of special needs in ordinary schools.* Routledge

Jowett J *et al.* Building bridges: parental involvement in schools. NFER

Kennedy J 1990 Inspection and advice within the wider education authority. *Head Teacher Review* Spring

Knight B 1989 *Managing school time.* Longman

Kogan M 1973 English primary schools. In Fowler G *et al* (eds) *Decision-making in British education.* (p. 145) Open University Press

Kogan M 1975 *Educational policy-making.* Allen and Unwin

Laws J, Dennison W F 1990 Researching the role of the primary head. *Educational Studies* **16**(3)

Lawton D (ed) 1986 *School curriculum planning.* Hodder and Stoughton

Lawton D 1989 *Education, culture and national curriculum.* Hodder and Stoughton

Lawton D, Gordon P 1987 *HMI.* Routledge and Kegan Paul

Leask M 1990 Planning for the future. *School Governor* March

Lees S, Scott M 1990 Equal opportunities: rhetoric or action. *Gender and Education* **2**(3)

Lessem R 1985 *The roots of excellence.* Fontana

Macbeth A 1989 *Involving parents.* Heinemann Educational

Maclure S 1989 *Education re-formed.* Hodder and Stoughton

Maclure S 1990 Beyond the Education Reform Act. *Policy Studies* Spring

Maclure S 1991 *Missing links: the challenge to Further Education.* Policy Studies Institute

Marland M 1983 *Sex differentiation and schooling.* Heinemann Educational

Marsh P 1991 Bounce in the showroom. *The Higher* 850. Nov 1991 (p. 16)

Matharu J 1990 Campaign for maximum class size. *Parents and schools* **57**(8)

Meighan R 1989 The parents and schools: alternative role definitions. *Educational Review* 141:2

Morgan A 1990 Parent governors? That doesn't mean a lot does it? *School Organisation* **10**(1)

Morgan C, Hall V, Mackay H 1983 *The selection of secondary school headteachers.* Open University Press

National Economic Development Office and Manpower Services Commission 1984 *Competency and competition* National Economic Development Office

National Forum for Management Education and Development 1991 *MCI in action*. London, Shell UK Ltd

National Institute for Careers Education and Counselling 1985 *Guidance in open learning*. NICEC, Balls Park, Hertford

NCC (National Curriculum Council) 1989 *Curriculum guidance 1: a framework for the primary curriculum*. NCC, York

NCC 1990a *Curriculum guidance 3: the whole curriculum*. NCC, York

NCC 1990b *Curriculum guidance 6: careers education and guidance*. NCC, York

NCC 1990c *Curriculum guidance 8: education for citizenship*. NCC, York

NCC 1990d *Curriculum guidance 5: health education*. NCC, York

NCC 1990e *Curriculum guidance 4: education for economic and industrial understanding*. NCC, York

NCC 1991 *EIU: managing economic and industrial understanding in schools* NCC, York

NCES (National Council for Educational Standards) 1981 *Secondary Schools 1965–79*. NCES

NCES 1983 *Standards in English schools*. NCES

NCES 1985 *Standards in English schools: second report*. NCES

Nias J 1989 *Primary teachers talking*. Routledge

Nightingale D 1990 *Local management of schools at work in the primary school*. Falmer Press

NUT 1990 Keeping track of LMS. *The Teacher* December

Nuttall D N 1981 *School self-evaluation: accountability with a human face?* Schools Council

Oppenheimer L (ed) 1990 *The self-concept*. Springer-Verlag

Owen J 1973 *The management of curriculum development*. Cambridge University Press

Oxford Delegacy of Local Examinations 1989 *General Certificate of Education 1991 Regulations and Syllabuses*. Summertown, Oxford

Packwood T 1989 Return to the hierarchy. *Education Management and Administration* **17**:(1)

Passow A H 1989 Designing a global curriculum. *Gifted Education International* **6**

Peaker G F 1971 *The Plowden children from years later*. NFER

Platt S A 1990 Hands-on-heads. *The Teacher* October

Plummer J 1991 Training turns into 24 bad jokes. *Times Educational Supplement* no 3899, 22 March:14

Polytechnic South West 1989 *A policy for in-service education*. Rolle Faculty of Education, Exmouth

Poster C, Day C 1988 *Partnership in education management*. Routledge

Ranson S 1990 *The politics of reorganising schools*. Unwin Hyman

Ranson S, Taylor B, Brighouse T 1986 *The revolution in education and training*. Longman

Reynolds D (ed) 1985 *Studying school effectiveness*. Falmer Press

Rudduck J 1991 *Innovation and change*. Open University Press

Rumble G 1986 *The planning and management of distance education*. Croom Helm

Rutter M *et al* 1979 *Fifteen thousand hours: secondary schools and their effects on children*. Open Books

Sallis J 1980 *The effective school governor*. Advisory Centre for Education

Sallis J 1988 *Schools, parents and governors: a new approach to accountability*. Routledge

Sallis J 1991 *School governors: your questions answered.* Hodder and Stoughton

Saran R Trafford V 1990 *Research in education management and policy.* Falmer Press

Sayer J 1989 *Managing schools.* Hodder and Stoughton

Sayer J Williams V 1989 *Schools and external relations.* Cassell

Schools Council 1968 *Enquiry 1: young school leavers.* HMSO

School Development Plans Project, see DES 1989e

SEAC (Schools Examinations and Assessment Council) 1990a *A guide to teacher assessment Pack A.* Heinemann Educational

SEAC 1990b *A guide to teacher assessment Pack C.* Heinemann Educational

SED (Scottish Education Department) 1989 *Talking about schools: the main findings.* HMSO

Shah S 1990 Equal opportunity issues in the context of the National Curriculum: a black perspective. *Gender and Education* **12**:3

Shaughnessy M 1989 Monitoring the active child, adult and prodigy. *Gifted Education International* **6**:22–4

Shipman M 1990 *In search of cramming.* Blackwell

Simons H, Elliott J (eds) 1989 *Re-thinking appraisal and assessment.* Open University Press

Slater F 1985 *The quality controllers.* University of London Institute of Education

Sinsarchuk R, Nicholl N V J 1990 APA and portfolio development: a review. *The vocational aspect of education* XLII. 113

Smith P, Kelly M 1987 *Distance education and the mainstream.* Croom Helm

Smithers A 1991 *The vocational route into higher education.* School of Education. University of Manchester

Southern Universities Joint Board 1988 *Regulations and syllabuses GCE 1990.* Bristol

Southworth G 1988 The glue of schools. *Times Educational Supplement* 20 May:B27

Stewart V, Stewart A 1982 *Managing the poor performer.* Gower

Swann Report 1985 *The education of ethnic minority children.* The Runnymede Trust

Taylor F 1989 Planning a head. *School Governor* March

TES 1990 Let them all settle for a new set of initials. *Times Educational Supplement* no 3886, 21 Dec:11

TES 1991a Matters arising. *Times Educational Supplement* no 3888, 4 Jan:4

TES 1991b Unperturbed by bias claim. *Times Educational Supplement* no 3888, 4 Jan:4

TES 1991c Another triumph for historic compromise. *Times Educational Supplement* no 3888, 4 Jan:13

TES 1991d Budgeting by creative inertia. *Times Educational Supplement* no 3892, 1 Feb:19

TES 1991e Fears grow over rise in truancy. *Times Educational Supplement* no 3902, 12 April:8

TES 1991f Pay criteria rejected. *Times Eduational Supplement* no 3935. 19

The Teacher 'Ten questions to ask your Governors'. December 1990:11

Thompson P, McHugh D 1990 *Work organizations: a critical introduction.* Macmillan

Thody A 1989 Me and my shadow. *School Governor* March

Thomas N 1990 *Primary education from Plowden to 1990s*. Falmer Press

Tizard B, Burgess T, Francis H, Goldstein H, Young M, Hewison J, Plewis I 1980 *Fifteen thousand hours: a discussion*. University of London Institute of Education

Torrington D, Weightman J 1991 'Too powerful' secondary heads reluctant to delegate. *The Guardian* no 3722, 4 Jan:6

Torrington D, Weightman J, Johns K 1987 Doing well but could do better. *Times Educational Supplement* 30 Oct:23

Trethowan D M 1991 *Managing with appraisal: advising quality schools through performance management*. Paul Chapman

Tulloch M 1990 Home school relationships. *Parents and Schools* **58**:11

Versey J 1989 The national curriculum and TVEI. *Education in Science* **134**:21–3

Wallace M, Hall V 1989 Management development and training for schools. *Educational Management and Administration* **7**(4)

Warburton F W, Southgate V 1969 *Ita: and independent evaluation*. Murray and Chambers

Waters D 1979 *Management and headship in the primary school*. Ward Lock

Watkins P 1987 *Modern approaches to the secondary curriculum*. Longman

Watson L E 1980 *Current issues in the management of education*. Sheffield Polytechnic Department of Educational Management and British Educational Administration Society

West M, Bollington R 1990 *Teacher appraisal: a practical guide for schools*. David Fulton

Whyte W H 1956 T*he organisation man*. Simon and Schuster, New York

Williams G 1987 Using MIS to keep the college under review. *Coombe Lodge Report* **19**(8)

Williams M 1991 *In service education and training*. Cassell

Winkley D 1985 *Diplomats and detectives: LEA advisers at work*. Robert Royce

Wolfendale S 1990 *Parental involvement*. Cassell

Young M 1988 NCC – a catalyst for social change. In Paine N (ed) *Open learning in transition*. pp. 11–12. Cambridge National Extension College

Young M, McGeeney P 1968 *Learning begins at home*. Routledge

INDEX